JUST CAUSES

*Notes of an
Unrepentant
Socialist*

JUST CAUSES

Notes of an Unrepentant Socialist

GERALD CAPLAN

ECW PRESS

CANADIAN CATALOGUING IN PUBLICATION DATA

Caplan, Gerald L., 1938–
Just causes : notes of an unrepentant socialist

ISBN 1-55022-204-3

1. Canada – Politics and government – 1984– .*
2. United States – Politics and government – 1981–1989.
3. United States – Politics and government – 1989–1993.
4. Right and left (Political science). I. Title.

FC630.C37 1993   971.064'7   C93-095194-8
F1034.2.C37 1993

Published with the financial assistance of
The Canada Council and the Ontario Arts Council.

Design and imaging by ECW Type & Art, Oakville, Ontario.
Printed and bound by Kromar Printing Ltd., Winnipeg, Manitoba.

Distributed by General Distribution Services,
30 Lesmill Road, Toronto, Ontario M3B 2T6.

Published by ECW PRESS,
1980 Queen Street East,
Toronto, Ontario M4L 1J2.

Table of Contents

Foreword   vii

I   My Brilliant Subversive Career   1
II   Moral Victories   7
III   Just Liberals   21
IV   So This Is Power   33
V   Brian Mulroney —
      The Opportunist as Ideologue   49
VI   The Friends of Brian Mulroney   71
VII   The World of Brian Mulroney   83
VIII   Following the American Leader   101
IX   The American Way   113
X   Bombs Bursting in Air   130
XI   Distant Causes   138
XII   Native Wrongs   163
XIII   Women's Equality: The Never-Ending Story   174
XIV   Values   191
XV   Culture versus Industry   214
XVI   Socialist Dreams & Nightmares   238

Foreword

OTTAWA, LABOUR DAY, 1993

I began writing a weekly column at the beginning of 1985, an endeavour that, to my surprise and pleasure, continued virtually non-stop until early in 1993. That adds up to some 400-plus columns over a little more than eight years, of which some 20 per cent are included between these covers [occasionally in slightly revised form].

If there is a greater privilege than to be able to mouth off every week in writing about any subject that grabs your fancy, I can hardly imagine what it is. If there is any exercise more challenging for a member of the chattering classes than to be forced to organize one's thoughts into 700–800 more-or-less coherent words, that too is not easy to conceive. At the same time, my awareness that I was one of a ridiculously tiny handful of certified left-wingers whose views were prominently and regularly featured in Canadian newspapers added powerfully to the responsibilities I was conscious of carrying. So while working on these columns was never my primary vocation during these years, it was invariably my central intellectual preoccupation.

It so happens that my column-writing began soon after Brian Mulroney won his first election and Ronald Reagan won his second. It ended around the time Mulroney resigned after almost nine years as Prime Minister and George Bush was defeated after 12 years of Republicans in the White House. In one way or another, most of the pieces in this volume revolve around my reactions to the beliefs and policies of those three self-described conservatives and their governments.

Of course the subject matter herein inevitably reflects my own varied interests over the decades: the past, present and future of democratic socialism, as befits both an historian of the old CCF and life-long NDP activist; the Third World and its relationship to western society, emanating from my doctoral work in African history in the

1960s to my 10 years teaching third world development to my involvement in umpteen third world support groups; women's equality, my long commitment to which has, I hope, matured into something approaching a thoughtful feminism, thanks largely to my wife Carol Phillips; native rights, a subject that I, like so many other Canadian progressives, ignored for decades as we concentrated on racism and social injustice south of the border instead of right here in our front yard; the tobacco racket, and my most unforgiving contempt for those involved in it in any way, shape or form, presumably a legacy of my days as Director of the City of Toronto's Health Advocacy Unit; the world of Canadian broadcasting and culture, about which I received a crash course several years ago thanks to the unlikely bestowal upon me by the Mulroney government of the co-chair [with my now dear friend Florian Sauvageau] of the Task Force on Broadcasting Policy. Evidence of all these interests can be found within.

Most of these columns first appeared in the *Toronto Star* or the *Sunday Star* and were also carried in the *Moncton Times-Transcript*. I am happy to express my gratitude to John Honderich in Toronto and Mike Bembridge in Moncton for opening their papers to me. Others appeared in the *Globe and Mail*, the *Financial Post* and the *Calgary Herald*. I am grateful to Jack David of ECW Press for believing that my columns merited collection in book form.

I also owe a debt to Rosemary Speirs, Ottawa bureau chief for the *Toronto Star*, who alone in the world ever offered me advice on how to write a column: keep each one to a single subject, and say something new each time. I hope she'll agree I tried faithfully to follow her counsel.

Needless to say, I alone am culpable for all those bold predictions and forecasts that, readers will have no difficulty discerning, proved in the end less than entirely accurate.

Finally, these columns began at the same moment as did my life with Carol Phillips. She has been, from the first, my editor, advisor and conscience. Except when we were separated by entire continents, no column saw the light of day without Carol's scrutiny. If I served as a voice for many who espoused these just causes, she shares the credit. This work is as much hers as mine, and is dedicated to her with love and gratitude.

This book is also dedicated to our son, Dylan Aitken, our inspiration for continuing the remarkably frustrating, heartbreaking, venerable struggle for a more just and equal society.

My Brilliant Subversive Career

1989 I MAY AS WELL COME CLEAN: I've been humiliated.
Utterly, shamefacedly, humiliated. June Callwood's
security file is bigger than mine. Paul Copeland's is bigger than mine.
Some radical I've turned out to be; not even the Mounties cared
enough to pay much attention. Oh sure, you can say I shouldn't
worry about keeping up with the Junes. But you're not a laughing-
stock in your own home. My only hope is that my secret files are so
explosive that they haven't dared release them.

Frankly, Copeland and I weren't sure they'd release anything when
we decided last June that it'd be neat to see what hidden files our
government had on us. So Copeland, a lawyer, applied under the
Privacy Act for our various files, including our National Security
Records. Lo and behold: After a few formal letters were exchanged,
some material actually arrived last month.

Now what we still don't know is what they didn't send us. The
Solicitor-General's privacy co-ordinator refused us access to some of
the requested files, and John Grace, the privacy commissioner of
Canada, has concurred with that decision. Not that either official
acknowledges that any information about us exists in those files.
Maybe it does. Maybe it doesn't. They aren't obligated to tell us. But
we can't have access in either case. So even if nothing ever existed,
we still can't be told.

Maybe our missing files are among the 150,000 that the Canadian
Security Intelligence Service says it's already destroyed of the
500,000 files illicitly collected by the Mounties in their rip-roaring,
liberty-trampling, barn-burning heyday; but naturally they're not
even allowed to tell us that those files no longer exist. Is this quite
clear now? Call it Catch-22.

I

Copeland, I must confide, is quite proud of his large file — the parts not blacked out, I mean. He's always been actively interested in the government's security operations, and it's gratifying that they took him seriously enough to spy on him for 25 years. Here's a 1978 Mountie profile prepared by one Cpl. Schmidt: "He first came to the attention of the Security Service in 1964 when he visited Cuba under the sponsorship of the Fair Play for Cuba Committee . . . He is recognized as one of the best (immigration) lawyers in Toronto . . . He has supported every progressive cause over the years, from the anti-Viet Nam war movement to Prisoners Rights . . . He is very upset by what he views as excessive police powers and consequently he is quick to condemn police activities in any given situation . . .

In the past, Copeland has not advocated or condoned violence . . . He has a genuine desire to assist people and sincerely believes in bringing about positive social change (but) it is unlikely that he will sacrifice his material comfort by committing any illegality in pursuit of his goals."

Except for the snarky final remark, Copeland preferred this memo to a 1977 one by another Security Service officer who obviously didn't appreciate the subject's mischievousness: "He examined my badge very thoroughly in a manner of uncertainty, as if suspicious of the identity provided . . . Copeland asked if I did any other work beside my security screenings . . . He stated it must be a very boring job . . .

"He is a small man with a large ego, who is excited and volatile and with a high degree of paranoia." No wonder Copeland was seen as a security risk.

Now there is a subtle difference between being paranoid and being persecuted, as this very file indicates. As did Copeland's many encounters with the RCMP both before and after this appraisal was written. As he long insisted, for example, and the 1981 MacDonald Commission on the Mounties' dirty tricks finally confirmed, Copeland's phone was tapped for six months in 1972.

Then there's the three-page 1976 Security Service biography of him — stamped "secret" by the RCMP, but now "declassified" by CSIS — that concluded: "He has become one of the leading radical lawyers in Toronto supporting every progressive cause that comes up . . . He is going to be of continual and growing security service interest, because of his position of influence . . ." Paranoia indeed.

So even though, as Cpl. Schmidt duly reported, Copeland never "advocated or condoned violence," his very public activities were deemed worthy of frequent surveillance — that's spying to us, folks — from 1964 right to the present. In fact, not the least curious parts of his file are press clippings from RCMP files dated as recently as October, 1988, outlining a case Copeland was handling for an Armenian whom CSIS wished to deport. CSIS now swears it's interested only in counter-terrorism and counter-espionage, yet the Mounties are keeping clippings on Copeland's present legal career. What don't we understand here?

We come, then, to my own unworthy record. It covers, I'm afraid, a mere five years of my sordid subversive career, ending two decades back. Does it mean I've failed in everything since? Did I never again agitate the powers-that-be? Have I done nothing worth spying on for 20 years? Can I not even have my name spelled properly? Kaplan indeed!

It's true those few years in the late 1960s were kind of special. It's sweet nostalgia to read of my arrest and brief imprisonment in 1966 by the Rhodesian security police, of my subsequent cross-Canada speaking tour to raise support for majority rule in Rhodesia (now Zimbabwe), of my 1968 participation in a demonstration on Parliament Hill to demand that Canada promote a ceasefire in the Nigerian Civil War, of my role in creating the Waffle movement (though some of my friends would properly resent the description of me as "the major Waffle group theoretician"). But frankly, all that's old hat. Hell's bells, my mother could've told them all that.

But not even my mother could have known that in 1970 I was apparently blackballed for some forgotten position or other with CIDA. "I doubt if he is the proper type of person to represent Canada overseas on a CIDA project," one Mountie concluded.

Whereupon, "Director, Security and Intelligence," wrote "Confidentially" to CIDA repeating the notorious facts laid out above, but including this statement: "According to the press, Caplan was suspected of preparing to use violence in opposition to white supremacy policies" in Rhodesia. I'm reluctant to admit it, but there was no truth whatever to that accusation, as two minutes of real police work would have revealed even to Inspector Clouseau.

The letter to CIDA concluded: "While we attach no particular security significance to Caplan's activities at this time, we are nevertheless providing you with the details in view of his potential as a possible source of embarrassment to your Department and the Government of Canada." Well that's not bad for a start, eh Comrades? And, one prays, it is merely a start. Copeland is already launching new appeals to get the rest of the goodies that — remember? — may or may not exist about us; I'm confident I'll easily catch up with him when all is ultimately revealed.

Look, it's not so much that the Mounties saw themselves as thought-control police. It's not their complete failure to distinguish between dissent and subversion or between treason and open opposition that gets us. It's this: Since so many Mounties spent so many hours clipping all those newspaper stories about us, collecting all those meeting notices and attending all those dreary leftie meetings, writing all those tedious profiles of us, and especially since everything we've both done has been deliberately as public as possible — well, surely the least we can do is try to get hold of all that bumph?

We radicals are, after all, nothing if not compassionate.

* * *

1990 FOR MANY DECADES, the responsibility for protecting our nation from subversion and treason lay in the trusted hands of the Royal Canadian Mounted Police. So dedicated were our Mounties to getting their man — and woman, too, if duty demanded — that hundreds of them spent thousands of hours pouring over such confidential sources as daily newspapers in their staunch pursuit of notorious menaces to national security like trade unionists, peace activists and contributors to small, financially precarious left-wing magazines that often survived thanks largely to RCMP subscriptions.

Like me, my old lawyer pal Paul Copeland is a well-known humanitarian, and we decided last year that all that devoted Mountie effort shouldn't go to waste. So he applied for both our files and, lo and behold, each of us eventually received a highly-edited and much blacked-out selection of once confidential and secret documents like newspaper articles proving conclusively that we had spent our lives doing exactly what we always proudly claimed we had spent our lives doing. After writing about our experience, I received letters from numerous envious readers demanding that we explain how they too can show their appreciation to the Mounties for those years of thankless slogging. We are happy to oblige.

4

You can actually follow much of this process without a lawyer at all. Up to a point it's quite straightforward and government departments themselves, when they respond to you, will often helpfully explain the next choices you can make. So here goes:

1. You need a Personal Information Request Form. They should be available from the post office but naturally are usually not. So write for yours to the Privacy Commissioner of Canada, 112 Kent St., Ottawa KIA 1H3.

2. You need to decide which of the many possible data or information banks you want to try to locate with this form. The government of Canada publishes, under the Privacy Act, a thick Personal Information Index in which each government agency lists its own data banks; there are plenty. You can find one at the Central Reference Library or buy it at the government book store. You can apply for as many data banks as you want, but send in a separate Request Form for each one.

While data banks from the Solicitor-General and the RCMP may contain security-related information, Copeland believes that the most fruitful data bank at the moment is the Canadian Security Intelligence Services (CSIS) Records #SIS/P-PU-015. It contains material that CSIS is in the process of destroying, since it is now considered to have been in bad taste to have collected it in the first place. So this is probably the data bank many people will want to aim at, and they should do so pronto.

Write to Departmental Privacy Co-ordinator, CSIS, P.O. Box 9732, Ottawa Postal Terminal, Ottawa K1G 4G4. You don't have to say Paul and Gerry sent you.

3. The government must reply to your request in 30 days, but is entitled to a 30-day extension. You can complain about the extension to the Privacy Commissioner at the above address.

4. If you're refused access to the data bank or consider the documents you receive incomplete — Copeland's files were so much more voluminous than mine that I was sorely tempted to hang up my red sweater — you can complain again to the Privacy Commissioner. But don't be unrealistic: The Privacy Act affords the government an abundance of excuses to refuse you access to your own files, or, in a perfect Kafkaesque situation, to refuse to tell you whether or not there are even any files on you that you can't have.

5. If you're unhappy with the way the Privacy Commissioner handles the matter, you can still appeal to a federal court judge for a review of the denial of access. But at this stage, Copeland advises, you really need a lawyer's help and financing this adventure then becomes an issue you must consider.

Look, let's talk straight here. Over the years, the Mounties cared enough to collect some 500,000 files on risky Canadians. The very least you — and 499,999 others just like you — can do is to show you're grateful enough to want to see your own personal collection. Why not write today? Show the government how much you appreciate being spied on to keep Canada glorious and free.

✻　✻　✻

Moral Victories

1985   NEW DEMOCRATS across the country will be watching the resumption of Parliament with mixed reactions. Rarely has the eternal dilemma of Canadian socialism presented itself with such clarity.

Certainly there is much good news. The party's standing, according to the polls, is up since the September 4 election last year. The leader is perceived to be doing a highly effective job as head of his party. The federal caucus is functioning well and deserves much of the credit for undermining many right-wing government initiatives. On universality, on equality for women, on indexed old-age pensions, on Star Wars, New Democrat MPs have made a concrete contribution to greater Canadian well-being. This is an exciting truth reflecting what democratic socialism is all about in Canada.

At the same time, the NDP has won the government of Yukon, has a real crack at British Columbia, could hold Manitoba and is growing in popularity across the Maritimes.

This is a genuine success story, but it needs a larger perspective. After all, much of this good news can be turned on its head. The NDP has apparently not succeeded in replacing the Liberals as the second party, as many expected after the last election. And the Liberal Opposition undeniably had a share in keeping the Government close to the centre of the spectrum.

As for the provincial electorate picture, it is at best murky. The NDP could lose British Columbia again, blow Manitoba, fail to win back Saskatchewan, remain negligible in Quebec and lose the momentum in the Atlantic provinces. Most precarious of all is Ontario, where the Liberal triumph and the NDP-Liberal pact destroyed a generation of NDP mythology that has not been replaced by a coherent set of credible alternative assumptions.

There is another, more fundamental, concern that disturbs some of us self-styled realists in the party. Although many New Democrats

7

50th anniversary convention of the CCF, *Regina,* 1983.
Tommy Douglas, Caplan (federal secretary), Alan Blakeney,
leading a rendition of "Solidarity Forever."
PHOTO FEATURES LTD.

dream of forming a government, too little serious analysis is attempted to explain why the NDP has remained in third place nationally since its inception as the Co-Operative Commonwealth Federation some 53 years ago.

In the 1980 election, the NDP won 20 per cent of the national vote; a year later the polls showed it sailing at 26 per cent. On the eve of the 1984 election, it was 11 per cent; it actually won 19 per cent and it now stands at 26 per cent again. But what is more important than these dramatic fluctuations is that the party leadership can't account for them.

Put another way, the party does not know how to maintain or to surpass its present level of support.

In fact, the problem is profound. Precisely what is unique and honorable about the NDP — indeed, without which its entire raison d'être would disappear — is its commitment to an ideology, a vision of Canada, and policies that are, as a package, anathema to the large majority of Canadians: a significant redistribution of wealth and power, hostility to the business world and its ethics, greater state intervention in the economy, some nationalization, centralized economic planning, abolition of capital punishment, affirmative action for women and for many minority groups, more rights for workers to join unions, the right of public-sector employees to strike, withdrawal from the North Atlantic Treaty Organization. That's why most Canadians respect New Democrats for their principles and social conscience and do not trust them to run the store.

What too many New Democrats want, in other words, is the best of all worlds. They want to espouse unpopular causes, yet win electoral support at the same time. It is a contradiction many in the NDP are reluctant to admit, even though it profoundly affects the party's behaviour in the political arena.

Here is the dilemma of the NDP in Canada: to remain true to its principles at the probable expense of permanently eschewing political power, or to move further to the centre where it risks losing its soul and becoming indistinguishable from other "liberal" opposition parties. As long as the NDP can remain effective in its dual role as the nation's conscience and the source of creative new ideas, that is its most influential — and honorable — contribution. That other New Democrats disagree only makes the debate more fascinating. The important truth is that the present political reality makes this the opportune moment for the party to launch that debate.

* * *

1986   IS IT NOT CURIOUS how we revere them once they are
────────   gone? Heaven knows they were not so universally
appreciated in their primes. It would be satisfying to say the powerful
establishments they fought all their lives suddenly discovered their
virtues only when they were safely out of harm's way. But the
undeniably sad fact is that even the common folks in whose name
they battled failed to embrace them much of the time.

Tommy Douglas, David Lewis, Andy Brewin: all gone now. Stanley
Knowles and Grace MacInnis: well out of the action. They were the
architects of a new and, to some, heretical political philosophy which
has come to play if not precisely a central role in Canadian political
life, at least an indispensable one.

If J.S. Woodsworth was the Moses of democratic socialism in
Canada, his successors were the pioneers, the creators, the builders.
First they established the Cooperative Commonwealth Foundation,
the very name reflecting a great deal more idealism than P.R. skills;
did 5% of Canadians ever know what the initials CCF stand for? Nor,
mostly, did they care; except for Saskatchewan, where Tommy
Douglas created his island of socialism in a sea of North American
capitalism in 1944, the party/movement failed to make significant
lasting electoral gains anywhere. Canadians may respect movements;
in the end they vote for parties.

True, there were those thrilling war-time years when the CCF
seemed to embody the hopes and aspirations of a people sick of war
and depression, and true too there were the endless little successes
piled one on top of the other which led to a social welfare system
that almost befitted a civilized nation. But when even Stanley
Knowles was defeated in the Diefenbaker sweep of 1958 — although
I never found a Winnipegger who fessed up to voting against him — it
was time for a vaguely modernized version of the CCF to emerge from
the ashes.

So they tempted Tommy out of Regina and put him on a stage that
proved too large for him to ever to master. Andrew Brewin, the most
personally lovable of them all as well as a man of courage and
integrity, ran for the dozenth time, and finally had to discard his
reputation for making the best loser speeches in Canada.

But Tommy was defeated in 1962 in his very own Regina, and his
provincial government toppled without him. He moved ignomini-
ously to British Columbia, but even there he suffered another
personal electoral defeat before he resigned as leader.

David Lewis had at last taken his rightful place in parliament in 1962. But the very next year the Pearson Liberals drove an anachronistic Tory party out of urban Canada, sweeping David away in the tide. He returned, thank our blessings, in time to stand with Tommy and Andrew against Pierre Trudeau's diabolically gratuitous imposition of the War Measures Act, and in so doing their generation of Canadians gave mine our pride in our party and our cause.

But having succeeded Tommy as leader, having given us the magnificence of the Corporate Welfare Bum campaign in 1972, having forced on the vulnerable Trudeau minority government the most progressive legislation it ever passed, Lewis was defeated once again in his own seat in the run-off election two years later.

What always struck me most about the entire little band was the absence of bitterness. Oh sure, there was profound weariness, a permanent failure to understand why their message never seemed more credible to the masses at whom it was directed. But they never succumbed to the so-easy temptation of cynicism. They never quit. They never dismissed their defeats as evidence of the unworthiness of ordinary Canadians. They never even resorted to simplistic conspiracy theories, blaming the capitalist media and their lackies. Instead, they just went on fighting, right to the end.

Yet if anything should have made them cynical, it was the glory that came from their life-long foes after the battles were over. I've been to the memorial services now for Andy, David and Tommy, and it's always impossible not to wonder how their memories can be so glowing, yet their cause so unacceptably dangerous. And through all the reverential platitudes bestowed by the old-boys' network, the gap between haves and have-nots in Canada continues to grow.

We've never needed their kind more than we do today.

1987   "MOST CANADIANS have viewed socialism as an ideology designed to stifle their most precious aspirations." So I wrote in an MA thesis more than 25 years ago, trying to explain the consistent electoral failure of the old CCF movement/party as it lay on its death bed.

A dozen years later, after three highly disappointing federal election campaigns, the words seemed entirely suitable to repeat in a book that attempted by inference to explain the failure of the CCF's successor, the New Democratic Party.

And a mere two and a half years ago, after an election campaign in which the NDP was deemed to have pulled off a miracle by winning 19% of the popular vote, it seemed to me demonstrable that, as I wrote, the NDP has "an ideology, a vision of Canada, and policies which are, as a package, anathema to the large majority of Canadians ... Most Canadians respect New Democrats for their principles and social conscience [but] do not trust them to run the store."

Something, clearly, has changed dramatically, even qualitatively, over the past few months. For many months, I remained a skeptic, despite the NDP's remarkably high showing in public opinion polls. I am now convinced, however, that the political phenomenon we are witnessing may well be an enduring rather than an ephemeral one.

There is reason to believe we are in the midst of a genuine historical revolution in Canadian politics.

Not everything has changed, of course. Some of the notions that matter most to New Democrats would by no means meet with widespread public enthusiasm, and research by both Gallup and Angus Reid Associates demonstrates that the NDP is still trusted far more on human and social issues than on economic and managerial ones.

But the difference today is this: these factors are no longer seen by 80% of Canadians as constraints against supporting the party. On the basis of a considerable amount of private and public research, two new propositions can be stated with some confidence: In comparison with the other two parties, the NDP no longer looks like such a risky venture for voters. And increasingly, voters are focusing on those aspects of the NDP they find attractive rather than being put off by those they find dubious. This constitutes a revolution in political perceptions in Canada.

Voters seem to be seeking three main attributes from their politicians at the moment, reflecting their great disillusionment with the Mulroney government and their growing jadedness with the political system as a whole; these are trust, fairness and competence.

Both polling research and general impressions tell us that the Mulroney government is perceived as being neither competent nor trustworthy; the question of fairness never even arises.

The Liberals, as their failure to cash in fully on the government's woes indicates, have a major encumbrance in their leader. Voters have not yet forgotten or forgiven John Turner's unparalleled ineptitude in the 1984 campaign. They greet with growing cynicism his rhetoric about straight talk as they witness his stubborn refusal to articulate clear policy positions. And they are skeptical as they try to reconcile his former Bay St. connections with his present reincarnation as a progressive reformer.

On the other hand, New Democrats have always been seen as politicians for whom fairness was an overriding characteristic — that is why the party has been rated so highly for its concern with human values that mattered to ordinary Canadians — and about whom hints of personal corruption or conflict-of-interest have rarely been raised.

For many years, these long-standing views of the NDP were not deemed as salient to voting intentions as the negative perceptions. Now the performances of the other parties have substantially increased the centrality of these positive characteristics.

So has one other factor: Ed Broadbent. The NDP leader became something of a folk hero during the 1984 election, and the process is now complete. He embodies in a way that a majority of Canadians find increasingly appealing the virtues of integrity, straight talk and fairness.

But he has begun to do something else as well: he is starting to be seen as not only a decent and trustworthy person, but as one of substance, who knows how the system runs and who would not threaten Canadians' desire for stable government if he ever had to operate it — especially compared with the alternatives. In other words, the risk factor that has always imposed a low ceiling on NDP support has been significantly reduced.

It would, of course, be foolhardy to predict that the New Democrat's Golden Age is truly beginning. But if my analysis of the reasons for the present situation is roughly accurate, and if the party plays it cleverly — as it has certainly been doing to this point — the NDP's future is open in a way that has never been true before.

✳ ✳ ✳

1989   "WE'RE REALLY WORRIED about the rural areas," one of the NDP's brightest prairie lights told me. "They just don't like some of our policies: our support for gay rights, for example, or for choice on abortions. And they don't love our opposition to capital punishment." So should the NDP drop its commitment to these causes?

Are they unnecessarily offensive to lots of otherwise potential NDP voters? Is the embrace of such positions central to contemporary socialism, or are they merely the obsession of narrow special interest groups? And how does the NDP calculate the right balance between principle and politics when the two are in conflict, as they seem to be with wearisome regularity?

The dilemma is hardly a rural one alone; it has defined the evolution of socialism within the capitalist democratic world for the past century. Other than some relatively trivial matters — formulating a wealth-creating national economic policy for a globalized universe, reconciling anglophone and francophone views on Quebec, devising structure to redress western Canadian alienation, and producing realistic policies to deal with such shameful phenomena as poverty in Canada, the status and condition of aboriginal peoples, child and women abuse, and Third World re-development — no issue is more central to the future nature of democratic socialism in Canada than how the NDP deals with fundamental positions when they are known to be politically unpopular.

The first question, logically, is to determine when a principle is so fundamental that to surrender it is to surrender your very raison d'être. For me, the right of a women to choose whether or not to have an abortion is a precondition of women's equality in our society. The right to choose one's own sexual orientation seems vital to a free society, while state executions intrinsically violate all that socialism implies about human development.

Or take that other symbolic issue, NATO. Beyond question, most Canadians firmly believe Canada should remain in the alliance; most New Democrats, including me, disagree profoundly. Remaining in an American-dominated instrument that inherently perpetuates the lunacy of the arms race seems self-evidently irrational for Canada. Most of us also reject a defence policy that would be as costly as this government's. These views may have unfortunate electoral consequences, but they're why, after all, we're in this party where the necessary pursuit of power must always be rooted in policies based on our principles.

There has been some curious talk of late in the NDP that winning government must be the party's central goal. It's really a red herring, since no serious New Democrat wouldn't cherish the opportunity to govern, while it's equally obvious that if the party had a magical formula to achieve that end — other than becoming Liberals — it would've done so long ago.

It also debases the historic contribution of the CCF-NDP, and its leaders, to imply that forming a government is the overriding criterion by which they should be judged. Look at two of the examples that Ed Broadbent himself uses to demonstrate the party's influence: the extorting by J.S. Woodsworth of Canada's first old age pensions from Mackenzie King in 1926 and by David Lewis of PetroCan from Pierre Trudeau in 1973. Woodsworth's caucus consisted of precisely two members, including himself; David Lewis', of 31. Yet, they wielded real power.

Or look at that legendary moment in October, 1970, that remains for so many New Democrats the proudest in their political lives: the party's courageous opposition to the imposition of the War Measures Act by the Trudeau government, with fully 90 per cent of all Canadians staunchly behind Trudeau's harsh crushing of civil liberties. It did not then seem unworthy to be the conscience of the nation, nor embarrassing to be part of a movement that put principle ahead of popular favour.

Of course, no one, not even navel-gazing socialist purists, seek defeat as a noble end in itself. It remains crucially important that the party articulate an economic policy that merits credibility and deep-sixes some of its anachronistic hobby horses such as nationalizing a bank or the cable industry. And perhaps Ed Broadbent's most lasting achievement is to remind party activists that they must reconcile their proper anti-business biases with economic policies that include the productive aspects of a market economy as an integral component. It is so, after all, in revered Sweden.

The socialist struggle for a more egalitarian and just society never ends, whoever leads the NDP. But the need to refine the means to that utopia has now become paramount for the Canadian left.

✳ ✳ ✳

1989   NOT EVERYONE IN CANADA will regret Stephen Lewis' decision not to go after the NDP leadership. Other candidates can now get on with the race. Reporters can relax and put away the dictionaries that are obligatory when covering Lewis; one fan urged him to run since Canadians would follow anywhere a leader who spoke in sentences. Our reactionary government can look forward to future question period sessions with rather less terror in their hearts.

Lewis' handlers can now stop stewing about how they would deal with his egregious corduroy suits. And I myself can cease fretting about whether I could get my terrific new slogan accepted by the party's right-wing:

DISGUSTED WITH CAPITALISM?

DON'T GET MAD.

GET EVEN.

GET STEPHEN.

Everyone by now presumably understands that Lewis agonized excruciatingly before making his final, irreversible decision. ("Are you okay?" I asked just before last week's press conference. "Of course," he replied. "I'm having a nervous breakdown.") But a remarkable truth about the wooing process of the past months has not yet been noted.

Not once, not in a single conversation, did Lewis ever reflect on the probable electoral consequences of his decision. I was assured by both astute journalists and pollsters that Lewis was a snap for official opposition and — who knew? — maybe even beyond, and by Liberal insiders that he would cause a major defection of progressive Liberals to the NDP. I faithfully reported these conversations to him, after which they were never again discussed nor, I believe, considered. The outcome of the next election was simply not the issue.

The high point of the draft-Lewis endeavors came on a Saturday night in April. In our living room, to meet with Lewis and his indispensable partner Michele Landsberg, assembled every prominent New Democrat in Canada who was being touted as a possible leadership candidate — Alexa McDonough, Roy Romanow, Bob White, Bob Rae — plus former Saskatchewan premier Allan Blakeney and Manitoba leader Gary Doer. For Canadian socialists it was as if, a generation ago, David Lewis, Tommy Douglas, Andy Brewin, Grace MacInnis, Stanley Knowles and Frank Scott had all gathered for an evening.

In that memorable, historic session, with the guests using every conceivable argument to persuade Lewis to run, not once did any participant even allude to electoral considerations. Every argument came down, finally to the point made perfectly by Blakeney: "The question for people like us," he said, "is how you make the most effective contribution to socialism."

Not: how to make lots of dough. Not: how to become CEO of some fancy corporation. Not: how to be famous. Not: how many seats you're going to win. Only: how a socialist helps make the world a more just and decent place. Lewis simply decided that he wanted to pursue this goal not in Ottawa but internationally.

What even I had not fully understood until recently was the full magnitude of Lewis' impact outside Canada. In his years at the U.N. and since, Lewis forged a literally unparalleled global reputation as an eloquent champion of the wretched of the Earth. He has remained the Secretary-General's special representative on African economic recovery — unpaid, by the way — and is a treasured friend of Africa for his contribution to the continent's development plans. In May, both the *Wall Street Journal* and the *Guardian* of Britain reported his key role at a Paris meeting where the Economic Commission for Africa launched a major, and substantially successful, critique of the World Bank. Nor does anyone doubt the centrality of his influence in Brian Mulroney's now discarded crusade against apartheid.

International development agencies like UNICEF, peace groups and environmental associations alike look to him for support and leadership. Influential officials even of countries where he is less cherished — a couple of unnamed superpowers, for example — pay him earnest attention. The man counts out there. It's where he now belongs. Only his own and his family's lifelong commitment to Canadian socialism even made the NDP leadership an issue to be wrestled with. There's a larger arena that needs him.

Canadians will have repeated opportunity over the coming years to be proud that one of their own is playing a star role in global affairs. But Canadian socialists will be even prouder: Stephen Lewis will be there, all right, fighting against exploitation and oppression and inequality and for that more just and decent world to which he has given his life at whatever level he's operated. Those grieving his decision not to run should be consoled that people like themselves beyond Canada are today rejoicing.

*　*　*

*Election night, 1975. The Big Blue Machine loses
its majority for the first time in years; and the* NDP,
*under Lewis, became the official opposition.
Caplan as* NDP *campaign manager for provincial campaign.*
TORONTO STAR SYNDICATE

1990   CAN I INTEREST YOU IN A BOOK on Eastern European
————————   Jewish socialism before the Russian Revolution? What
about a study of the social gospel tradition in Canada? Care to learn
why Cambridge in the 1930s, instead of Oxford, produced all those
Communist spies? Or which international figure has the most repul-
sively chewed fingernails?

Now all these glorious tales and countless more can be yours all in
one fat and fabulous volume written with great panache by Cameron
Smith and called *Unfinished Journey: The Lewis Family*. It is a
genuine saga, a monumental work of scholarship and research, and
as eccentric and fascinating as the three generations of Lewis men it
describes. It's one of the best Canadian non-fiction books we have.

Smith's style is equal to the subject matter. Here's his description
of the romance between David and Sophie Lewis: "It was a love that
shimmered, not like moonlight across quiet lakes, but like heat waves
rising from a summer road." But once they came back to Canada
from their idyll in Oxford and David became my most illustrious
predecessor as first federal secretary of the old CCF, Smith writes:
"Rarely were there long walks or concerts or outings together, or the
extravagant pleasures of letting a whole afternoon, dappled in
intimacies, drip slowly through their fingers."

In fact, Lewis' utter dedication to the cause of Canadian socialism
was paid for by his family, and Smith treats the subject with
uncommon sensitivity. The notion that "sacrifice, however much it
hurt, was honorable," he sees as a male value, and notes that being
so purely, so selflessly dedicated to a cause, is, ironically, a male form
of selfishness and self-indulgence. "So, I shan't see you for two
weeks," David typically writes home to Sophie. "It makes me sad.
But duty is duty. And I know that you . . . won't mind." It was as if
her role was to accept that his role was to sacrifice her and the family
for the greater good of the cause. But in fact she bitterly resented the
position that he, in typical male fashion, unilaterally assigned to her.

Unfinished Journey has two overriding lessons for Canadian
socialists. Smith observes that no Lewis ever believed he would live
to realize the dream of a socialist Canada. Obviously, Stephen told
him, David would've loved to see the CCF or NDP in power, but "he
never imagined it possible. Just as I never imagined it possible and
thoroughly accepted that. Accepted his analysis that there's an awful
lot to achieve on the road to Utopia. You don't have to be the one
who ushers it in." This remains a cardinal truth about present

Canadian political realities, even though some New Democrats, disdaining the plain lessons of history, consider it a form of defeatism, almost a betrayal of the cause.

But there's a far more profound lesson here. Although David Lewis offended party purists by pragmatically advocating approaches and rhetoric that altered with changing circumstances, he never ever lost his passionate, driving fury at the inherent immorality of capitalism. Even as he accepted the necessity of a mixed economy and the role of the market, he never forgave the profit motive for those it cruelly turned into economic losers, nor for making moral losers out of all of us.

"We do not," he never tired of repeating — and you can almost hear the Old Testament severity — "we do not believe that profit is the be-all and end-all of life. On the contrary, we believe the profit idea is immoral . . . and that people are capable of being motivated by things other than profit and that society ought to appeal to these other sources of motivation rather than to their self-seeking search for private gain. . . ."

Idealism's not the worst sin in this world, and Canada may never have needed it more desperately than now, as we are endlessly entreated to worship the values of the marketplace, to embrace competitiveness lustily, to pursue individual greed as a positive good.

Maishe Lewis had an alternative dream, a dream of "a free world, a new world, a world of justice, a world of equality." Truth is, we're not much closer to it today than when he was born in Poland 102 years ago. But the journey's not abandoned; it's just unfinished.

✳   ✳   ✳

Just Liberals

1986   IT IS NOT TRUE, widespread gossip to the contrary notwithstanding, that Brian Mulroney and Ed Broadbent clandestinely launder money to the John Turner leadership campaign. It is true, however, that both of them would love to do so, because Turner is regarded by both camps as one of their secret weapons.

This, of course, is precisely the argument being made by that supreme political hardball player, Marc Lalonde, now busily playing Brutus to John Turner's back. Loyalty and fair play are fine in their place, he acknowledges. But ask yourself, he invites the 3,000 delegates to the Liberal leadership review at month's end: "Who would the Conservatives and the NDP most wish to see as leader of the Liberal Party at the next election?" In fact, the answer is not as self-evident as Lalonde indicates. After all, John Turner's possible replacement matters to the argument. Keith Davey, point man for the old-guard disloyalists, offers us Lloyd Axworthy, Paul Martin Jr., Jim Coutts, and Dennis Mills. A list to conjure with. Others throw in the Liberals' next president, Michel Robert, Lloyd's little brother Tom Axworthy, and Don Johnston for a second try. And then there's PET himself.

I have news for Lalonde. Both the Tories and the NDP would kill to have any of the men listed replace John Turner. Since the name of the game is winning — the sum and substance of Lalonde's position — Turner's foes are shrewdly offering their party, and the lucky voters, a veritable cornucopia of these irresistibly charismatic figures. Personally, I intend to throw the legendary Caplan machine behind Dennis Mills.

In fact, what we are witnessing in the old-guard leadership of the anti-Turner forces is a shameless, unabashed conceit that their self-interest is identical to the self-interest of Canada itself, and a determination either to regain control of "their" party or to take it into oblivion with them. That's why Lalonde's letter to the delegates is bereft of a single issue of substance, policy or principle.

Reacting to the letter, Turner's Quebec lieutenant, Raymond Garneau, understood that "Marc, by his tone and his pontifical 'I,' has brought back that image of arrogance, that divine right to govern, that Canadians, with good reason, have been trying to get rid of for a number of years." Boy, do I wish I said that first.

The irony of Lalonde's position is that only one candidate fits his bill, Jean Chrétien. Yet Lalonde supported Turner against Chrétien for the leadership, and brutally cut Chrétien and his people out of decision-making roles in the 1984 campaign. Typically, he has never hidden his contempt for Chrétien's shallowness, and considers him intellectually deficient for the Prime Minister's job.

Yet the single alternative to Turner that both Conservative and New Democrats fear is Jean Chrétien. He alone could steal support from both left and right. He would end any hope of Mulroney holding on to Quebec as a base, and would re-attract to the Liberal camp those many citizens who, dismayed by John Turner's lack of personal appeal and Brian Mulroney's apparently infinite untrustworthiness, have been "parking" their support with the NDP.

The stakes in the Liberal leadership review are, therefore, unusually significant. We are at a potential watershed in our political history, where, for the first time ever, the NDP has an opportunity to break out beyond its traditional ceiling of less than 20% of the vote. With Turner (or Dennis Mills?) as Liberal leader, and the Mulroney government's reverse Midas touch, the next election would certainly see a minority government with the NDP not only holding the balance of power, but quite plausibly electing 60 or more MPs, some of them from Quebec.

Which is precisely why we can be confident that John Turner will not be allowed to stay around long enough to fight the 1988 election.

*   *   *

1986   THE CONSERVATIVES, the New Democrats and the media are having the time of their lives. When has the world last witnessed Canada's Natural Governing Party in such public turmoil, riven by precisely the kind of dissension, disloyalty and internecine warfare that, for so many glorious decades, characterized the hapless Tories.

Allow me to answer that question: the last time was smack in the middle of the 1984 election campaign, when members of the John Turner team and members of the former Trudeau team were shooting at each other in public. You remember: under great pressure from Marc Lalonde and other Trudeauites — but not Jean Chrétien, whom Lalonde ruthlessly cut out of the campaign's inner sanctum — Turner's man Bill Lee was turfed out in a highly unceremonious manner to be replaced by that renowned miracle worker, the Rainmaker himself, Keith Davey.

Bill Lee was a true gentleman, and the three national campaign managers — Lee, Norman Atkins and I — all had high regard for each other and all kept in touch to make sure the campaigns of our respective parties, so far as we had control over them, stayed at a relatively high level.

In the event, Davey focussed the Liberal campaign more than it had been, yet he confused the electorate even more by introducing a John Turner who, first, was no longer accessible to the media, and, secondly, had suddenly moved to the left of the political spectrum. Turner, who had been uncomfortable in his return to public life even saying things he believed in, was palpably unhappy in his new role as Keith Davey's progressive puppet. Voters, who are not always as pliantly manipulable as some political strategists would like, clearly sensed the awkwardness of the new Turner, and the campaign ended, as you will recall with a huge grin, in a debacle for the Liberals of unparalleled proportions. How sweet it was.

And is. Having in their turn largely been cut out by the new Turner team — Turner asked Michael Kirby, instead of Keith Davey, to start preparing for the next general election — the Trudeau old guard has decided that they're either going to regain control of the party they still think of as theirs, or they're going to leave it but in a horrible shambles.

Detached observers, such as this humble scribe, cannot help noticing the mischief the old guard had created even before their latest campaign of de-stabilization. They have successfully imposed on Turner and his advisers their preposterous proposition that the Liberals must position themselves on the left-of-centre if they are to return to their mythical glory days of yore.

In fact under no previous leader were they anything but a mish mash of left, right and centre. But they had, as an immutable base, their vast repository of safe Quebec seats — which had absolutely nothing to do with ideology one way or another — and it was not in fact such a herculean task to boot home enough other seats in the Maritimes, Ontario and B.C. to give them more than the self-destructive, undisciplined Tories.

In the face of that truth, the Liberals still were able to win majorities in only 3 of the 11 elections held since 1957, while the Tories did it twice. Without that Quebec Liberal base, the perception of a natural governing party would be very different indeed.

As it is, the ostensible need to be seen as left-of-centre is haunting John Turner now as it did during his pathetic election performance. His awkwardness as a progressive is apparent to all, and together with his impossible television style makes voters turn off him in droves. That he runs far behind his party, and far behind the other two leaders, is in no way surprising. But part of the responsibility must go to those who have persuaded him that he must try to be something that is wholly unnatural to him.

John Turner will win a majority of the delegates to the weekend Liberal convention, although many of them will cast their votes for him with the utmost ambivalence and lack of enthusiasm. That will make it irresistible for the old guard to continue undermining him for the next two years, which in turn will ensure that Tories, New Democrats and the media continue to have the time of their lives.

*　*　*

1986　SO CANADA has a new national hero. "Good luck and take care of yourself," Montreal radio interview show host Pierre Pascau saluted him. "I've always thought of him as a Boy Scout in the best sense of the word," an older professor pal explained — "the fraternity, the loyalty, the idealism." Gourmet Gandhi Backs The Kids, read the headline on a column by *Ottawa Citizen* editor Keith Spicer.

They were all referring, of course, to Senator Jacques Hébert, now in the 11th day of a hunger strike aimed at forcing the Government to restore funding to the Katimavik youth program.

Senator Hébert is a man of courage and conviction. He was a crusading human rights advocate against the authoritarian Quebec regime of Maurice Duplessis. He made a significant contribution to Canadian reform. Katimavik was his baby. He importuned his friend Pierre Trudeau to create it, and it is plausible that the Brian Mulroney Government has scuttled it out of partisan pique.

On Hunger Strike For Youth, proclaimed one Quebec paper in a bold red headline. He "has pushed youth and its shattered post-recession hopes to the top of the nation's agenda," according to Mr. Spicer. He "reminds us . . . how rare it is for any man or woman in Canadian politics to care this much about anything . . . it's beautiful to behold."

Nuts! Not to any responsible citizen who has the slightest respect for parliamentary government, it isn't. Senator Hébert is seriously challenging the principle of political democracy by threatening to kill himself by starvation if his particular concern is not met by the elected Government of Canada.

What does his hunger strike mean for our democratic process? Mr. Spicer asks. "It means . . . that the traditional parliamentary ways have failed. Hébert . . . exhausted all of them — speeches, lobbying, publicity, even a straight-from-the-heart public letter to the PM."

Imagine that. Even a straight-from-the-heart letter to Brian Mulroney failed to change the Government's mind. No wonder the man decided he must stop eating.

To draw a parallel with Mahatma Gandhi is to sully the name of the greatest proponent of civil disobedience in this wretched century. To be sure, Gandhi protested through hunger strikes. But there were two circumstances that make even the hint of comparison with the tactics of Senator Hébert ludicrous. In the first place, Gandhi developed his strategy of civil disobedience for a people suffering under foreign domination. Canadians can blame only themselves for this Tory Government.

In the second place, Gandhi fought, and fasted, for the freedom of his country, indeed precisely to establish the kind of self-government Canadians take for granted. To equate the Indian struggle for political independence with the maintenance of the Katimavik program is irresponsible nonsense.

Most people can barely discuss Katimavik knowledgeably for longer than 40 seconds. It was a pretty useful minor project that the Government was foolish to scupper. But the Government has done more foolish things than this and will, we can predict with lugubrious confidence, do far worse before it is finally turfed out.

It may well restore capital punishment. It will significantly increase the level of hardship for the poor in Canada. It is cutting foreign aid.

It is exacerbating the arms race by not banning the testing of cruise missiles in Canada. Do you blackmail the Government by threatening to kill yourself each time your side is in danger of losing?

Did Senator Hébert starve himself to death when Mr. Trudeau introduced the War Measures Act, by any democratic standard one of the truly infamous acts in Canadian history? And what happens when an hysterical physician tries a similar trick to force the Ontario Government to back down on extra-billing, or when someone from the National Citizens' Coalition decides to fast until the federal civil service is reduced?

These are not frivolous analogies. Senator Hébert has no right to demand that each of his personal causes be adopted by the elected Government of Canada. Civil disobedience in a democracy, let alone the threat of self-destruction, is acceptable only under the most extreme circumstances. The preservation of Katimavik hardly applies.

Senator Hébert's friends say he is capable of dying for this cause. Whether he does or whether he blackmails the Government into temporary capitulation, it will be a black day for democracy in Canada.

*　*　*

1987　　CREDIT WHERE CREDIT IS DUE. The other side is not invariably wrong, after all. Heaven knows that the Tories have been wrong often enough in the past while: a destructive and opportunistic postal policy; a cold war defense policy; a gratuitous and inflammatory debate on capital punishment (although the Prime Minister's personal intervention was splendid).

Yet in the midst of this deplorable record comes the news the Government is introducing a new Emergencies Act to replace the notorious War Measures Act. Every government requires provisions for special police and military powers in legitimately extraordinary circumstances, from natural disasters to war. But no democracy needs an act as miserable as the one Canada has endured for the past 73 years.

As the Defence white paper put it, "The broad and sweeping powers of the War Measures Act are excessive in relation to national emergencies in peacetime . . . It incorporates few safeguards against abuse." The new legislation is intended by this government, to its eternal credit, to be consistent with the human rights and civil liberties guaranteed in the Charter of Rights and Freedoms.

What I now wonder is whether the Liberal Party of Canada will support the new bill, since it has been Liberal governments that have invoked the War Measures Act in two of Canada's most dishonorable spectacles.

One was the deportations and expropriations of Japanese Canadians early in World War II by the Mackenzie King government, as great a stain on Canadian honour as can be found.

The other was during the Quebec crisis of October 1970, when Pierre Trudeau used the Act allegedly in the face of an "apprehended insurrection." A crisis there unquestionably was; the threat of a genuine insurrection never existed. Trudeau knew it. John Turner, then Liberal Justice Minister, knew it. Both promised one day to reveal the information they then claimed at the time they could not make public. That day has never come; not one new piece of evidence has ever been brought forward. This continues to embarrass John Turner whenever it is raised, as well it should. Nothing, of course, ever embarrasses Pierre Elliott Trudeau.

Using the extraordinary powers granted under the Act, 497 Quebeckers were arrested, of whom only 18 were ever convicted of anything, and none of whom was connected to the kidnappers of James Cross or the murderers of Pierre Laporte. Most of them were likely separatists, the real objective, in fact, of the Trudeau government's policy. While they were at it, however, police as far away from the action as British Columbia happily used the Act to harass various political dissidents they found unpalatable.

When it was all over, the Trudeau government, and Mr. Turner specifically, promised to replace the War Measures Act with something less draconian. In their next 13 years in office, they failed to make good on this commitment, a far more telling part of the Trudeau record, I have always believed, than the ultimate passage of the Charter, whose spirit Trudeau blithely violated when it suited him. The Conservatives made the same pledge in the 1984 campaign, and are now delivering.

For someone like me, these two incidents provided some of the moments in Canadian history of which I have been, ironically, most proud. And for the same reason in each case: the readiness of my political party to stand up against such intolerable repression whatever the political consequences. The attack on Japanese Canadians was, I'm afraid, wildly popular, yet CCF leaders across the country denounced the deportations categorically and courageously.

By the 1970 crisis, we of course had polls, so we knew that fully 88% of Canadians supported the government's position. Perfectly appreciating this disappointing truth, the NDP made the occasion one of its finest hours. Led in parliament by David Lewis and Tommy Douglas, they fought a futile but honorable battle. It cost the party a significant amount of support in the short run, but it saved something of the soul of Canada.

In Ontario, David Lewis' young son Stephen had become NDP leader literally only days before the crisis hit, and one of his first acts was to come out against the imposition of the Act, regardless of public opinion. I was part of that moment in history, and our refusal to contemplate even for a moment compromising on an issue of such fundamental principles has always been one of the highlights of my own political career.

*　*　*

1990　　TWO HIGHLY RESPECTED FIGURES on the political left, historian Ken McNaught and publisher Mel Hurtig, have both been calling for an electoral alliance between the Liberals and the New Democratic Party.

The country, they argue, can't afford another election in which the two parties split the anti-Tory vote and give Brian Mulroney the opportunity to complete the ruination of what's left of our country.

It's a persuasive proposition on the surface, but I have to say, guys, you'd better take a second look at that Liberal bunch.

For a New Democrat, a Liberal convention is as alien as Addis Ababa. There are no fundraising appeals for Nicaraguan relief. No impassioned tributes to Nelson Mandela. No condemnations of U.S. evil-doing in the Third World, biting attacks on free-market ideologues, declarations of solidarity with the trade union movement, calls for the dismantling of NATO and for massive disarmament. Nothing, in short, that nourishes and motivates NDP activists everywhere.

According to pollster Martin Goldfarb, Liberal delegates in Calgary last week explicitly situated themselves smack in the middle of the political spectrum, with Tories to the right and New Democrats well to the left. As it happens, academic studies entirely confirm this judgment.

Using surveys taken at all three parties' conventions, political scientists Alan Whitehorn and Keith Archer concluded recently that on many of the issues dearest to the hearts of New Democrats, the differences between them and Liberals was greater than that between Liberals and Tories.

And even though many Liberals are indeed moderate progressives, the research demonstrates that the passion to win, not philosophical conviction, is the primary motivation of Liberal activists.

Maybe this explains certain features of the Liberal party that have long perplexed reformers, such as:

- Why the Liberal party gratefully accepted $8.4 million in corporate donations in 1988;
- Why in its leadership campaign real spending by the two front-runners probably totalled $3 million each (Tom Wappell alone spent more than all the NDP leadership hopefuls combined);
- Why it spent only a few hours over four days discussing crucial policy matters, none of which binds the leadership in the slightest;
- Why the Martin and Chrétien organizations campaigned with such reckless disdain for democratic processes, including the ultimate cynicism of making deals for delegates with so-called Liberals for Life who had accused both men of being "pro-death" on the abortion question.

Are these our people, Ken McNaught?

And that's why, finally, they chose John Turner in 1984 and Jean Chrétien in 1990, although for the second time in a row the party might have outfoxed itself.

After all, notes *Le Devoir* publisher Lise Bissonette, Jean Chrétien is now "the most discredited politician in Quebec." A pretty provocative act, to rub the noses of Quebec nationalists in Chrétien's anachronistic federalism. More important for the left, Chrétien long ago said adieu to the little guy from Shawinigan.

His pose, of course, was always suspect. Behind the populist posturing lay essentially conservative instincts. He was always a right-winger in cabinet, former health minister Monique Begin fessed up last week, to which former Alberta Liberal leader Nick Taylor cheerily replied: That's what we like our leader to do — talk populist and act right-wing.

Two of Chrétien's former deputy ministers reassured *The Financial Post* that as finance minister he was "instinctively drawn to conservative economic views." And he himself wrote in his best-selling *Straight from the Heart* that as minister of industry, trade and commerce "I was even considered soft on the issue of foreign ownership." Are you listening, Mel Hurtig?

Ah yes, P'tit Jean, straight from the heart. Like your millionaire status. Your fancy Bay St. law firm. Your high-rolling Toronto investment house. Your directorships at the TD Bank and Consolidated-Bathurst. Your flights on Power Corp.'s private jets. Your all-male advisers. Your failure during the leadership campaign to spell out your views on most of the key issues of the day. Your breathless cynicism in the past month refusing to take a stand on the constitutional crisis. Yep, it's just like you told the convention: "We must restore honesty and integrity in Canadian life."

Sure we've got to stop the Tories and their destructive conservative agenda. But Ken and Mel, shouldn't we try to do so working with those who share our principles?

* * *

1990　　I, TOO, STILL CAN'T GET PIERRE TRUDEAU out of my system. I harbour toward him such visceral hostility that my amiable Liberal adversary, Michael Kirby, believes me deranged on the subject. I beg leave to disagree.

To begin, many of us will simply never forgive Trudeau for introducing the War Measures Act during the October Crisis of 1970, the greatest single violation of civil liberties in Canada since the expulsions of the Japanese Canadians during World War II. Mysteriously enough, in Stephen Clarkson and Christina McCall's new study of Trudeau, you'll find only one paragraph in 400 pages on this vital matter.

On the other hand, Clarkson and McCall do provide abundant evidence of Trudeau's unhealthy and almost contemptuous attitude toward women, which I find equally unforgivable. Trudeau, the supreme cradle-snatcher, was still dating girls — not women, girls — when he was in his 30s. When he finally married Margaret, he was

51 and prime minister, she 22 and the quintessential flower child. As everyone but he instinctively knew, they were doomed from the start.

This was no union of equals. He openly treated her as an ornament, and though he was pained when they began coming apart, it was invariably Margaret who was expected to make all the adjustments. Though even his friends considered his treatment of her to be "too harsh and unforgiving," according to Clarkson and McCall, to the bitter end he blamed the breakdown entirely on her. If only *she* changed, if only *she* could become the kind of wife and mother *he* demanded, the marriage could resume — on his terms. It was a demeaning performance by a man renowned for his brilliance and his ostensibly rigorous rationality.

In the end, Trudeau loved his own conceits more than he cared for his young wife. And the world, the media especially, let him get away with it.

No boast was more inaccurate than the assertion that for him, reason always took precedence over passion and emotion. It was never true. Clarkson and McCall show how often he engaged in verbal combat not with reasoned argument but with "the Jesuitical tricks of sophistry and rhetoric." In fact, he could be a cruel and wildly unreasonable antagonist, both simplistic and extremist in his arguments, demagogic in his debating tricks, invoking the tools of formalistic logic while shunning basic common sense.

Never was this trait more destructive than in his intransigent insistence that Quebec was a province "comme les autres." A reasoned belief in federalism as the best political structure for the Canadian state became a pathological and unreasoning loathing of Quebec nationalism, for which we're still paying the costs. A sensible concept was transformed into an inflexible dogma, from which no deviation could be tolerated. To the theologies of Catholicism, Marxism and Freudianism, add a rigid Trudeauism.

Yet, though he was a harsh and demanding judge of others, he allowed himself more latitude. Once an outspoken critic of the Liberal party's proclivity for political opportunism and eloquent advocate of participatory democracy, it took only one political beating, in the 1972 election, to place himself in the hands of the most manipulative backroom wheeler-dealers in the business.

The result was the 1980 election, one of the most cynical of modern times, in which Trudeau said almost nothing of substance, and, on the explicit advice of his handlers, certainly not a word on matters constitutional. Whereupon, regaining majority government, he obsessively turned his attention to these matters, making the personal, arbitrary decision to repatriate the Constitution unilaterally if necessary. "We could tear up the goddam country by this action," he informed his kowtowing cabinet, "but we're going to do it anyway." It was the authentic voice of Pierre Trudeau.

And when large numbers of Canadians protested bitterly his approach, he gave his hateful, arrogant shrug and announced that if Canadians didn't like it, they could throw him out at the next election.

Sound familiar? Sound like Brian Mulroney, whom the Liberals trash viciously for taking precisely the same line?

Is Mulroney's unyielding insistence on the GST any less arbitrary than Pierre Trudeau's implacable one-man crusade to impose on us his view of constitutional reform at any cost, a crusade then championed by the very Liberals who now denounce the Tories for usurping Canadian democracy?

He raised our expectations to the skies, and disappointed us on every count. How can we ever forgive him?

* * *

So This Is Power

1990   WELL, it only took 17 elections and 56 years, but that
curious Canadian party-cum-movement called the
CCF–NDP finally won the big prize in Ontario last week. After several
generations of moral victories, don't blame your friendly local
socialists if they're still pinching themselves in euphoric shock.

Of course, all New Democrats will be saying silent prayers for the
luck of the splits. Traditionally in Ontario elections, the NDP has lost
the closest races; this time the party won far more seats than its share
of the popular vote would normally warrant. But while the new
government should prudently note that far more Ontario citizens
voted against than for it, it's also true that such results are commonplace in our wildly imperfect voting system.

After all, many more voters opposed than endorsed free trade in
the 1988 election, which didn't deter Brian Mulroney from implementing the deal for one nanosecond. So before the disgruntled
Tories and Liberals expend too much indignation over the unfair
outcome, let me invite them to join this column in a crusade for a
sensible proportional representation system that will apply to every
jurisdiction in Canada.

Now, let me share this truth with faithful readers. Not only did no
New Democrat anticipate this traumatizing turn of events until
about two days before the election, many of us, in our heart of hearts,
never expected to form a government in Ontario in our lifetime.
Being the conscience of the province may not have been as effective
as direct power, but, as some argued volubly for years, it was not an
ignoble contribution to the public weal. As a result, a major psychological rethinking must now occur, and fast. As it happens, Premier-
elect Bob Rae — my, how it trips liltingly off the tongue — was never

among that band who thought permanent opposition was a satisfactory way for grown-ups to spend their adult life.

For all New Democrats, the long decades of opposition at least served to create a clear sense of whom we existed to represent. Let the other parties, we loudly proclaimed, speak for the successful in our society, the powerful, the wealthy, those who had it made. Our raison d'être was to try to make life better for everyone else, those for whom the system did not work properly or, worse, whom it actively ground down. Now that the magic of real political power is in our hands, we must not fail those to whom our entire lives have been devoted until this very moment.

But in the process of speaking out on behalf of the natural constituency of social democrats, we often neglected to talk about the tough economic realities of how the economy of Ontario really works. Frankly, that was simply not the priority until now, so if many Ontarians have a certain lack of confidence in the NDP's ability to manage the economy in an effective manner, it's no big surprise.

Similarly, if the business community in particular fears it now faces — for the first time ever — a government that is actively hostile to corporate interests, that too is an entirely understandable perception. It is also wrong.

For the fact is that the Rae government — there it is again; isn't it lovely? — must, absolutely must, demonstrate not only that it can run the peanut stand efficiently, but also that it understands business is and will remain the engine that drives — but shouldn't run — this province and this country.

And that, unless business remains strong and confident and expansive, it will be impossible to deliver the goods to all those who need a supportive government so desperately. This is, after all, the working premise of those Scandinavian governments that, for decades, have delivered some of the world's most efficient AND progressive administrations to their peoples.

The business community will find Bob Rae a perfectly compatible premier, so long as he finds them good corporate citizens who treat their employees with dignity and fairness and make their appropriate contribution to the general well-being of this community. And business leaders better understand that the rest of Ontario will consider this an absolutely reasonable trade-off, and one many businesses should have been making a whole long time ago.

The world should get the message loud and clear. New Democrats didn't wait half a century for power to blow it now that it's here. Of course, not every expectation can be met, or every wrong quickly righted. Still, this can be the best, the most exciting decade this province ever had — the impending recession notwithstanding.

It will take every group of our citizens working together to make it happen so that all of us benefit. The new government will do all it can; but please — just be a wee bit patient for a few days or so.

＊　＊　＊

1990　AT FIRST it reminded me of old-time university mock parliaments: somewhat surreal, play-acting really. But there was this difference: We didn't cry then.

So when the first-ever Ontario NDP cabinet finally entered the University of Toronto's Convocation Hall, led appropriately by Frances Lankin — a strong, confident woman who'd once been a prison guard and now had become one of the most powerful political figures in Ontario — the crowd erupted in a sustained outpouring of exultant, emotion-wrenching cheering and applause. It reflected the sheer elation and pride of men and women whose cause had never before found public sanction. There we all were, 2,000 of us, grown-ups, with a lifetime of moral victories and lost crusades behind us, many weeping unashamedly, too choked up to utter a word if our lives depended on it.

Anyways, how could it be model parliament, with the grand old hall chock-a-block with real, live working people — not exactly the folks who cluttered up university assemblies in my day, or, indeed, now. I know the autoworkers best, and everywhere the eye roamed it fell on CAW activists, from London and Windsor and Scarborough, Kingston, Oshawa and St. Thomas, come to cheer on the NDP members they had helped elect, some of them actually to be sworn in as cabinet ministers.

And that's exactly what the new cabinet represents for the first time in decades — a more accurate slice of the real Ontario. Teachers, blue-collar workers, environmental activists, social workers, union supporters: no corporate leviathans here, no massing of downtown lawyers. Just a band of pretty ordinary folks, really, determined to demonstrate that you don't need Bay Street credentials to run a sensible, compassionate government.

In fact, the most inexperienced of Bob Rae's new ministers could look at the record of the Brian Mulroney and David Peterson administrations and legitimately wonder how they could do any worse.

Rae's two-pronged message was clear enough, as it had consistently been since election night. He repeated yet again his reassurances that his government was committed to working partnerships with business as well as other community groups, especially for the purpose of beating the recession. And certainly the new team understands that they need from the best of Ontario's business people all the creativity, ingenuity and initiative they can marshall to meet Ontario's economic plight successfully.

But with new ground rules. There's a new game in town, and it's called putting people first. The values of the new gang are perfectly clear; they're exactly what New Democrats have fought for all these long, long years. Rae summed it up simply: The most important impact of recessions isn't on governments or businesses, he reminded the world; it's on ordinary folk. And that's who this government represents.

Nothing infuriated New Democrats in southern Ontario more than the assertion in recent months that we could deal with our pressing housing and transportation and social problems only when they became incidental by-products of the vast megaprojects of Expo 2000 or the Olympics.

Rae shared this outrage.

Why, he wondered aloud, if our community could mobilize its best efforts for such ephemeral projects, such unessential indulgences, why can we not do so now to tackle the great urgent tasks that this province faces. That's what his government is determined to do.

And there's so much to do. There are so many areas of Ontario life that haven't been examined freshly for decades. There are so many windows to be opened, walls to be torn down. There are so many people who have never been allowed to participate in the processes of government.

This administration has been deluged by offers of assistance from people in every walk of life, from the highest level of Corporate Ontario to the very grass-roots, all dying to be involved. Specialists in all fields of public policy can't wait to be plugged in. The Rae government really is in a position to offer genuine people power to Ontario, to be a government that musters the best of all its citizens.

At his swearing in, Bob Rae ended his speech with a quote from his hero, Tommy Douglas. Tommy, after all, had also known real power. Tommy was inspiring, idealistic, crusading. Tommy's government in Saskatchewan was also efficient, modernizing, innovative, humane, open and incorruptible.

Tommy was re-elected four times.

Not a bad role model for Premier Bob.

* * *

1991
    NO, I AM NOT GLOATING. Not me. Why should I be? Just because half the face of Canada has now been painted a resplendent pink by vanquishing socialist — well, social democratic — hordes? Nope, my bleeding heart is going out to those business people whom the recent election results have made nervous wrecks.

When you observe the seething over-reaction of so many in the business community to Ontario's eminently moderate NDP government, you have to doubt whether even the relentless centrism of Mike Harcourt and Roy Romanow can temper their knee-jerk paranoia. So guys, and Audrey, you'd better start ducking, pronto.

The Canadian corporate world, after all, has never been shy about defending its own interests. Way back in 1920, Canadian business raised a million dollars — big bucks, then — to wage a major propaganda campaign against — wait for it — rising free trade sentiment and its main proponent, the Progressive Party.

A quarter century later, with the CCF striking a chord with Canadians dreaming of a better world after World War II, business mobilized again. Between 1942 and 1945 business launched the largest single propaganda campaign in Canadian history to discredit the CCF. There was barely a corporation in the country — the names remain familiar today — that did not actively throw itself into a vicious and hysterical smear campaign that was almost American in its nature and intensity.

Conservative and Liberal politicians joined with prominent businessmen to accuse CCFers of being fascists, Nazis, Communists, or all of the above. Dictatorship and regimentation, they screeched, were inevitable under a CCF government; both individual freedom and private property would be in dire peril. Businessmen didn't hesitate to stuff employees' pay packets with pamphlets denouncing socialism and notices warning that their jobs were at risk under the CCF. And, smack dab in the midst of the war against Hitler, anti-Semitism was hurled against the CCF's David Lewis.

So pathological was the fear of a CCF victory that the Ontario Tory government, headed by George Drew, actually maintained during those years a secret police agency to spy on CCFers and other left-wing political figures.

But never mind such ancient Canadian history. As recently as the 1988 election Corporate Canada intervened monolithically in a ferocious effort to re-elect the Mulroney government and save the free trade deal. The amount of money spent may never be known. One hundred and sixty-two corporations made donations to the Alliance for Trade and Job Opportunities, the deftly named pro-free trade lobby, but despite the commitment to open its books, in fact even now 61 donor corporations refuse to divulge the amount of their contributions.

But we know that CP, Alcan Aluminum and Shell Canada each gave $250,000; Noranda, Royal Bank and Imperial Oil, $200,000 each, and just about anybody who's anybody on Bay St. chipped in with tens of thousands more. The Alliance itself admits to a $5.24 million war chest, though heaven alone knows the amount spent by local businesses, let alone the value of the threats made by untold numbers of businesses to their employees — the old stuffed payroll envelope gambit — that they'd likely close if free trade lost.

And of course, their fear-mongering worked beautifully, just as it did against the CCF 50 years ago. And obviously many business people hope it's working again now in Ontario, that they'll be equally successful in forcing the government to back down on virtually every progressive move it wants to make.

But in fact their real success is far more destructive and counter-productive to their own interests than anything the government's even remotely contemplating. What they're achieving is the undermining of business confidence in Ontario itself, the poisoning of the investment climate of the province.

Look at the shoddy deceits being resorted to. Last week the "All-Business Coalition," representing 42 businesses, called a press conference to release a report on business reactions to some changes trade unions wanted to the Ontario Labour Relations Act. Their ominous, menacing, headline-making findings: these changes threatened up to 480,000 jobs and $20 billion in investment in Ontario over the next five years.

Except for this: those changes had never even been endorsed by the government, and weeks earlier a government document had become public showing that many of the most controversial proposals about which business people had been surveyed were not on the government's agenda at all. Did that stop the coalition from releasing its fraudulent, scare-mongering figures? Did they consider the damage they were doing to business confidence in Ontario by such dark, dishonest propaganda?

Here are two things I don't get: Why are such people trying to subvert the well-being of all Ontarians in this way? And how can they expect the government to listen to their legitimate concerns if they behave in this irresponsible and destructive manner?

* * *

1991   SOME IMPORTANT NEW PRINCIPLES of governance have merged in the wake of the Ontario NDP government's first budget. It's important they be understood clearly.

1. Many critics, led by Prime Minister Brian Mulroney, have chastised the NDP for being out of step with the economic policies of Ottawa and most provinces. This novel notion calls on individual governments to repudiate their own philosophies and election promises and govern instead according to the ideology of the governing federal party. I expect his innovative proposition will be interestingly tested once Audrey McLaughlin becomes prime minister.

2. Regardless of your own record in office, you are free to kick the bejabbers out of another government — especially if it's NDP. So Michael Wilson, whose high interest rate, high dollar policies have caused a major recession and resulted in the largest per capita deficit by far of any government in the country, rebukes Ontario because its budget will prolong the recession and keep interest rates high. This is what my old bubba would call chutzpah city.

Note, too, similar attacks by various provincial governments. By Grant Devine in Saskatchewan, where Alan Blakeney's NDP government brought in 11 consecutive balanced budgets, while neo-conservative Devine has chalked up 10 consecutive deficits. By Alberta's very conservative Conservative government, with one quarter of

Ontario's population to deal with, which has recently racked up deficits of $4 billion (1987), $2 billion (1989), and $2.3 billion (1991); try multiplying those figures by four, and see how Ontario's $9.7 billion deficit really stacks up. Is the Ontario government so far out of line?

3. A province's credit rating, normally the esoteric terrain of insiders, has now become the fashionable touchstone for judging the competence of a government — at least when it's NDP. This interesting principle, if carried to ridiculous extremes by being applied to other governments as well, produces unexpected results. After all, David Peterson's government lost its AAA rating in Ontario in 1985 after sober Bob Nixon's very first budget, and didn't have it restored for three years. And Grant Devine's government has had its credit rating reduced on 10 separate occasions by four different bond rating agencies.

Remember too that Ontario is now the only province with a Standard and Poor's AAA rating in all of Canada. The unstable Socreds in B.C. earn an AA+, deep blue Alberta AA, and the dependable, cautious Quebec government of Robert Bourassa an AA−. I'm sure there's a coherent pattern here somewhere, but I'm afraid it confuses a simple soul like me.

4. Beating up the civil service has emerged as a foolproof new test of government earnestness. The bureaucracy is, self-evidently, a group of privileged, overpaid, slothful hangers-on, and not the vital machinery that makes governments tick. Non-wimp, i.e. non-NDP, governments are those that single out and penalize civil servants in ways that are guaranteed to undermine administrative morale and dedication.

5. A responsible government demonstrates its mettle by the savagery of its attack on the innocent victims of tough times. Thanks to the reckless demagoguery of certain commentators, welfare cheaters are seen by many as the great scourge of our society. Never mind the billion-dollar rip-offs by corporate welfare bums. Never mind the recession, or massive job losses, or the bread lines, or indeed that all serious evidence indicates that the rate of welfare fraud is very low.

Never mind the indisputable facts: That 42 per cent of all those on social assistance are kids and that 60 per cent of all households receiving assistance are made up of families of the ill, the disabled and single mothers. And that in Metro Toronto the average cost per welfare case is a lavish $611 a month and the average stay is precisely 3.9 months. REAL politicians know who the enemy is.

Sure it's a gamble for Ontario to run up such an enormous deficit. But what was the alternative? Almost 90 per cent of that deficit is a direct consequence of the recession and drastically decreased transfer payments from Ottawa; the Peterson government, if re-elected, would have been stuck with at least an $8 billion deficit. As it was, the NDP budget provides only modest benefits — far, far less than are needed, as the government well knows — to some of Ontario's most vulnerable and needy citizens.

There's been much talk all week of the great damage the Ontario deficit will cause our grandchildren. But this government, as I see it, decided that the urgent priority was to do at least something for the many kids who are hurting today. Right now. For my money, any other approach would have dishonorably betrayed everything the NDP has always stood for.

✳ ✳ ✳

1991   A GREAT DEBATE in public policy everywhere in the world continues to rage: have we run out of the means, or merely the will, to continue trying to improve the human condition?

One side — the other side — argues unceasingly that in this harshly competitive, globalized economy, nations and provinces must be lean and mean to survive. Major expenditures on "non-productive" social programs can simply no longer be afforded.

But this oft-repeated mantra begs some questions. After all, as this column has frequently documented, there are unlimited resources for some initiatives, like fighting a war or developing new weapons systems or bolstering dictators or giving generous tax breaks to the rich.

It's this sense of twisted priorities that runs through two important recent documents, one domestic, the other international. The first is the Canadian Council on Social Development's annual review of social development in Canada for 1990, a period it characterizes in three simple words: "Year of frustration."

Reviewing the major developments in the areas of income security, employment, food and housing and social justice, the assessment is unrelievedly bleak. "The main theme emerging from 1990," the Council summarizes, "was the overwhelming effect of the recession: close to 1.5 million Canadians are unemployed and more and more are homeless and visiting food banks. Several federal government policies, such as cuts in transfer payments to provinces, reductions in social housing, changes to unemployment insurance and the claw-back of federal benefits to individuals with incomes over $50,000 have only served to exacerbate the effects of the recession.

"Some provincial policies have done the same. Those who earn minimum wages, which are not indexed to the cost of living, lost 1 per cent of purchasing power last year. Social benefits increased by an average of only 0.4 per cent across Canada while inflation hovered around 5 per cent.

"Times were tough, but instead of responding to people's increasing needs, governments were preoccupied with balancing their budgets."

The problem, it appears, is not insufficient resources but inadequate will and distorted values. There's the awful sense that society is going backward, that we've become startlingly like the Dirty '30s.

Most of us grew up believing in the inevitability of human progress; the Great Depression seemed a terrible aberration. It was unthinkable that we could ever again witness in Canada bread lines and food banks. Yet to that shameful condition we have regressed. Have we run out of resources that we once took for granted or are we the victims of false ideologies?

Yet whatever problems Canada faces, we still seem a paradise to most of the rest of the world. In its Human Development Report for 1991, the United Nations Development Program itemizes the magnitude of the problems facing the Third World in terms of poverty, malnutrition, poor health, illiteracy, gender inequities. And they are truly, depressingly awesome.

But the report, which is about financing human development, is anything but pessimistic. In fact, UNDP states baldly: "The lack of political commitment, not of financial resources, is often the real cause of human neglect . . . The potential is enormous for restructuring national budgets (in poor countries) and international aid in favour of human development." It concludes that "Much current spending is misdirected and inefficiently used. If the priorities are set right, more money will be available for accelerated human progress."

The report documents the enormous amounts of money that could be released for productive purposes if Third World countries reduced their scandalous military spending, halted the flow of capital to the opulent West, reduced widespread corruption and lessened the oppressive burden of servicing the humongous debts they owe Western countries and banks.

The UNDP then acknowledges what all of us have come to understand, that "human development requires economic growth, for without it, no sustained improvement for human well-being is possible." But it adds the all-important qualification that free market conservatives everywhere ignore so recklessly: "But while growth is necessary for human development, it is not enough. High growth rates do not automatically translate into higher levels of human development. And firm policy action is required to forge a closer link between economic growth and human development."

So, the right is obsessed with growth and has traditionally been indifferent or even hostile to policies for human development; observe the governments of Mulroney, Bush, Reagan, Thatcher, not to mention the IMF and World Bank. The left, on the other hand, has traditionally been preoccupied with distributing wealth but not sufficiently with creating it.

Can both these vital strands be woven into a single policy? Do we have both the wit to increase our resources and the will to distribute them fairly? This, above all, is the challenge in Ontario that Bob Rae's government must meet.

* * *

1991 LAST WEEKEND, the *Toronto Sun* was at it again, continuing its hatchet-job on Laura Rowe. Laura Rowe? Again? That's precisely the point. It is important that readers of this paper [*Toronto Star*] know that the *Sun* is waging a relentless, systematic campaign to drive a wedge between the Metro police force on the one hand and the Ontario government, the Metro Toronto Police Services Board, and Toronto mayoral candidate Jack Layton on the other. Laura Rowe is an innocent victim of this highly dangerous goal.

Laura Rowe is a new member of the Police Services Board (formerly Police Commission) appointed by the NDP government. A

43

community worker, Rowe's not a New Democrat but she is an avowed feminist who's helped sensitize police officers to the traumas faced by women who have been raped. She supported Susan Eng for chair of the Board.

Twice in the few weeks since she was nominated to the Board, Laura Rowe has been deliberately harassed and persecuted by the *Sun*. On May 4th, an article in the *Sun* stated that the police "are investigating an alleged sex assault at the home of newly appointed Police Services Board member Laura Rowe . . . in 1985 or 1986." Where did the *Sun* get this story? All we know so far is that it was based on leaks of a report given by Metro Police Chief William McCormack to a supposedly confidential meeting of the old board, including its previous chair June Rowlands, and that reporters were actually given the exact words McCormack had spoken.

Then, on May 18th, a huge front page *Sun* banner headline proclaimed "COP COMMISSIONER PART OF OPP PROBE." The inside story was so bizarre that no schlock thriller would have dared invent it. At 12:30 a.m. on the night before Rowe was sworn in to the Board, she — of all the people in the entire city — was identified as being a passenger in a car driven by Franklina Langford, an ex-hooker and ex-lover of ex-Toronto cop Gordon Junger, who had quit the police force for running a sex-for-money operation with Langford. An unnamed police officer who stopped the car, the story said, believed the passenger was Laura Rowe; the next day at the swearing-in he identified her as the passenger.

Empathize with Laura Rowe's nightmare. Not only had she been tormented by the earlier story, but two different *Sun* reporters had trespassed on her home and property, as Rowe's lawyer Clayton Ruby formally stated, in an "unacceptable" manner. This time Rowe, who has never met Franklina Langford and who was asleep at home with her two young kids at the time of the incident, was being framed, plain and simple.

The next day in the *Sun*, Rowe's other lawyer, Ruby's partner Marlys Edwards, denounced the allegation as "utter, unmitigated nonsense . . . I cannot conceive how this kind of leak comes out at this time, without it being for some purpose, and I'm shocked by it." Chief McCormack responded that Edwards's allegation that police were out to get Rowe was "absolutely incorrect." Maybe. But then exactly who leaked this incredible hoax, and why?

Finally, on Victoria day, the sudden truth: "MYSTERY WOMAN STEPS FORWARD," read the *Sun* banner. "Teen says she, not police commissioner, was car passenger." Even the *Sun*'s Christie Blatchford, who had led the paper's unprincipled campaign to incite the police against their alleged antagonists, noted the difficulty in confusing the two women. While Laura Rowe is "pale, middle-aged, thin-lipped and average height," the actual self-confessed passenger, Franklin's friend Lara Hoshowsky, was a "leggy, full-lipped, rather gorgeous six-footer all of 19 years old." What they had in common were similar first names, period.

How can such a cruel, outrageous injustice have happened here? How can such an unthinkable accusation have been publicly levelled at all? Who leaked it to the *Sun*? Why is Laura Rowe being smeared?

Christie Blatchford herself glibly describes "the undeclared but very real state of war that exists between the new, NDP-appointed members of the police board . . . and the great majority of the metro force." Baloney. The only war is the one the *Sun* is methodically fomenting.

The only board members appointed by the NDP, Laura Rowe and Father Massey Lombardi, have never demonstrated the remotest hostility to the force. Susan Eng, appointed to the Board by David Peterson and promoted to chair at the behest of Bob Rae, knows she must work closely with the force. Roy Williams, the member who has just angered the police union, was a Peterson appointment.

I have faith that the great majority of Metro police officers will be appalled by the dirty tricks the *Sun* has twice now played on Laura Rowe. I believe the great majority will also condemn scurrilous attempts by malicious trouble-makers everywhere to inflame relations between the police and civil authorities, especially in these difficult times. If I'm wrong, this city is in for big, big trouble.

NOTE: Because *The Toronto Star* claimed to have a policy not to refer to other papers, this column was never printed.

* * *

1991   HERE'S A TIDBIT I'll bet you didn't know: it was actually on the recommendation of official representatives of the police community in Ontario that the NDP government decided to drop the Queen from the police oath.

Here, for the first time, remarkably, is the inside story.

Under the Peterson government, the antiquated 1945 act that regulated policing in Ontario was finally updated. As Mal Connolly of the police union told me, the old act "no longer reflected modern-day policing, and it was completely rewritten from A to Z."

To advise it, the government assembled an External Consultative Committee consisting of three representatives from each of the three organizations that constitute this province's police community: the Ontario Association of Police (the police union), the Ontario Association of Chiefs of Police, and the Ontario Association of Police Services Boards, which includes all the local police commissions in Ontario. It functions to this day.

John Whiteside was appointed to the Windsor Police Commission six years ago by Bill Davis; one of three members chosen by the directors of the police boards association to represent it on the consultative committee, he recently described it as "providing a cross-section of authoritative opinion within the police community upon which the Solicitor-General is entitled to rely in formulating proposals."

After extended discussions, consensus was reached among these groups, and in June 1990, the Ontario Legislature under the Peterson government passed the new Police Services Act. Then regulations had to be formulated to implement the principles enshrined in the legislation.

So in the summer of 1990, the External Consultative Committee was reconvened, chaired, as usual, by the deputy solicitor-general, a senior civil servant, and the process of drafting the regulations began.

On September 6th, Ontario changed governments.

But as Sandi Humphrey, executive director of the Police Boards Association, told me, "Nothing in the process changed as a result of that change."

The oath, John Whiteside wrote, "was one of several proposed regulations considered by the committee at meetings held from September to December, 1990, including use of force, employment equity (within police forces), political activity and other matters."

The question of rewording the oath that all officers must swear was discussed at three separate meetings, but the decision to drop the reference to the Queen was agreed in principle at the very first; the subsequent two discussions simply, and amicably, debated the exact new words to be used. "During these discussions," John Whiteside wrote, "no comment was made nor objection taken by any member to there being no explicit reference to the Majesty . . ."

Both Sandi Humphrey of the Police Boards Association and the union's Mal Connolly told me that no one on the consultative committee considered the oath change a big deal or ever anticipated its becoming a political hot potato. Nor was it by any means the most contentious matter dealt with. Jake Barber, chief of police of Brantford and a committee member selected by the Police Chiefs' Association, told me that "it was surprising to us that it became such a controversial issue."

One police union representative on the committee has been its long-time president, Detective-Sergeant Neal Jessop of the Windsor police force; Jessop told me that "when we finished this discussion, all three associations were satisfied with the results."

So the Queen was removed from the official oath and replaced by the words: "I solemnly swear (affirm) I will be loyal to Canada and that I will uphold the Constitution of Canada." John Whiteside of the police boards association said: "I cherish . . . the fact that Canada is a constitutional monarchy . . . (Regarding the oath) it seemed to me two things were essential: first, that at a time when severe strains have been placed on national unity, the declarant affirms loyalty to Canada, and secondly, that the central ethos of the Police Services Act be reinforced by swearing allegiance to the Constitution, which encompasses allegiance to the crown as well as those human values we are sworn to uphold."

The police union's Neal Jessop: "I'm a working police officer and the new words met all the needs that I had to perform my job loyally. Canadian society is getting more and more diverse. We wanted to reflect that. Our make-up isn't going to be based on those from Britain or even Europe. It's more and more universal. We do respect the Queen and meant no disrespect of any kind to that part of our heritage. I apologize to those who disagree . . . but we tried to look into the future, and this oath will satisfy the future."

So when the cabinet received this recommendation, John Whiteside points out, it "quite rightly in my view considered that it had the approval of the majority of the police community." And it was quickly accepted.

In other words, according to Mal Connolly of the police union, the changed oath had nothing whatever to do with the government's decision to promote Susan Eng as chair of the Metro Toronto Police Commission; "it was coincidental." Given the make-up of the consultative committee, he added, it's obvious no one ever intended to "beat up on the police."

So that's the story, sports fans; no NDP government conspiracy against the police, no perverse desire to rent the fabric of the nation, no bid to protect Susan Eng, no intended disrespect for the monarchy. Simply an attempt by all those concerned, as Neal Jessop said, to reflect the new realities of Ontario.

Surely all those Chicken Little editorial writers and columnists who hysterically proclaimed that the sky was falling when the new oath was announced will now give equal time to admitting they were all wet. But isn't it something that not a single journalist in all Ontario bothered to find out the truth before going berserk?

∗　∗　∗

Brian Mulroney —
The Opportunist as Ideologue

1988   AMONG THE STARK FAILURES of almost all Western governments since World War II has been their utter inability to eradicate poverty. However prosperous in general the West has become, no country has been able to rid itself of a substantial minority of very poor people, even though, until the era of Ronald Reagan and Margaret Thatcher, that was considered at least a desirable goal of governance.

The entire electoral fortunes of the Mulroney government today rest on the assertion that his policies have been responsible for the economic well-being that has shone upon us lucky citizens for the past several years. One might speculate, however, that at least some of "us" will not so easily be persuaded, say in Newfoundland, where more than one in five families lives in poverty, or Saskatchewan, where the figure is 16.4 per cent, or Quebec with its 15.3 per cent.

It is not inconceivable that the 3,689,000 poor in Canada may remain unmoved by the Tories's propaganda (although since more than a million of them are kids they are highly unlikely to vote). Over 50 per cent of all female-headed families live below the poverty line, as do more than four out of every 10 single women, most of them widows, over the age of 65. Many of the disabled similarly can barely make ends meet. Some of these folks may be unimpressed by the Mulroney economic miracle.

A very substantial number of the poor in fact work for a living; indeed, the Prime Minister can congratulate himself that there are now 128,000 more working Canadians living in poverty than there were in 1980. Just about anyone trying to make it on the minimum wage lives well below the poverty line. Families headed by women who work have a very good chance of knowing poverty intimately. Those increasing numbers of employees in the service sector, particularly in accommodation and food, retail and personal services, can expect a life of austerity.

Many poor people, however, live on social assistance — that's welfare, in plain talk — of one kind of another, and it's among the most shameful characteristics of our society that they must endure not only the scourge of poverty but also the withering scorn of demagogic, welfare-baiting politicians. Whether motivated by uncontrollable battiness (Bill Vander Zalm), or fatuous business shibboleths (Robert Bourassa with his welfare police, the BouBou Macoutes), or ideological dogma (Grant Devine), the witchhunt for alleged welfare cheaters rarely knows a moment's peace. Yet, the "blame-the-victim" accusations of these privileged bullies are simply baloney.

In fact, children, single parents (overwhelmingly women) and the disabled account for 90 per cent of all those who depend on social assistance. In Ontario last year, no more than 2-1/2 to 3-1/2 per cent of total welfare payments were based on fraudulent claims. In Toronto, only 1-1/2 per cent of all recipients were even under suspicion of fraud. The figures are comparable from sea to shining sea.

One jurisdiction where the heroic efforts of welfare-hounding vigilantes have been stalled is Ontario. Among the many positive achievements of the Liberal-NDP accord that ended when David Peterson won his majority government was the creation of a special committee to investigate Ontario's $2.3 billion social assistance system. The committee's massive report, issued last week, substantially, if not completely, survives the high expectations many held for it.

Almost more important than the committee's hundreds of laudable recommendations are the implicit philosophical underpinnings of its approach. On the basis of the vast mountains of evidence it accumulated, the committee in effect repudiates many of the key tenets of neo-conservative economic theory. Trickle-down capitalism doesn't trickle very far. Poverty is a systemic problem. Private initiative and the marketplace offer few rewards to the poor. Only government intervention can succeed in rescuing them from the virtually inescapable traps into which they have fallen. Many welfare recipients are anxious to work. Most of the working poor prefer work to welfare.

Initial reactions from the Peterson government, no longer vulnerable to the pressures of minority rule, have been encouraging in principle but sadly disappointing in terms of commitments. It appears that our rulers consider another Christmas dinner courtesy of food banks an acceptable burden for a million Ontarians to bear.

The poor in most other Canadian jurisdictions will simply have to grin and bear it for the foreseeable future. And plausible fears abound that a renewed Mulroney majority will mean a renewed attack on the federal social service system. Next time the PM waxes rhapsodic about his government's economic record, give at least 30 seconds' thought to the Canada he so complacently ignores.

*　*　*

1988　　"FOR THE GOOD OF THE PARTY," Tory MPs Michel Coté and André Bissonnette are not running in the next election, no longer to be awkward embarrassments to this government. "For the good of the party," Suzanne Blais-Grenier is likewise under enormous pressure to step down, and probably will, but Sinclair Stevens certainly will not.

Why should he? He acknowledges no a shred of culpability even though a judge found he had violated the Prime Minister's conflict-of-interest rules a mere 14 times in two years, demonstrating at least vigour and energy that Tories show under certain circumstances. In any event, why should Stevens be a sucker? Other senior members of the government have hung in even though their sins were at least as venal. Indeed, the minister responsible for one of the single most egregious acts of this government is even less remorseful for this deed than Stevens is for his. He is the Prime Minister.

Three years ago, the government announced that a new federal penitentiary was to be built in Quebec to replace the archaic and violent pen in Laval, one of Canada's most notorious and dreaded maximum security penal institutions. Laval is just north of Montreal; of the 200-odd prisoners who would be transferred out, 80 per cent hail from the Montreal-Quebec city corridor. Corrections Canada planners had chosen Drummondville as the site of the new facility. It's only 85 kilometres from Montreal. It would permit inmates to be close to their families and to established community support services, as Corrections Canada policy demands. And in Drummondville it could share facilities with an existing penal institution, this one medium-security.

Which is why, naturally, the Mulroney government decided to build the new pen in Port-Cartier, which just happens to be — wait for it now — in Brian Mulroney's own riding. Heaven knows Port-Cartier, which is 725 kilometres from Montreal, needed help. It had been badly hurt since a cellulose fibre plant was closed, and the Prime Minister was unapologetic, openly crowing that the new prison would create jobs and inject some $13 million a year into the town. Of course, he didn't exactly affirm the tips from anonymous government sources insisting that he personally intervened to have the site moved from Drummondville to Port-Cartier, but I would love to discuss some prime land I have for sale in Florida with anyone who believes the PM wasn't involved in the decision.

Auditor-General Kenneth Dye has said that this little political gambit by Mulroney would cost the rest of us suckers an extra $41 million in the coming years. Building the prison in Port-Cartier costs $11 million more than building it in Drummondville, while operating it will cost $3 million more a year. In fact in his 1986 report, Dye cited this decision as a flagrant example of wasteful government spending. The government, however, was unmoved. It was, after all, the Prime Minister's riding we were talking about.

Nor were they impressed by the universal condemnation that emanated from every single group that was affected by the move other than the citizens of lucky Port-Cartier — the inmates themselves, their friends and families, criminologists and prisoners' support groups — nor by the tension that's palpably been increasing within the Laval pen. Last month there was a serious riot in the exercise yards that both penal experts and guards attribute substantially to the prisoners' resentment at being transferred to the remote isolation of the North Shore.

They know they'll receive far fewer visitors in Port-Cartier. While any disturbance at an institution like Laval is bound to have multiple causes, many criminologists believe, in the words of one, "There is a very real connection between prison violence and unpopular transfers." But the government is unmoved. Obviously in today's atmosphere, prisoners' rights are not exactly high on the priority list of this kind of government. But whatever happened to the concern for law and order that's supposed to be a Tory hallmark?

And what about the families of the inmates? Most live in the Montreal area. Yet Port-Cartier is a numbing 14-hour bus ride, or an expensive flight, away. As one inmate's sister said, Port-Cartier means double punishment for her and her family. And still the government remains unmoved.

This isn't an issue that directly affects millions of Canadians (although violent prison riots do make news). But it speaks eloquently of those who now govern this country. For the good of the country, it is an episode to tuck away for election day.

✳   ✳   ✳

1988   VERY SOON, a bitterly divided Parliament will pass the government's two repressive immigration and refugee bills, C-55 and C-84, whereupon the United Nations will announce that Canada has dishonoured the Nansen Medal we were awarded two short years ago for our humanitarian treatment of the world's refugees. It will be a fitting symbol of the Mulroney government's harsh rejection of an unhappily brief tradition in Canadian history when we showed some generosity to the wretched of the earth. Some will be humiliated by the UN's action. Many more, I fear, will rejoice.

It is among the least attractive of Canadian characteristics, this disdain for and fear of other newcomers that we have demonstrated from the very beginning. Our aboriginal peoples aside, each generation of us has shown a remarkable lack of sympathy for the next group banging at the door. In fact for four-fifths of our existence as a nation, our immigration laws have been blatantly exclusionary and racist.

Most Canadians have forgotten this ugly truth. Yet as historians increasingly expose our abysmal record on blacks, Japanese, Jews, Chinese, Asians and others, we typically continue to see ourselves as humane and welcoming, appropriate winners of a UN award. Indeed, so deeply entrenched has our smugness become that we are self-indulgently outraged at the disgraceful episode of the "Voyage of the Damned," the 907 German Jews whom we, along with the Americans, turned away in 1939, dooming them to return to the death camps of the Nazis.

Oh sure, we're all now properly humiliated about that past for which we weren't responsible. But then why's the government going to get away with this new legislation that returns us to the policies of those dreaded days? And why do some two-thirds of Canadians at any given time believe there's too much immigration into Canada? And why do more than 80% of us apparently support the new legislation?

Of course Canadians are typically ambivalent on the question. In fact three-quarters of us believe we should continue to accept legitimate refugees. The question, then, is why the government has chosen to exhibit the most misanthropic of Canadian impulses instead of offering courageous leadership and addressing our more generous sentiments.

There are three apparent reasons. The first is simple political opportunism, a not very subtle attempt to exploit some of the ugly public mood towards foreigners.

The second is ideological, based on the harsh Darwinian premises of marketplace ethics. Since the liberalization of the 1960s, Canada has been trying to balance its immigrant flow between those successful outsiders whose economic situation would most immediately benefit us and those who were fleeing political repression, economic deprivation and religious intolerance.

In a report overseen by former Tory heavyweight Erik Neilsen in 1985, the government was strongly encouraged to make narrow economic self-interest the overwhelming criterion for entry onto our sacred shores; humanitarianism would become an afterthought in cases of last resort. This harsh neo-conservative approach is contained in Bills C-55 and C-84.

The third flows from Ronald Reagan's twisted view of Central America, which is reflected in the U.S.'s own immigration policies. Because Nicaragua is seen as evil incarnate, the Administration is loathe to acknowledge the unspeakable human rights violations that are still commonplace in El Salvador and Guatemala. As a result, the Americans don't recognize fleeing Salvadoreans and Guatemalans as legitimate political refugees.

It's these terrorized Central Americans who are the real targets of the government's legislation more than the Sikhs and Tamils whose two small boats provided the flimsy excuse for the Tories to create a panic about an impending national emergency. Under the new legislation, refugees will be returned to "safe third countries" while awaiting Canada's decision — a safe country like the United States, for example, which so brutally rejected them in the first place.

Every organization in Canada involved in assisting refugees has bitterly, passionately, and apparently unsuccessfully fought these two bills. While our government is hell-bent on closing our golden doors to the oppressed of the world once again, everywhere in the third world refugee numbers are increasing, literally by the millions. I bet our grandkids are going to be really humiliated when they read about it fifty years from now.

* * *

1989   IN THE END, after several roller-coaster rides and expenditures of unprecedented millions by Corporate Canada, the Mulroney government succeeded last November in persuading 43 per cent of Canadians that it could probably provide more competent management of the nation's business than the alternative. The embodiment of this sterling capacity has been, of course, Mr. Integrity himself, Finance Minister Michael Wilson, behind whose indefatigable recitations of dreary stockbroker mantras, we are incessantly assured, lie the moral strength of a saint and the financial acumen of a wizard.

It's well past time to demystify this laughable proposition. Michael Wilson is the most overrated person in public life in this country, certainly an appropriate representative of Corporate Canada but hardly in the way Tory flacks want us to believe.

During the 1988 election, Wilson never so much as whispered the word "deficit:" the day after, he enthusiastically became Chicken Little, warning of impending doom if the deficit weren't drastically cut. Where Mr. Integrity was before the election when his government lavishly promised some $15 billion worth of election goodies, remains, I'm afraid, a state secret.

This is the same man of unimpeachable honour who let himself be trotted out during the campaign by desperate handlers to terrify Canadians with the outright deceit that the U.S. would unilaterally tear up the auto pact if the free trade deal were threatened.

He then proceeded to insist that because Tories were the government, their campaign promises were not really promises at all but "commitments" that didn't have to be costed as oppositions' promises did. Among Canadian Tories, this shameless opportunism passes for integrity; imagine what constitutes baseness.

Then there's Wilson's vaunted competence. This is, after all, the finance minister whose last budget predicted that this year the average rate on short-term interest would decline by almost 1 per cent from 1988 to under 8 per cent. Easy come, easy go: Since the rates are in fact above 12 per cent, he was, as it turns out, merely 50 per cent wrong.

Then there's the unusually ingenious way the government is waging its fierce war against the scourge of inflation. Each time the Bank of Canada, encouraged warmly by the minister of finance, raises interest rates in order to suffocate inflation, in fact inflation actually increases in places like Toronto and Vancouver — diabolically clever, no? And Wilson himself stated last week that his proposed new national sales tax will boost inflation even more — by around 3 per cent.

At the same time, as everyone knows, each increase in interest rates that the government applauds increases significantly the deficit the government is so boldly determined to reduce. Moreover, the combination of tax hikes and spending cuts expected to be central to Wilson's budget next week will very likely cause a recession. Unemployment will soar, productivity will fall, tax revenues will decline, and the deficit will increase. Are you not struck dumb with awe at the sheer genius of it all?

Mr. Integrity has already hired outside PR experts to help con Canadians into believing that the budget will be bad for all of us regardless of race, creed, gender — or class. Especially class. "Everyone," he announced earnestly last week, "except for the most needy among us, must be prepared to share in the effort (to tackle the debt situation) in a tangible way." But don't start organizing tag days yet for those 18 Canadian executives who, according to *The Financial Post*, earned — well, let's say received — more than $1 million each in fiscal 1988, or the 50 who hauled in more than half a million dollars each.

In fact, as the Pro-Canada Network has just pointed out in an excellent report, Corporate Canada has had a field day under Michael Wilson's benevolent trusteeship. Corporations actually have been allowed to withhold tax payments in this fiscal year totalling a staggering $30 billion, enough to wipe out the year's deficit.

And — believe it or not — while Wilson's budgets lowered the basic tax rate for the wealthy so that families earning more than $117,000 a year actually pay $3,750 less in taxes, a family earning $35,000 pays $840 more. And, as if the new regressive national sales tax won't penalize lower-income Canadians enough, the National Council on Welfare calculates that $100 million has been cut — so far — from social programs under the Mulroney-Wilson government.

Count on this: Interest rates will not be cut, a recession will ensue, unemployment will increase, taxes will remain wildly unfair, the social security net will be shredded, and the government's paid flacks and hacks will assure us once again of Michael Wilson's unparalleled integrity and peerless competence. Come to think of it, if you're rich enough, they're probably right.

$$* \quad * \quad *$$

1989   "TWO NATIONS WARRING in the bosom of a single state." Lord Durham's famous 1838 description seems eerily applicable to Canada today, but not merely in regard to francophones and anglophones. Canada increasingly seems two nations also in the lamentable way Disraeli used the concept to characterize Victorian England: the rich and the poor.

Nor is this an accident. It is the inevitable consequence of considered Progressive Conservative government policy, of which the proposed goods and services tax is just the latest example. Whatever its final shape, the GST will be yet another regressive tax which clobbers poor people most.

For Canada's least privileged citizens, being beaten up by this government is not big news. Yet, opponents of the GST have, I'm afraid, failed to make most Canadians understand the tax is just another in a long, unrelenting series of Tory blows against the vulnerable and the poor.

It's all being done in the hallowed name of deficit-cutting and trickle-down economic theory, even though this theory has been discredited only about a zillion times. Somehow, the benefits never quite dribble down to those most in need. But don't take my word. The fact is this gloomy truth has rarely been as definitively documented as it has recently. The cup of depressing data runneth over.

The flood of information actually began last year with the publication of *A Choice of Futures: Canada's Commitment to Its Children*, by seven organizations dedicated to improving the well-being of all Canadians, including the Canadian Council on Children and Youth, the Canadian Council on Social Development (CCSD), the Child Poverty Action Group, and the Vanier Institute of the Family. The document is nothing less than a searing indictment of Canadian society; it should break your heart. To choose just two appalling facts out of countless dozens, in our Canada today kids make up the largest group of poor people. At last count, more than a million children — about one in every six — were growing up in poverty.

Then in June, the CCSD released its devastating *Canadian Fact Book on Poverty, 1989*. Written by social economist David Ross and statistician Richard Shillington, the 100-page report will shock you. Two million Canadian households now live in poverty. A job by no means guarantees immunity from poverty, especially among women. And only continuous increases in government transfer payments — the precise programs the government is systematically undermining — have, until now, kept the problem from becoming even more horrendous.

This summer, the CCSD featured Ross and Shillington again, this time analyzing the Tories' fiscal and tax strategy since their victory in 1984. The government's long-term objective, they demonstrate, is "to reduce tax burdens for higher-income persons and corporations while shifting the burden to lower- and middle-income households."

At the end of August, the dogged CCSD jumped in once more with a column by its director, Terrance Hunsley, documenting the desperate plight of single parent families in Canada, which he described as a "national tragedy and national emergency." For readers wondering if Hunsley was guilty of melodrama, he made this unnerving observation: In Sweden, 9.9 per cent of children of lone parent mothers live in poverty; in Canada, the rate is 61.8 per cent — fully six times greater.

In mid-September, hard on the heels of Hunsley's jolting piece, came the latest report from the government-appointed National Council of Welfare. It had analyzed the clawback provisions of the last Wilson budget, focussing on baby bonuses and old age pensions. The council expressed its verdict in no uncertain terms: "There is no question that the clawback put an end to universality of social programs in Canada."

The list, as you see, never ends. Just think of native people and the disabled. Last week Havi Echenberg, the head of the National Anti-Poverty Organization, demonstrated to a parliamentary committee that the bill to gut the Unemployment Insurance Act will inevitably most hurt those most in need — the Tories' neat little policy formula, it appears. The Conservative majority on the committee could hardly have cared less. Soon she will attempt to show the finance committee why the GST is not simply too high but hurtful in principle for needy Canadians.

But she, like her colleagues, is feeling overwhelmed, angry, barely able to cope each day with the latest of a hundred battlefronts as the government inexorably proceeds with its systematic onslaught on Canada's most vulnerable citizens. For those dedicated souls who run these admirable organizations, the futility and despair may soon become unbearable. So what must life be like for those they represent, those who actually inhabit The Other Canada?

*　*　*

1990　　IF THE RAIN didn't make contemplative discourse too uncomfortable, the Campaign Against Poverty (CAP) marchers trudging across soggy Ontario all week might have mused about this curious irony: In Canada, it is the left-wing opposition that is seeking sophisticated new policies rather than the dominant Conservatives whose exertions have created the very conditions the CAP exists to challenge.

While fatuous tycoons denounced Pierre Trudeau as a ComSymp, in fact most of his government's economic practices were distinctly pro-business. From time to time — during minority governments, for example — NDP policies were invoked to humanize the system somewhat, and progressive rhetoric was routinely marshalled during election campaigns to camouflage Conservative policies. Under Brian Mulroney, while caring-sharing clichés are nauseatingly repeated, the policies are unashamedly those of Corporate Canada.

In short, our present condition is the responsibility of mainstream politicians implementing the prevailing capitalist dogmas of their time. So it is they that Canadians have to thank for:

- The new generation of "food bank kids," in Metro Toronto alone numbering some 72,000;
- The 18 per cent of working people, the working poor, who are forced to resort to food banks;
- The minimum wage, which guarantees poverty to those who live on it;
- The homeless men and women who live on the streets of every large Canadian city;
- The 20 per cent of Canadian kids who live in poverty;
- The feminization of poverty, including the 50 per cent of all female-headed families and the 82.3 per cent of elderly women living alone — yes, that's 82.3 per cent! — who live in poverty;
- The 30,000 families in New Brunswick who are in desperate need of even half-decent shelter. According to the co-author of a recent report entitled *Home Sweet Home?*: "We saw cases with people living in conditions like we often see on TV from the Third World — no water, no sewer, no electricity, and a baby crawling around on a mud floor";
- The East Asian farmworkers in British Columbia, who earn $2.50 an hour berry-picking, work 13 hours a day, travel another 2–3 hours to the farms in crowded, smelly buses, wash in filthy water, get raspberry leaves for toilet paper, and begin the tortuous grind again after only a few hours sleep;
- The Ontario native children whose death rate is four time non-natives', a direct consequence of the wretched conditions in which they live.

This decade has witnessed not only the greatest average level of unemployment in Canada since the dirty '30s, but the genius of capitalism also conferred upon us stagflation, combining simultaneously a world-class recession and sky-high inflation.

At the same time, no other industrialized nation in the world is marked by such intense concentration of corporate ownership as Canada, not merely lessening competition but dangerously amassing more and more real power over all our lives in the hands of fewer and fewer business giants with no public responsibility whatever. And let's not even raise for now our pillage of the Third World.

And with what innovative solutions are capitalist sages attacking this proud record? Why, trickle-down private enterprise, as the Throne Speech reassures us. Cutting the deficit while applauding the Bank of Canada's high interest rate policy that systematically

Inasmuch as my friend is the leader of the NDP, I thought she would be interested in paying heed to the comments of one of Canada's most distinguished NDPers who said on *Canada AM*—

An hon. member: It is old.

Mr. Mulroney: No, it is new. I am not going to quote Stephen Lewis. I will quote Gerry Caplan who said:

It is creating—

This is the NDP now.

—a terrible, terrible precedent, that one day the rest of us will rue, for these Liberal senators to say that they have the right to stop the functioning of the elected government.

Listen to the people and listen to Gerry.

Some hon. members: Hear, hear.

* * *

Hansard Commons Debates, October 2, 1990, p. 13680.

increases that deficit. Jockstrap capitalism with its self-parodying locker-room rhetoric about going mano to mano with the Yanks. Cutting back on unemployment insurance while deliberately increasing unemployment itself to foil the wage demands of the labour movement. Belt-tightening for the needy and market-driven opulence for the privileged.

A personal note: In recent months, I've publicly called on the left to do some serious policy rethinking. For this political indiscretion, I've earned something of a cult-hero status on the right. I've been quoted ecstatically by a Tory cabinet minister in the Saskatchewan Legislature and been invited to discuss items of mutual interest by David Somerville, president of the right-wing National Citizens' Coalition.

Buzz off, gentlemen; we have nothing to discuss. While the left at least recognizes the need to keep up with changing times, right-wingers keep peddling the pious platitude that what's good for Corporate Canada is automatically good for ordinary Canadians. For decades there has been a profound bankruptcy of economic thought among Conservatives, who keep reworking their discredited nostrums and ignoring the inexorable tendency of their cherished market-place to produce a society whose human values range somewhere between Social Darwinism and Hobbes. Ask the hunger marchers who showed up at last at Toronto's Queen's Park. What was trickling down on them was nothing more than cold rain and the vacuous Conservative clichés of the Mulroney Throne Speech.

* * *

1990   MUCH OF THE HISTORY of the Canadian left in the past decade has been a tale not only of lost elections but of lost intellectual debates. For a variety of reasons, ideological conservatives and lovers of market-driven economics for years have been allowed by progressives to get away with intellectual murder. While some conservative positions have a certain merit, none deserves the mindless, exuberant acceptance that often seems the case.

It is not true that the public sector is invariably inefficient and unproductive. It is not true that the deficit is our all-consuming economic crisis. It is not true that trickle-down economics works. It

is not true that inflation is more harmful to Canada than unemployment. It is not true that market economies and political democracies
axiomatically go hand in hand.

And it is absolutely not true that it's time to put the golden age of
universal social programs behind us. Let's examine this particular
conservative contention. Those who have led the attack on universality assert that it makes no sense to be giving government handouts
to very wealthy Canadians: It's a luxury we can't afford, given the
challenges of international competitiveness. So if we really cared
about the poor we'd target them directly.

In fact, none of these arguments stands up to scrutiny. It is true that
our social programs are in a shambles and badly need radical repair.
Those of us who believe passionately that an attack on poverty and
the present immoral distribution of wealth in Canada must be
launched with unprecedented commitment and vigour can hardly be
satisfied with the patchwork of inadequate policies that constitute
our bare-bones welfare system.

But the co-ordinated attack by business and political conservatives
on the principle of universality, and the specific steps taken by the
Mulroney government to claw back family allowances and old age
pensions from Canadians above a certain income threshold, seriously undermine an already inadequate system without in any way
refashioning a more equitable one.

Let the left stand on the following forthright statement: "Our
position is simple and straightforward. We are in favour of universality in social programs and it shall not be touched." Thus spake R.
Hon. Brian Mulroney, March 7, 1984.

The arguments for universality are both philosophical and political. Universality should be seen as part of an implicit Canadian social
contract: The state provides all citizens, as a matter of entitlement
and regardless of their wealth, a series of public services and programs ranging from hospitals to material security to schools and
libraries, and in return, each of us contributes to their costs in
relation to our ability to pay through a system of progressive
taxation.

The theory, of course, has been implemented with woeful inadequacy; but in itself it represents the best of Canadian values that
many of us rightly feared would be jeopardized by the free trade
agreement.

Politically, it's been the case throughout the Western world that
wherever social programs were universal, they disproportionately

benefited middle class recipients, who in turn became fierce uphold-
ers of the programs. Programs that primarily targeted the poor were
invariably the first to be slashed by unsympathetic governments. In
other words, the best way to help poor families and kids and poor
seniors has been programs for all families and seniors. And since
these payments are taxed progressively, the poor, quite properly, gain
more than the wealthy.

Finally, the federal budget is about $150 billion. It gives titanic
corporations multi-million-dollar tax credits and billions more in
countless subsidies and grants. It proposes to increase tax-deductible
limits on retirement savings plans for the wealthy at a price to the
rest of us suckers of $350 million a year. It lets you (well, somebody)
make $100,000 in capital gains, entirely tax free. Its tax rate at the
very highest end has been reduced from 34 per cent to 29 per cent at
a cost of a cool $2 billion a year. Its regressive tax structure and
myriad bountiful corporate exemptions cost us untold billions and
billions in foregone revenues.

Now ask yourself this. How come, therefore, the best place our
ingenious government could find to claw back an extra $500 million
a year to reduce its self-inflicted deficit were programs directed at the
elderly and at kids? That's what Tories mean when they attack
universality.

* * *

1990   THE VICTORY OF THE NDP in Ontario on Sept. 6 has been
———   greeted so far with an unexpected degree of enthusiasm
from almost all corners. Much of that expansive reaction, I think, is
because so many Ontarians believe Premier-elect Bob Rae — lord, it
still makes me weak all over — is a very smart man. For ordinary
folk, that means he's smart enough to bring both efficient and just
government to the province.

To many business people, however, I fear it means that they're
confident Rae is smart enough to jettison his party's "cockamamie
socialist schemes" to ravage Ontario's economy, like his preposterous election campaign cry that the corporate sector pay its fair share
of the tax burden. After all, as business flacks tirelessly warn, fairer

taxes would merely mean that Corporate Ontario would pack its kits and caboodles and trundle off to Bolivia or Bangladesh before you could say Friedrich Engels.

However, it's not just NDP politicians who take a tough stand on the operation of the Canadian tax system. One of the most important recent analyses was presented this summer to the Senate Committee by Mel Hurtig, publisher extraordinaire, successful businessman, and indefatigable Canadian nationalist.

Hurtig's 47-page document is a superb tour de force of rigorous research based on the most impeccable possible sources. This brilliant document, available from the Canadian Senate, should be required reading for every university, community college and high school social science and economics course in this country. It reveals more profound truths about the real way Canada works than a dozen text books.

"The Canadian tax system," Hurtig irrefutably demonstrates, is "characterized by enormous tax concessions for giant corporations and wealthy individuals. Huge, very profitable and powerful banks, trust and insurance companies, petroleum and mining companies have been paying remarkably low real rates of taxation on real profits, well below the rates of most small and medium-size Canadian business.

"The Mulroney government 'tax reform' has increased the tax burden for the overwhelming majority of individual Canadians and their families and decreased it for the very wealthy." (But so, too, as Hurtig's data also reveals, did the tax policies of the Trudeau government.) "At the same time effective corporate tax increases for the largest, most profitable corporations have been modest . . . the result is a shocking concentration of wealth and power in Canada and an excessive tax burden for the overwhelming majority of Canadians." By comparing relative taxes paid by Canadian and Japanese corporations, Hurtig also effectively punctures the cherished corporate myth that if we tax corporations fairly they won't be able to compete in the global market.

But you don't have to trust Mel Hurtig either. Late in the Ontario election campaign, a resourceful Canadian Press reporter received through the Access to Information Act a remarkable government document bearing the innocuous bureaucratic title *Final Report of the Committee on the Restructuring of Compliance Programs*. It proves to be the explosive work of Revenue Canada tax experts in Ottawa, who, after long study, concluded that giant corporations in

Canada are among the least likely to pay their full share of taxes. "Very large corporations tend to be chronic non-compliers (with tax laws) . . . (They) can also afford to use the services of expert advisers to help them plan and implement their tax minimization . . . (These) highly paid advisers ensure that very large corporations pay as little tax as possible, either by arranging their business in favorable ways or by challenging every gray area of law that could be to their benefit. Even if the advantage sought is denied, a deferral of tax payment is often achieved since the assessment, audit, appeal and court procedure can take several years."

In total, Revenue Canada estimates, Canadians in 1987 owed a staggering $10 billion in unpaid taxes, about one-third of the entire current deficit.

That's why Bob Rae's campaign was so much more compelling than Tory Mike Harris' right-wing populism. Canadians understand that tax increases can't be avoided. They simply demand that the system become fair and progressive. That's why we can reasonably expect Rae's colleagues in the House of Commons to pick up the same issue and run hard with it. The truth is there's enough scandalous information just in these two documents to take a determined political party right through until the next federal election.

∗ ∗ ∗

1991   YES VIRGINIA, there are Canadians who just won't enjoy the holiday season for fretting about the size of the deficit. So, as my yuletide gift to them — call them the Noisy Minority — herewith a wee fable about how that pesky deficit could be eradicated in its entirety. Call it Scrooge's Christmas Carol.

Recently, *Our Times*, an independent, pro-union monthly, dramatically illustrated how the corporate agenda for slashing the deficit might actually be implemented, taking as an illustration Ontario's $9.7 billion deficit. Even if its calculations aren't dead on, they give a good sense of what this modest little exercise would involve.

It's actually easy as pie. First, you simply slash the Ontario deficit in half by increasing government revenues by almost $5 billion. Mainly that means hiking taxes. So you boost the provincial sales tax from 8 to 9 per cent, raise individual taxes by 14 per cent and jack up taxes on luxuries such as gasoline, booze, cancer sticks and the like by another 14 per cent. Presto and poof! There goes about half the deficit. That didn't hurt much, did it?

Since the remaining $5 billion can only come from cutting spending, and since three-quarters of the entire provincial budget goes to health, education and social services, they each have to take a very big hit.

So let's go to it. Health loses $1.7 billion. Schools at every level, just under a billion. Social services, $.75 billion. Then, all the 20 other ministries — women, transportation, environment, culture, trade and technology, etc. — would have to cough up the remaining $1.5 billion.

Since the NDP is a big believer in fairness, these cuts would necessarily be allocated evenly across the province. As a case study, *Our Times* looked at the consequences for the 75,000 residents of Brantford, but they'd be similar in dollar terms for Peterborough or Oshawa (never mind GM) or the Sault (never mind Algoma), and proportionately similar for both smaller and larger places.

Now, naturally, everyone would be hit by the hikes in personal income tax, the sales tax and on selected items, so that would mean dramatically fewer bucks left to spend on buying goods and services around the community.

Then, according to *Our Times'* estimates, health spending in Brantford would decline by $13 million. Just think of all the hospital beds — or entire hospitals — or community care facilities or nurses that would eliminate.

Education would take a $7 million wallop in Brantford. Visualize it in terms of teachers laid off, infrastructures deteriorating, class-rooms closed and kids crowded together, innovations postponed indefinitely, high-tech training put on hold until the next century.

Social services in Brantford would lose more than $5 million, even though about 40 per cent of the beneficiaries are kids. But these are tough times, pal. And Brantford's local government can't make up the difference, either.

Remember that Ottawa has sharply reduced transfer payments to the provinces — especially opulent ones like Ontario, even though Ontario has been battered hardest by the depression that the Mulroney government deliberately engineered.

So Queen's Park must, in turn, be miserly in its transfers to municipalities in order to slash its own deficit. In other words, even though Brantford's problems would increase gargantuanly, it would get peanuts from the province.

Nor can wretched social assistance recipients be forced to work since there are no jobs for them. Since the smash-the-deficit crusade would mean little cash left over to spend or invest, the economy would continue to stagnate. And since the job-creating programs the Ontario government initiated in its first budget would have to be eliminated entirely — just too costly, chum — in fact 500 more jobs would probably be lost immediately in Brantford.

If they had worked long enough, the unfortunate victims in this Christmas fable would join the already long list of UIC recipients. But since Ottawa cut the length of time that UIC is available, they would, very soon, join the swollen welfare lists and, thereby, the ranks of Canadians living well below the poverty line and reduced to dependence on food banks.

Sure, it's a tough job, but social democrats have to be mean hombres. By pursuing the corporate agenda, the NDP government would clean up Ontario's deficit in one fell swoop, and soon the entire country would follow suit; indeed, some jurisdictions are well on the road.

Within a very few years we would find a Canada unencumbered by the shackles of deficits, free of the albatross of social services and medicare, lean, tough, uneducated, awakened from its entrepreneurial stupor by the cold bath of budget-slashing, its belt tightened to the last notch, ready to take on the world. We can do it, Canada.

Alas, this harmless fable must be taken deadly seriously.

As we dive into our Christmas turkeys, let's remember that already in each city of the land we can overflow the local sports stadium with the kids who won't have enough to eat this holiday. And let's reflect for a moment on the Canada that might be if we follow the prescriptions of our Canadian Scrooges.

*   *   *

1991   AS IF THIS CITY didn't have enough troubles on its own, Canada's most gruesome oxymoron invaded poor Toronto this week. I mean, of course, the Progressive Conservative Party of Canada. But their party's outlandish name wasn't the only contradiction that characterized the delegates to last week's convention.

The modern PC party — Brian Mulroney's remarkable creation — is a triumph of expediency over conviction, lust for power over principle, free market ideology over territorial loyalties. It unites at the trough those anti-francophone, neo-conservative westerners who felt violated by the supreme indignity of bilingual cornflake boxes and those neo-conservative francophone Quebeckers who are instinctively sympathetic to the sovereignist goals of both the Parti and Bloc Québécois. One defeat, and poof! there goes the coalition.

Yet this unnatural creature has survived far longer than most of us anticipated, and even now, standing sixth in the polls behind even the undecideds, only the rash would yet count them out. Whatever else you may say about Brian Mulroney, with him it really ain't over till it's over.

Which is a great, possibly irreversible, tragedy for this country by the time his gang gets through with it. For like Dr. F. himself, Brian Mulroney has become the prisoner of his monster and its destructive ideological nature.

Personally, Mulroney is no hardened, heartless neo-con. In fact he's the essential pragmatist, wildly ambitious, yea, even power-hungry, a guy who stopped at little to get where he is. In other words — and I know he'll never forgive me for this ultimate insult — Brian Mulroney is as natural-born a Liberal as this country every threw up — if you'll pardon the expression. But as a born compromiser in a party of sectarians, having won the 1983 leadership convention, he chose to follow those he now leads.

Now the prevailing ideological convictions of the party he'd inherited weren't exactly a state secret at the time. On the contrary, the political scientists who surveyed the delegates at that convention found — in a nutshell, you might say — a P.C. party that was proudly and unabashedly ultra-conservative and not a jot or tittle progressive. The results have been documented in essays by professors Donald Blake and Richard Johnston in George Perlin's *Party Democracy in Canada* and with beguiling detachment by two prominent Liberals, Martin Goldfarb and Tom Axworthy, in their book *Marching to a Different Drummer*.

In the words of Goldfarb and Axworthy, "the activist base of the Conservative party is close to being a clone of the Republican right wing" in the United States. Not just the Republican Party, observe, but the right-wing of the Republican Party, heaven help us.

In fact, nearly 60 per cent of the Tory convention delegates cheerfully described themselves as right-wingers, and they proved it repeatedly with their views on continentalism, the welfare state, universality, immigration, cruise missile testing, foreign aid; you name it, they had neat, simple-minded, mean-spirited, knee-jerk responses to them all.

Just as, only three decades ago, Barry Goldwater and William Buckley seemed relegated to the American right-wing lunatic fringe, a mere eight years ago the reactionary sentiments of these Tory activists seemed downright un-Canadian, far out of the Canadian mainstream. Yet, just as Goldwaterites and Buckleyites became the heart of the Reagan-Bush governments, so the Mulroney government has largely implemented the agenda of its right-wing dinosaurs. And got itself re-elected in the process!

You can, by the way, see their influence not just on domestic issues but on the central issues of foreign policy as well; not easy ones like South Africa, where Brian Mulroney did fleetingly shine, but those of war and peace and our relationship with the United States. Shortly after Mulroney won the leadership in 1983, Douglas Roche, then a Tory MP, publicly described "two competing foreign policy philosophies inside the Tory caucus."

One, the minority, was Canada's traditional, moderate, Pearsonian, United Nations-oriented position. The second was "dominant both in numbers and intensity. Espousing the same form of neo-conservatism that marked the Reagan administration . . . the centrepiece is massive military spending. The possibility of a limited nuclear war is not ruled out . . . Foreign aid is slashed, repressive military regimes are bolstered."

As in domestic policy, here, too, the extremists prevailed. The result was the government's Defence White Paper of 1987, a document so anachronistic, so perversely unbalanced in its cold war belligerence that it made us a laughingstock around the world.

Now Tory spin doctors are beginning to soften us up for the 1993 election. They want to persuade us that the government's unpopularity is a direct consequence of its courage in implementing tough but crucial policies. If they succeed again, we'll deserve everything that will surely be coming to us.

*　*　*

The Friends of Brian Mulroney

1985   THE DEMOCRATIC LEFT is the victim of endless negative
stereotypes. Most of them are demonstrable miscon-
ceptions but they nevertheless are widely held and seriously limit the
electoral prospects of the New Democratic Party.

One venerable anti-socialist myth pits the vaunted productivity of
private enterprise against the alleged inefficiency of government
operations. Crown corporations, it is asserted, are notoriously ill-run
while civil servants are lazy and inept. They lack the motivation of
the mystical "bottom-line" which invigorates the private sector.

If only we cut back government operations, got it off the back of
industry, de-regulated and sold off our crown corporations — then
we would really see something. But what?

One of the unintended consequences of the role of Auditors-Gen-
eral in our public life is to reinforce these wildly simplistic clichés.
Every Auditor-General rigorously scrutinizes the operations of the
complex, multi-billion dollar organisms that constitute the Canadian
public sector, and inevitably finds countless examples, both large and
picayune, of waste, incompetent management, poor planning and
simple foolishness. Proof again, crow the business propagandists, of
the innate inefficiency of government and all its works.

But hold on. Where is the Auditor-General for the private sector?
Who has access to the confidential documents of the business
community? Who provides the public with a regular accounting
from the corporate side?

As it happens, Lee Iacocca has just been thoughtful enough to offer
us "a realistic picture of the excitement and challenge of big business
in American history." In his best-selling autobiography, Iacocca
speaks with some candour of the two companies which he knows
intimately, the Ford Motor Corporation and Chrysler Corporation,
respectively the third and tenth largest industrial corporations in
America.

According to Iacocca, the Ford Company was run by a capricious, insecure, cruel and ignorant tyrant, Henry Ford II, grandson of the original Henry Ford who had himself left the company in ruins. "Henry was an old pro at spending money, but he never understood ... what made the place tick." Behaving "like a spoiled brat," Henry Ford's arbitrary decisions meant the company's small, front-wheel drive cars, Topaz and Tempo, went on sale five years after the public wanted them.

Yet the Ford Corporation was a model of efficiency compared to Chrysler, Iacocca reports. Taking over Chrysler after being humiliatingly dumped by Henry Ford, Iacocca found it "in a state of anarchy ... I took one look at that system and I almost threw up ... Chrysler executives had a better reputation for their golfing ability than for any expertise with cars."

Caveat emptor. Now he tell us. From the people who brought us the Edsel, more lemons from The Big Three. Who can forget Ford's 1957 Fairlane 500 or its 1971 Pinto, Chrysler's 1975 Aspen and Volare, and GM's Corvair, which, Iacocca acknowledges, "really was unsafe." And who can forget that in 1983, the heads of GM and Ford received respectively 1.5 and 1.4 million dollars in combined bonus and salary?

It is self-evidently ridiculous to generalize from such outrages to the incompetence of all corporate capitalism. But equally ludicrous are the frequent extreme attacks by representatives of the private sector on the public sector.

The miracle of Canadian survival has been achieved in substantial part by the unabashed use of the power and resources of the state. In every aspect of our lives, Canadians enjoy and appreciate the services provided by government and crown corporations, from garbage collection to hospitals to hydro-electric power.

So let us redress the balance upset by the excellent work of Canadian Auditor-General Kenneth Dye. For the sake of fair play, I suggest this bold New Year's resolution to the most outspoken critics of the public sector: Name an Auditor-General for the private sector.

Name a Canadian in the Lee Iacocca mould: outspoken, independent, respected, tough, a bottom-line guy. Give him access to your key documents and let him give an annual public accounting of how efficiently the private sector works. Let Canadians compare the horror stories of the two sectors.

Let me even presume to recommend the perfect person — you might even say he is the Lee Iacocca of the working class. Why not choose Bob White? Now that would be the kind of entrepreneurial daring that could truly make Canada great again.

* * *

1986 HISTORY, MR. MULRONEY ALLOWED with typical under-
statement, will probably judge Michael Wilson to have been one of Canada's greatest finance ministers. The problem with Canada, Mr. Wilson has allowed, is there are not enough rich people. This statement is unlikely to help Mr. Wilson attain his immortal status. He is, alas, wrong.

It was North America's greatest left-wing gadfly of this century, I.F. Stone, who discovered that the most credible and devastating way to attack the capitalist establishment was to use its own tools. For decades, Izzie Stone's *Weekly* would expose the underlying motives and the hidden truths of American big business with facts and figures from — where else? — the *Wall Street Journal* and the *New York Times.*

There he discovered everything a fine researcher needed to document his continuing indictment of the brutality, the hypocrisy, the war-mongering of American monopoly capitalism. And who would dare dispute the reliability or meticulousness of his sources?

Now Canada's own *Financial Post* may not quite have the stature of the *Times* or *Journal.* But if you want to learn some truths about Canadian capitalism from an unimpeachable authority, the *Post* is a fine place to begin. Too bad no one told our Finance Minister.

On April 26, the weekly edition gave us a long, detailed article called "What our top executives earn." It presented a list of 31 Canadians who "earn" more than $500,000 a year.

Then its monthly magazine for May was good enough to follow up with another comprehensive look at "The Top Forty: Our richest people and how they grew." The story also included a long side-bar titled "They Almost Made It," a listing of 34 other individuals and families "who might qualify if we had information about them." The wealth of this also-ran group, so far as is known, begins at $80 million with Allan Slaight, the new owner of Standard Broadcasting.

This is a serious problem indeed for Canadian researchers, for much of the necessary data for assessing wealth accumulation in

Canada need never be publicly revealed, according to our laws. But Canadians operating in the States must spill their beans to the U.S. Securities and Exchange Commission, and it was from that source that the *Post* compiled its top earners.

(How come, do you think, the States demands so much more openness from its capitalists than we do?)

Among the most remarkable aspects of the *Post*'s two groupings was that not a single person or family overlapped between the list of the 31 top earners and the list of the 40 richest Canadians, while only one among the 34 who almost made it appears among the top 31 earners — Frank Stronach, head of Magna International, who took home in 1985 in salary and bonuses a trifling $1,853,000.

But that leaves many unanswered questions. How is it that Edgar and Charles Bronfman are in the highest earning list and not among our richest citizens? How come Kenneth Thomson and the Reichmanns and the Eatons and the Irvings and Galen Weston and the Blacks — Conrad Black, for heaven's sake — are only found in the list of the richest and not among the highest earners? (Are they paying themselves inadequately? Should we have a tag day? Organize a union?)

And where is Trevor Eyton, the controller, it appears, of most of the great Canadian family treasuries and *Toronto Life*'s choice as the Most Influential Person in Toronto? Or all the bank heads on the *Toronto Life* list of Toronto's most influential 50?

That means, in the words of the *Financial Post* itself, that "Canada does not suffer a shortage of wealthy people. In proportion to its population, Canada has almost as heavy a concentration of very well-to-do people" as the States. The 40 richest individuals and families on the *Post*'s list have holdings worth $18 billion (Cdn.), "slightly more than 1% of Statscan's total estimated national wealth of $1.7 trillion (Cdn.)."

Here's the question the *Post* has not yet answered, however: What does it say about Canadian democracy that a few people have such unthinkable riches and concomitant influence and power while most others just get by and some don't even have enough to eat much of the time? Come to think of it, Izzie Stone never got those answers from the *Wall Street Journal* either.

* * *

1988   THE DEBATE UNLEASHED by the government's free trade
———   deal is really about a far broader, more pivotal issue: it
is nothing less than the kind of economic strategy Canada should
follow as we prepare for the 21st century.

James Laxer, in his important new book *Decline Of The Superpowers*, conceptualizes it as the choice between the market-driven
"enterprise" economic system that characterizes American and British capitalism, and the "enterprise-intervention" system of Europe
and Japan where the state and private sector jointly determine
economic and social development.

Until recently, there has been an historical consensus in Canada in
favour of the enterprise-intervention model. Whether for pragmatic
or ideological reasons, most politicians have agreed that this awkward country could not rely exclusively on market forces as the
primary engine of society. The question that has seriously divided us
has been not whether there should be a mixed economy, but on the
balance between the relative weights of the market and the state.

The counter-revolution that has now been launched by the Mulroney government is to shift the balance dramatically to the market
side. Although Laxer demonstrates empirically the reality of a
declining America and a surging western Europe and Japan, Canadian business is determined that this country should be run more and
more on the American model of jock capitalism and unbridled
individual initiative.

Since the erstwhile incarnation of such machismo economics, John
Turner, has (until after the next election at least) publicly repudiated
his old pals at Winston's restaurant, they are holding their noses and
turning to Brian Mulroney. They don't like him one single bit, but
he's offering them, through free trade, tax reform and in a dozen
other ways, the New Utopia of social Darwinism for which they
salivate.

And what a world it would be when a band of Bay Street barons
calls the shots for Canada. Take William Mackness, a Bank of Nova
Scotia VIP whom Michael Wilson handpicked as special advisor
when he became Finance Minister. Mackness believed that since all
growth came from business investments, corporations should not be
so heavily taxed. But besides tax breaks for the mighty, Mackness
wanted significant cuts in social programs for ordinary Canadians,
since these programs deprived business of investment capital. As
investigative reporter Linda McQuaig summarized his advice to the

Minister, "take the money from social programs and give it to business."

The Tories enthusiastically followed Mackness' tax advice, but have not yet felt it politically advisable to cut social programs drastically. But the Tory/corporate agenda remains clear. At the same time as Mackness was hired by Wilson, Canadian business, euphoric at the Tory 1984 sweep, felt free to be publicly candid about its real philosophical convictions.

The Royal Bank, for example, announced that unemployment would be decreased if employers simply could pay the lowest wage the market would bear without being constrained by unions or minimum wage laws, and if unemployment insurance were cut so workers would be less fussy about taking jobs.

The Canadian Manufacturers Association advised the government to loosen up expensive laws dealing with statutory holidays, minimum wages, health and safety standards, and — wait for it — child labour. It also recommended a guaranteed annual income of $7,000 a year for an individual and $10,000 for a family — well below the poverty line. Today, the ever-candid CMA praises the free trade deal because it will "move us towards the discipline of a market-based economy . . . and remove . . . counterproductive and discriminatory interventions" by government.

The Tories were dying to accommodate their corporate cronies, but the Prime Minister's opportunism, thank heavens, won out over his own profoundly entrenched branch plant mentality. Canadians, the polls shouted at him, wouldn't take it. But after another election victory? With free trade in place? American-style locker-room capitalism can triumph at last.

There's another way to go, of course. The model is one of the world's most economically and socially successful nations, Sweden. There, Jim Laxer points out, organized labour's voice is strong, while comprehensive social programs are seen neither as economically counter-productive nor as frills to be cut back in bad times, but as an integral component of a successful tripartite industrial strategy.

It is problematic just how adaptable the Swedish alternative is to Canadian circumstances. But given the real Tory/corporate agenda for Canada, it is surely the direction for which progressive Canadians must wage a mighty battle.

*　*　*

1988   THE HOUSE OF COMMONS Finance Committee has just handed the New Democratic Party a formidable election weapon. The Tory majority on the committee want to modify somewhat the capacity of Canadian banks to rip off their customers — that's us — through an endless variety of dubious service charges.

The NDP minority want to go further and take even tougher measures. In fact, the government won't go even as far as their own MPs want, let alone the NDP. That's bad news for Canadians but political gravy for the NDP.

It's a gangbusters political issue. Remember Stephen Leacock's charming little fable of the meek little fellow — your ordinary Canadian — reacting in terror to a huge, anonymous, soulless, heartless, inhuman bank. Since then it's gotten really bad.

Banks are an irresistibly glorious political target: Unimaginably rich and powerful, they have a major impact on every one of our lives. Is there a single Canadian breathing without some personal banking horror story burned in his or her memory?

Well before the intense focus of recent months on exorbitant bank service charges, our captains of the banking industry — those paragons of sophisticated, bottom-line capitalism, greedy at the sight of easy marks — had made egregious errors in lending so much money to Third World countries during the wildly inflationary years of the 1970s; indeed, some experts dare argue that they've raised their service charges to help ease the losses they've incurred by those foolhardy loans.

Of course there's always the little matter of interest rate spreads. Compare the interest rates they charge you on your loan or mortgage (or mine, come to that) with the interest you get on your bank account, and see what happens. Then there's the grand brokerage houses that, under Tory deregulation, each of our giant chartered banks has recently taken over, dramatically broadening the banks' already monumental power.

Or, to get back to the specific issue of the moment, service charges. By nickel and diming — that really means dollaring these days — every helpless sucker who comes through their doors with a bewildering array of so-called service charges, the Big Five earned no less than $750 million big ones in 1987. Not bad, since the way they get rich is by investing the money we deposit with them.

And how do they show their gratitude for the plunder the government allows them to loot from our accounts? Let me count the ways.

First, in 1984 — which just happened to be an election year — each of the Big Five generously contributed between $70,000 and $75,000 to both the Liberal and Conservative Parties; that's a cool $720,000. In between-election years, they fork over only half that amount — about $35,000 per bank to each party — although the Royal has been holding out on John Turner for the past year or so. (This curious discrimination may relate not to the Royal's Tory partisanship, but to the fact that it's the Liberals' own banker.)

Still, you will smartly observe that those sums do add up over the course of four years. I know some misanthropic folk who will question whether those parties will really want to get tough with their banker benefactors. Personally, I eschew such tasteless cynicism.

Secondly, there is the quaint matter of taxes. Well wouldn't ya just know that in the 1987 tax year, the mighty Royal Bank of Canada paid no income tax whatever, thanks to a special tax writedown provision the government has thoughtfully granted the banks. I bet you wish you had one, eh? And for 1988, because the Royal, like its competitors, must cover its Third World debt liability referred to earlier, its income tax bite is likely to be equally onerous.

Thirdly, there's the substantial but unknowable sums that our banks spend on the noble cause of saving their employees from the clutches of trade unions. Rest assured they are not wasting their precious profits on such profligacy as excessive wages for their staffs. Many tellers — overwhelmingly women, naturally — still make no more than $15,000 a year — on which they probably pay more income tax than their employers.

The political irony of the banking issue in recent months has been its virtual monopolization by the Tories, thanks to Don Blenkarn, chairman of the Commons Finance Committee and, it so happens, one of the most rabidly right-wing populist members of the Conservative caucus.

Enough is surely enough. The Tory government will inevitably cop out, and together with tax reform it's the most natural issue in the world for the NDP. Bring on the election.

∗   ∗   ∗

1990   IT'S MORE THAN A PLEASURE, it's a privilege, to be able
────────   to report that deserving Canadians are hanging in there
through these difficult times.

True enough, the combination of quasi-recession, deficit, GST and
free trade is taking its inevitable toll. Many large Canadian corporations have cut down on their charitable giving at a time when the
need is greater than ever. The food banks' Easter food drives have
been disappointing, especially in Toronto where there are — believe
it or not — three times the number of outlets providing meals to the
needy than there are McDonald's restaurants.

But the most ominous portent of tough times was reflected in a
recent *Financial Post* headline: "Top paycheques," it announced
starkly, "feel pinch." The *Post*, you see, found no more than a dozen
Canadian executives who made more than a million bucks last year
in salary, bonuses and stock options. Now that's a pinch.

But our tag day for Bay Street remains, happily, premature. In fact,
"base salary levels for most executives in 1989 climbed, despite a 13
per cent drop in corporate earnings." And jettisoning the archaic
notion that rewards should vaguely be related to performance, "the
earning squeeze is not expected to affect base increase in value
despite the sluggish economy and an anticipated 6 per cent drop in
corporate profits this year." In other words, the bottom line may be
hurting, but the bosses ain't.

Of course it's not all rosy down there on The Street. The pay of
D.J. Phillips of Inco, the *Post* reports, is down from $2 million in '88
to only $1.9 million last year. Seagram's Edgar Bronfman has tum-
bled from $1.9 million to $1.8 million. Frank Stronach, whose
Magna International has had a disastrous year, paid the supreme
penalty by falling from $1.4 million to a humbling $1.2 million.

These punitive sacrifices at the very apex of the corporate pyramid
may be responsible for a phenomenon called the Gold Parachute
Club, whose 10th anniversary is recorded this month by that unlikely
purveyor of Marxist analysis, *Toronto Life*. A golden parachute, for
those of you who don't travel the fast lane, is a lush severance
package of bonuses, pensions and stock options wangled by top
executives when they leave their companies.

Like the pay packets discussed above, it's not necessarily material
whether the executive's firm has thrived or withered, or whether he
left voluntarily or was forced out. The goal, as one Bay Street lawyer
earnestly explained, is "secure maintenance of lifestyle."

Lifestyle, of course, is in the eye of the beholder. So our friend Donald Phillips of Inco, to compensate for last year's disappointing salary, is entitled, when he departs, to a $3 million parachute. Victor Rice of Varity, who plunged entirely from *The Financial Post*'s 1989 million-dollar club when his salary slumped by 10 per cent to $898,646, will take home 3.5 million big ones. And so it goes.

Mark Witten, who wrote *Toronto Life*'s excellent piece, sees a curious correlation "between the size of a man's golden parachute and the number of employees he's terminated," pointing for example to Bill James, former head of Falconbridge who lost his job when the corporation changed owners. Of course there's job loss and job loss.

James slashed Falconbridge's Sudbury workforce by 40 per cent but is bearing his own loss with the help of a $4.5 million-plus parachute. Witten could also have included Varity's Victor Rice, whose restructuring of Massey-Ferguson cost 2,300 employees their jobs and more than 3,000 retirees their health-care benefits; you might say their parachutes failed to open.

"It's interesting to note as well," continues Witten, "that some of the most vocal critics of the government's UIC program, who are appalled because Newfoundland fishermen collect a few extra weeks of pogey, are members of the Golden Parachute Club. After all, what is a golden parachute if not the finest form of pogey in the world?"

What indeed? And why stop there? Many of the biggest, richest, most privileged executives in the land are also among those who complain most incessantly about greedy, powerful unions, who whine that workers are unproductive, who courageously advocate high unemployment and low wages for workers to keep Canada internationally competitive, who want to slash social programs while protecting tax write-offs for entertainment and minimum corporate taxes.

And as it happens, their reactionary wish list is precisely what the Mulroney government is delivering.

* * *

1992   FOR YEARS, I'VE BEEN MYSTIFIED by the dogged efforts of the Mulroney government to undermine the interest of the business community. Equally inexplicable is that business people generally consider the Tories to be their government, when in fact they've been served so poorly by it.

Of course, it's true that in a few meager ways, like the free trade agreement and tax reform, the government has been little more than the handmaiden of the Business Council on National Issues. But just look at all the scandalous ways the Tories have sold Corporate Canada down the river:

- Unreliable economic forecasts, making business planning exceedingly difficult. Even though Michael Wilson's predictions were substantially off base in every one of his seven budgets — his deficit forecasts were merely wrong to the tune of some $50 billion to $60 billion — the Tories, for some unfathomable reason, are still seen as competent managers. In fact, they wouldn't know a bottom line if they tripped on one.
- Failing to restore consumer confidence and purchasing power. All forecasts of better times ahead — about which the government has now been dead wrong for two long, difficult years — are based in some part on the premise of increased consumer activity. Yet last week's budget, by failing to take any steps to reduce unemployment or to instil confidence in the millions of Canadians who fear losing their jobs, has ensured continuing consumer non-confidence for the foreseeable future. So who will buy business's products and services?
- Transferring impossible burdens to the provinces. Business people should be railing against the budget's cynical scam of pretending to cut programs and taxes when, in actuality, it's merely transferred even greater obligations to the strapped provinces.

  Provincial governments, already reeling, now have no choice but to raise taxes, increase deficits or cut programs. And almost the only programs of any relevant scale are in the health and education areas. Will cuts to medicare or schools, colleges and universities serve the interests of the business community?
- Failing to prepare Canada for the kind of information or idea-based economy that's already supplanting our conventional manufacturing and resource-based economy. Like everybody else, the Tories prate endlessly about the need to compete in the tough new global competitive order through more research and development and better education. "One of the most important investments government can make is in education," reads one of last week's budget papers, and that's exactly what just about every other government in the industrial world is doing. Except Canada, where the feds have actually put a tight cap on education spending.

And while all our industrial competitors are jacking up spending on science and technology, our government has mandated a chintzy 3 per cent ceiling on such expenditures. Here we have blind dogma at work. Caught up in their own obsession with deficits, the government imposes short-term pain in return for long-term pain. This policy is in the interest of no Canadians, least of all those in the business sector who depend on a skilled work force and serious R&D for their own future prospects.

- Failing to strengthen the country's physical infrastructure.

Here is the most glaring example of opportunity lost in the budget. There's an abundance of serious evidence — little of it, please note, emanating from dubious pinko sources — that government investment in physical infrastructure works.

Public expenditures on deteriorating municipal services such as public transit, sewers, water and sewage plants, or on highways, bridges, airports and energy-efficiency programs, have proved in Europe, Japan and even free-enterprising America to boost productivity and job-creation substantially, while leaving a modernized nation for future generations.

In fact, in the words of the Organization for Economic Co-operation and Development, "Infrastructure is indispensable . . . It is essential for industry, forming part of the production process in the same way as fixed capita." Yet who will build or upgrade or repair these structures — without which business cannot operate productively — if not government? The answer, everywhere, is no one; it's the state or nothing.

Increasingly, in recent months, the value of crash, large-scale, national capital investment projects has been gaining converts from people of all political stripes. The synergy of multi-billion-dollar federal-provincial joint programs could have transformed the face of this country for decades. But with its single-minded fixation on the deficit the Tories have subverted the urgent task of forging a modern Canadian economy.

Is a single business in this country better off for this victory of dogma over common sense? The federal government has repeatedly undermined the best interests of all Canadians, not least those in the corporate sector. Yet business rants and raves about the socialist hordes in Ontario and prepares to re-elect the Ottawa Tories.

Seems that sometimes ideology triumphs over that old bottom line.

✳　✳　✳

The World of Brian Mulroney

1987   OKAY, CLASS, let's see if you recognize who made the
following statements:

- "The central fact [of international life] is confrontation in east-west relations."
- "It is a matter of fact, not a matter of interpretation, that the west is faced with an ideological, political and economic adversary whose explicit long-term aim is to mould the world in its own image. That adversary has at its disposal massive military forces and a proven willingness to use force, both at home and abroad, to achieve political objectives."
- "IN THE EVENT OF WAR [emphasis added], the Warsaw Pact could be expected to use its superior numbers to overwhelm NATO defenses."
- "The principal direct threat to Canada continues to be a nuclear attack on North America by the Soviet Union . . . Although Canada is unlikely to be invaded in a conflict, limited incursions . . . are conceivable."

Now, can you identify the source of these statements? Dr. Strangelove? Ollie North? The Air Farce? The ghost of John Foster Dulles? Wrong, wrong, wrong.

It's none other than last month's Defence White Paper, issued by Defence Minister Perrin Beatty on behalf of the Cabinet of this government, and it contains more bellicose Cold War rhetoric than anything Canada has heard for a quarter of a century. So far, most attention has been devoted to Beatty's plan for a fleet of billion-dollar nuclear submarines, a proposal so fatuous it has made us a laughing-stock among military experts abroad.

Much more sinister, however, is the premise that the Soviet Union is virtually exclusively responsible for international tensions in today's world. Since the Prime Minister himself has distanced his government from the blindly reactionary American dogma that Southern Africa and Central America are, for example, primarily east-west conflicts, the basic philosophy articulated in the White Paper is simply beyond credulity.

There are a number of major fallacies with this premise:

1. If the Soviet Union launched a nuclear attack on Canada (or on anyone else), we are all done for in any case. Yet a new war is treated mindlessly as simply an upgraded version of those we've survived before.

2. If the deterrent theory works, only a counter-threat of nuclear attack could deter the Soviets, yet even this government remains, thank heavens, committed to keeping Canada a non-nuclear nation.

3. If deterrence is in fact serious, the stockpiling of nuclear weapons could have been halted 20 years ago, when each side already had enough to deter the other.

4. Notwithstanding the endless propaganda of NATO and its allies, NATO and the Warsaw Pact actually have, according to the prestigious London-based Institute for Strategic Studies, functional parity in weapon and troop strength.

5. So-called conventional warfare is no longer a question of machine guns and rumbling World War II tanks. Conventional weapons have become such lethal killing machines that even without nuclear warheads, almost all troops on both sides would be slaughtered within a short time. A missile with no nuclear warhead is a "conventional" weapon.

6. That the Soviet Union remains a totalitarian nation is undeniable, notwithstanding the new era of reformism. But the demonstrable fact is that the Soviet Union has attempted no aggression or expansionism towards western Europe since the Greek civil war and the Berlin blockade, both in the late 1940s, or forty years ago.

7. The description of a superpower attempting to mould the world in its own image, and prepared to use force to do so, also sounds remarkably like the United States in Viet Nam, Central and South America, Africa, and indeed anywhere that American economic and

political interests are deemed to be in danger. Don't believe me; what else is the Iran-Contra scandal about?

8. The real threats to peace are not to be found in a direct Soviet-western confrontation but in the Third World, where dozens of ghastly wars are being fought at this very moment.

It was once the heart of Canadian foreign policy to offer our good services for the purpose of peacekeeping. It was once our boast that we had a role to play in limiting the spread of arms, not widening it. These roles are given perfunctory mention in the 89 pages of the White Paper, literally a page apiece.

Don't look now, but if you don't pay close attention, the Mulroney government will get away with reversing Canada's proudest traditional international role. I hope Ronny Reagan at least appreciates it.

✳   ✳   ✳

1988 "I CAN'T THINK," allowed General Paul Manson, chief of the Canadian Defence Staff, "of a single element of the recommendations of the department to the minister that has not been brought to the government's defence white paper." How comforting. While you sleep, Mr. Submarine stands on guard for thee.

Yes, it's Defence Minister Perrin Beatty himself, faithful mouthpiece of the military brass and benefactor extraordinaire of our defence industries, simultaneously determined to exasperate his American allies while rebuffing Soviet arms-cutting initiatives. But will we have new weapons coming out of our ears! Nuclear subs, frigates, battle tanks, minesweepers, jet-fighters, anti-submarine patrol aircraft — you name it. And all for a piddling $200 billion or so over the next 15 years.

The direct target, of course, is the evil Commie empire, which, according to the white paper, is the central threat to peace and justice in the world. Never mind Joe Clark's statement a year ago that "in terms of threats to our sovereignty in our north . . . the larger threat comes from friends, the United States." Yet the government resurrects a Reaganite Cold War caricature of the state of international relations and issues bellicose, jingoistic threats. The weaponry it's seeking, the white paper stresses, "must be bought not simply for its utility in peace but more importantly for its utility in war."

You'll therefore understand why the white paper's 89 pages waste only a page apiece on those tedious old Canadian traditions of peacekeeping and arms control. After all, last year the world spent some $1.2 trillion on armaments, fully $100 billion over 1986. Obviously that increase was necessary, since more wars were fought than at any other time in human history — 22 wars that took 2.2 million lives, no fewer than two-thirds of them civilians. Our Tory masters apparently now want Canada to play in the big leagues.

Thus, Mr. Submarine dismisses out of hand the latest Soviet peace initiative, even though it echoes remarkably a 1986 all-party joint House-Senate committee report on international relations: "We recommend that Canada, in co-operation with other Arctic and nordic nations, seeks the de-militarization of the Arctic region through pressures on the United States and the Soviet Union." So now that Soviet leader Mikhail Gorbachev has initiated explorations of precisely this notion — an Arctic "zone of peace" with reduced levels of arms plus co-operation on scientific and environmental issues — what does he get from Mr. Submarine? Skeptical interest? "I don't really trust you guys but what do we have to lose?" Exactly the opposite.

At first contemptuous silence, then a demand for significant uni-lateral Soviet disarmament. Hell, you don't get to be next leader of the Conservative Party by being some wimpy Com-Symp. So instead of peacekeeping and arms control, this government gives us red-bashing and the militarization of the Canadian Arctic.

First they're going to build a permanent military base in Nanasivik near the Northwest Passage in order to test equipment for Arctic warfare. The land in question, wouldn't you just know it, is presently being claimed by the local Inuit in negotiations with Ottawa.

Then they'll buy us a passle of those multi-billion dollar nuclear subs. But the Americans naturally want our subs — like the rest of our defence policy — under their de facto control. And since the U.S. alone challenges our claims to the Arctic, the Americans are also affronted by our intentions to protect Canadian northern sover-eignty at all. So they'll be damned if they help Canada build subs to guard against U.S. subs (by giving them tickets if they intrude into our waters?) and will likely refuse to authorize the British sharing the nuclear technology in their subs with us.

That then allows Brian Mulroney's new unelected Quebec saviour, Lucien Bouchard, to deliver to some of his former friends from his ambassadorial days in Paris a vast contract for French nuclear submarines, to be built of course by his new friends in the province of Quebec. An auspicious beginning for Bouchard, if not exactly your major contribution to world peace.

Personally, I have a better solution. Since the point of nuclear subs is their untraceability, let's not build them and say we did. We can save a good $15 billion yet announce to the world that no darned foreigner better intrude into our Arctic waters — or else. Who'll ever know the difference?

Anyway, the quintessential Canadian dilemma, as Ben Wicks reminds us, is not between nuclear and diesel subs, or even French and English subs. The real question, O Canada, is: roast beef or the pizza sub?

✳ ✳ ✳

1989   WHAT A TESTAMENT to the genius of capitalism is the state of the Third World. Over the centuries, western interests have been able to squeeze untold bounties from Africa, Asia and Latin America. Western economic development has been made possible, in substantial part, because we had their boundless labour and resources to milk for all they were worth. They, however, have had no Fourth World that they could similarly pillage.

For eons, through mercantilism, the slave trade, the great imperial companies, colonial occupation, and, finally, formal political independence, we blithely enriched ourselves. The history books taught of the modernization and civilization we brought to primitive, war-like savages. The truth was substantially different, as recent generations of scholars (including me, 20 years ago), have amply demonstrated. Dr. Walter Rodney called his groundbreaking book *How Europe Underdeveloped Africa*. Professor Andre Gunder Frank described the consequences of capitalism in Latin America as "the development of underdevelopment." Always we — rich beyond the dreams of avarice — grabbed, and grabbed, and grabbed. Always they — poor beyond our Dickensian imaginations — gave, and gave, and gave.

What's different now is only that the grotesque imbalance is widely acknowledged, thanks to the unholy alliance between corrupting foreign capitalists and corruptible local elites who together through the ages have casually sold the citizens of the Third World down the river.

During the '70s and early '80s, flush western banks provided eager military dictators and small-time tyrants with massive financing they could not conceivably afford for projects they did not remotely need. Gargantuan loans went to the rulers of the poorest countries on the globe who gorged themselves on world-class fighter planes and state-of-the-art missiles and nuclear plants and unproductive mega-projects, while billions more were simply skimmed off the top. Soon it became obvious these loans could never be repaid.

But fear not for our intrepid bankers. Most of them, thanks to a little creative entrepreneurial finagling, have benefitted handsomely from their own recklessness while, with only a handful of Asian exceptions, the Third World miserably stagnates. Between 1982 and 1987, the impoverished nations dispatched to the affluent West no less than $220 billion more than we provided them. In the words of Third World expert Susan George, "Never before in history have the poor financed the rich on such a lavish scale."

The consequences have been tragically predictable. UNICEF's 1988 annual report, *The State of the World's Children*, put it baldly: "For almost 900 million people, the march of human progress has now become a retreat. In many nations, development is being thrown into reverse . . . large areas of the world are sliding backwards into poverty." UNICEF calls for a massive increase in foreign aid, pointing out how remarkably easy it would be to save the lives of 5 million kids a year — let's say it again — 5 million kids, every year, using dirt-cheap vaccines and oral rehydration treatment.

Justifying their recent hateful budget, Tory propagandists concocted the clever line that each day the national debt costs us $80 million. UNICEF, coincidentally, has its own version of this device: In the past 24 hours, almost 40,000 kids under the age of 5 have died unnecessarily. After the Tory budget, we know that UNICEF and the kids lost — again.

The Third World's good friends, Canadian banks, won big. Having made a record $3.3 billion in after-tax profits in fiscal 1988, a persuasive bankers' lobby convinced their Tory chums to exempt them from some $500 million a year in new taxes that were widely anticipated in the financial world.

Many humongous corporations will still pay no taxes, victorious to the end. All wealthy Canadians win, retaining generous tax preferences on investment income such as capital gains, a triumph for market dogmas over fairness and common sense. The well-off in general are laughing, the extra surtax probably forcing them to cancel as many as two or three meals out at their favorite restaurants.

Of all the possible budget cuts before them, the Tories chose to slash foreign aid most viciously. Reneging on commitments repeatedly made to increase Canadian aid spending, and shamelessly regurgitating false promises that "Canada's aid contribution will continue to be the one of the most generous among developed countries," the Tory budget in fact puts Canada dead last among aid-givers from comparable middle-power nations in Europe.

Faced with the need to make difficult choices, the Mulroney government adopted a cherished western capitalist tradition and chose to clobber hardest those whose need is greatest. In the next 24 hours, another 40,000 kids will die in Third World countries. I bet Canada's contribution kind of makes you quietly proud, eh?

* * *

1990   FORGIVE ME if I'm not myself today, but I've been a nervous wreck all week. Partly it's the shattering news I've learned, but it's also my anxiety about whether to share it with you. Frankly, it's all because this damned Tory government is just too decent. But their paternalistic decision to spare Canadians a terrible shock has left this burden to me.

The Cold War, I greatly fear, is not over. And the Mulroney government has known it all the time while we deluded saps were revelling in the false hope that a new era was dawning. Sure, it's true they took us into their confidence in 1987 — two years after Gorbachev took over in Moscow — by the timely warning in their intrepid Defence White Paper that "The principal direct threat to Canada continues to be a nuclear attack on North America by the Soviet Union." By last year, however, they were trying to soften the blow; you had to search out the document revealing that "The most serious direct threat to Canada is a Soviet nuclear attack on North

America." This year, while the illusion spread of the disintegration of the Soviet Empire, the evaporation of any Soviet capacity to attack the West, and, therefore, the end of NATO's sole raison d'être, the vigilant Tories knew the bitter reality was different. But, ever sensitive, they chose again to reveal it most discreetly.

In fact you must unearth the volume on National Defence among the 87 volumes of the government's Budget Estimates for 1990–91, Part III, to find this forthright statement buried on page 22: "The most serious direct threat to Canada is a Soviet nuclear attack on North America." And we save typesetting costs too.

Of course the logic of this truth remains inescapable, and the government boldly faces it. Only NATO's nuclear weapons can deter a still-possible Soviet strike. Indeed, Canada endorses NATO strategy that calls for a pre-emptive NATO nuclear first strike if necessary. But since Gorby might at any moment launch the Red Army across Europe to invade the free world before he nukes us, Canada loyally "continues to commit conventional . . . forces to NATO in Europe."

This hard-headed realism is reassuringly reflected by those Canadians entrusted with safeguarding Canada's security abroad. Last month a Canadian Voice of Women delegation met in Vienna with negotiators from countries involved in the arms control meetings between NATO and the Warsaw Pact.

According to Janis Alton, VOW's United Nations representative, they found our Canadian guys without the false hope that characterized, for example, the bleeding-hearts who spoke for West Germany. The innocent Germans were filled with naïve dreams of new forms of common security for all of Europe. Not Johnny Canuck, though. Our boys recognized the West's dependence on nuclear deterrence for the foreseeable future.

Oh sure, they told Alton's group, it was exciting seeing the Warsaw Pact dissolve before their very eyes. But, Ambassador David Peel enlightened them, we must still retain nuclear weapons against possible other enemies such as Libya; otherwise they too, the VOW delegation solemnly learned, might well also nuke us. (Do you wonder I'm overwrought?)

So even though one of our military chappies good-naturedly joshed the little ladies of VOW about "Making love, not war, ho! ho! ho!", in fact they were assured we need NATO for at least another 10 years.

So if the bad news is that the Cold War still rages, the good news is that our government is on the case. That's why, you see, in a budget that reluctantly was forced to slash funds for battered women's centres and native newspapers to keep the deficit from strangling the entire economy, the Department of Defence was, thank goodness, able to emerge with a 5 per cent increase.

In fact in their first budget in 1984–85, the Tories devoted $8.7 billion, merely 9.3 per cent of all expenditures, to defence; in the new budget, they've prudently raised the ante to $11.8 billion or 11 per cent of the total.

So Canada maintains its proud record of pulling more than its load in keeping the world safe from Soviet Communist imperialist aggression; after all, we can boast we rank about 12th in the world in total military expenditures and 6th among the 15 countries of NATO. Personally, I salute our far-sighted governors. My family's feeling more secure already.

✳   ✳   ✳

1991   SO SADDAM HUSSEIN is "serene" and George Bush is "at peace with himself." Naturally. Both of them have clearly taken leave of their senses, or we wouldn't be plunging into this maelstrom of death and destruction. Saddam, no doubt serenely, has kept his terrible vow to retaliate at Israel — another good reason why this war should never have happened. And only the day before attacking Iraq, a tranquil Bush released $42.5 million aid to the Salvadoran government and its death squads, who could teach Iraqi soldiers a trick or two about savagery.

While it's true the international community is remarkably united against Saddam, there'd be no war now if American interests hadn't demanded one.

That's why Brian Mulroney's speeches in Parliament this week were so misleading. For all his pious invocation of the United Nations, the truth is he committed Canadian warships to the gulf the moment Bush asked him to, which was right after Iraq's attack on Kuwait and before the United Nations had met. His government's agenda has hardly deviated from lapdog subservience to Bush ever since.

There is now no retreat from full-scale participation by Canadian troops in an all-out offensive war conducted entirely by the United

States. Nor will this be a limited war confined to ejecting Iraq's forces from Kuwait. The Americans are in this to exterminate Saddam personally and to level his country.

Many will sympathize with these objectives. But they're not what the U.N. approved. They're not what this alliance is supposed to be about. And it won't be accomplished in a few short, sweet days.

The real tragedy in all this is how terribly the credibility of the U.N. has been undermined. Thanks to Washington's conniving, sanctions were never given a realistic chance to work. Incredibly enough, the U.N. never properly assessed the effectiveness of sanctions before handing Iraq its ultimatum and arbitrary deadline. Yet surely the resort to war should have been unthinkable unless it was conclusively demonstrated that sanctions would not work.

Under any circumstances, Mulroney's faithful parroting throughout these months of the Bush line profoundly undermined his moral authority last week when he declared war on behalf of Canada — as "a moral duty," no less.

But his position is further dramatically weakened by the contempt and loathing in which he's held by the overwhelming majority of Canadians, most of whom are opposed to committing Canadian troops to war. Ironically Quebec, the one province where Mulroney retains some stature, also embraces the greatest anti-war sentiment. With Canadians already bitterly divided on almost every other conceivable issue, we now are split asunder on tempestuous, fundamental issues of peace and war. Is there a Canadian less suitable to lead us through these dreadful times than Brian Mulroney?

Now what? The Big Guns may be placid and philosophical but, like everybody I know, I'm twitchy, frustrated, anxious, depressed. Helplessly watching it all unfold, hour by hour, day by day, has been almost macabre: Literally a death watch for mass murder.

This will be a trying time for those of us who are determined to continue opposing this unjustified war. As the Liberal party has already shown, once the battle begins it is difficult to resist the stampede toward unthinking patriotism: Now's the time for all good men to come to the aid of their country. Rally round the flag, boys. (How come it's always males?) My country right or wrong. We've got to stand up for our boys over there.

Nuts. What we owe our troops is our principles, our values, our commitment to peace. This war was wrong before it began, and it's wrong now. I am proud of my party for having the courage to stand alone in Parliament and say so consistently and clearly, and I'm proud it intends to speak for the ever-growing number of peace activists. There exists in Canada a gratifying universe of people who simply can't accept that the first act of the leader of the new international order is a catastrophic war. I'm proud my party will be their voice.

"You're the luckiest 9-year-old in the world," I teased our kid as he deftly stopped a sure goal. "Uh uh," he said earnestly, "9-year-old kids over there will be the luckiest in the world if there's no war there." It was the only glimmer of light in a bleak, black week.

* * *

1991   THESE ARE VERY TRYING TIMES for many of use who oppose the war in the gulf. Reconciling conflicting emotions and convictions is an agonizing experience. Watching Saddam Hussein shamelessly exploit prisoners of war makes your stomach turn. Waiting for his campaign of terrorism abroad chills the blood. And witnessing the missile attacks on Israel makes the heart sick.

So when anxious friends ruefully conclude that the painful duty now must be to help obliterate this menace, you sympathize. When Audrey McLaughlin candidly confesses that she can't guarantee that her stance is a perfect one, she reflects appropriate uncertainty and ambivalence.

Nevertheless, when McLaughlin finally argues that this terrible war will solve no real issues, that Canada is better equipped to pursue peace than to wage war, I must agree. In the end, reason and sanity tell me that no other role makes sense for this country in the long months to come.

After all, will the war be shortened by even a single second if every one of us endorsed an offensive role for Canadian troops? Will Iraq fall more quickly? Will the next attack on Israel be halted?

The logic seems clear: To end the conflict more quickly, you fight not for a bloodier war but for an earlier end to war. It may feel futile now, but it's the most important contribution that can be made by those of us who believe the war should never have happened.

But passion and emotion are in the saddle now. Take Saddam's use of POWs as hostages. Sure it's despicable and illegal. But what in the world did we expect he'd do? We go to war because we say he's a Hitler-like madman, and then we're outraged when he plays dirty.

And what fine distinctions we make between OUR acceptable and THEIR barbaric activities! Is carpet-bombing more honorable than misusing POWs? What about those obscene U.S. cluster bombs? The phoney, theatrical indignation about the POWs on the part of the American coalition is contrived to whip up patriotic hysteria, plain and simple.

Or look, most tragically, at the attacks on Israel. Terrible? Beyond words. Predictable? One hundred per cent. Saddam promised them, and he's keeping his promise. Everyone always knew that his major strategic option was to weaken Arab support for the alliance against him by attacking Israel. Please tell me: Why didn't Israel's supporters speak out in advance to stop a war that would inevitably lead to attacks on it? Why don't they now demand an early end to this war that otherwise must bring more and more Israeli deaths and destruction?

I understand completely the fear that Saddam would eventually have attacked Israel anyway. Now we'll never know. But we do know for sure, bizarrely enough, that our side deliberately escalated the crisis to the point where attacks on Israel were absolutely guaranteed.

Friends of Israel are properly shattered by what's happening there. Buy why don't they worry that the day after Saddam is crushed, a strengthened Syria — today's great ally — will rise to lead the anti-Israeli crusade? Why don't they demand a regional peace settlement that, however difficult, ultimately alone will assure Israel's continued survival?

And above all, where is the concern for the terrible suffering of other innocent victims? Contrary to American propaganda, this has been no antiseptic, victimless, video game exercise. Refugees fleeing Iraq are telling hair-raising tales of life — and death — under the unparalleled allied onslaught. The *Los Angeles Times* quotes escaping Egyptians, who actually had been harsh critics of Saddam, describing what happens when the bombs fall on Baghdad, "crushing children, maiming adults and paralysing all of them with fear." "People are screaming in the streets," said one. "I have seen it . . . It is destruction. It is not war." It "makes the children jump out of their skins," says a Palestinian, referring to "Screaming children in Baghdad's bomb shelters (who) cower in terror from the thunder of air raids and the roar of anti-aircraft fire." Those who are running this war are determined to carry on to the bitter end, until Saddam is dead or surrenders unconditionally. It won't be easy, but the job of those of us who hate this war must be to demand that it be ended before there's nothing left.

✳   ✳   ✳

1991   WHAT IF THEY GAVE A WAR and one side didn't show? What would you conclude about a great military showdown in which one side only intermittently fired a shot? What do we say about a titanic struggle between the allied coalition and "the world's fourth-ranking military power" in which there was only a handful of minor skirmishes and possibly not a single real battle?

How would you account for a casualty ratio of about 3,000:1 in favour of the coalition? For 28 Americans dying in combat, compared to perhaps 100,000 Iraqis? For "the biggest tank battle since World War II" taking only 100 hours and costing exactly two destroyed allied tanks? For the Iraqis' vaunted impenetrable bunkers proving to be flimsy shelters covered with corrugated metal roofs and some sand?

From the first day to the 42nd, this war has been a veritable target practice for allied forces, a real-life laboratory for trying out all those infernal weapons developed in the Reagan years, mostly with little risk of Iraqi retaliation. As one American fighter pilot explained, it was like shooting fish in a barrel — or Iraqis in their tanks.

Did the Americans understand in advance the magnitude of their military superiority? Absolutely. Did they grasp the vast gulf between their capacity and Saddam's? Without question. Did they know that Iraq could barely even pretend to fight back? Almost certainly. Did they tell their allies, like Canada? We can't be positive yet.

But they sure convinced the public, including those of us on the peace side who believed the $50 billion of armaments Iraq purchased over the decade would make this one of history's most savage wars.

Yet there has been no real war at all. Iraq's army has proved to be a sham, a paper tiger. There has been no Desert Storm. As *The Toronto Star*'s Richard Gwyn says, we have instead witnessed Desert Slaughter. Gwyn, in fact, argues that six weeks ago Iraq was little more than a minor military power. The wild hyping by the allies of

95

Saddam's military might was "one of the most brilliant campaigns of deception and disinformation in military history."

Virtually all allied depictions of the Iraqi war machine, claims Gwyn, were fraudulent. Most of its soldiers, including a majority of the "elite" Republican Guards, were raw conscripts. During the Iran war, the Soviets sold them first-rate tanks with second-rate electronic systems since the Iraqis routinely sold such systems to the CIA in exchange for U.S. satellite photos of Iranian positions. Nor were the Iraqis technologically prepared to use effectively all their costly new state-of-the-art weapons.

And did you never ask yourself why those notorious Iraqi chemical weapons failed to materialize? Why were they never used? Because, Gwyn's sources claimed, "Washington has known all along that Iraq had no chemical warheads for its missiles, thus no ability to deliver chemicals at a distance. And in the open desert, Iraq's chemical shells for its artillery would be scarcely more than a minor irritant militarily."

Gwyn is one of the few commentators who has attempted to explain the amazing mystery of the disappearing Iraqi military. But is he correct? The implications of his analysis, if true, are almost too appalling to bear: a fiendish, cynical, warped conspiracy by the White House to demonstrate George Bush's manhood and to reassert America's primacy around the globe. So a fight is deliberately picked against a tin-pot Middle Eastern dictator, who is then, for reasons of public opinion, pumped up into a world-class villain and his army into a world-class fighting machine.

If this monstrous plot is true, it would make a mockery of every casualty on both sides and every fleeing refugee and every moment of horror and panic of the past six weeks. It is a conspiracy theory bordering on the paranoid. Is it possible? Can the gulf war have been the mother of all deceptions?

Well, you know, it wouldn't exactly be the first time the U.S. has engaged in questionable international behaviour. Forget the coups it's organized and the tyrants it's supported. Think only of the direct invasions: Viet Nam, Cambodia, Laos, Grenada, Panama. With surrogates: Cuba, Nicaragua, Angola. Each was a brutal, immoral aggression masquerading as a sacred mission for justice and peace.

Does the gulf war now join this honour roll? And what lessons are there for Canadians about the new international order about to be forged?

* * *

1991   THE MONTHS AFTER THE IRAQI INVASION of Kuwait,
_____   culminating in the brief, bloody war against Saddam
Hussein, were uncomfortable ones for my family.

My outspoken opposition to the war led to an unprecedented
number of menacing calls and letters that actually led us to adopt
precautionary steps. Most came from fellow Jews, furious that I
dared betray what they saw as Israel's cause. Others were from the
usual run of bigots — "you gawddam Jew bastard you" called
regularly for months — affronted by my failure to stand up for Bush
and country.

On the other hand, our situation seemed mercifully uncommon.
We were never badgered by the Mounties or the Canadian Security
and Intelligence Service (CSIS), and it appeared there'd been relatively
little harassment of other Canadians during these anxious months
either by state security agents or by other Canadians.

How terribly wrong I was. How little we knew about what many
of our fellow citizens endured throughout that period. Now, thanks
to a little-publicized report issued last month by the Canadian Arab
Federation called "CSIS and the Arab Canadian Community," and a
new book due out next week by journalist Zuhair Kashmeri, *The
Gulf Within: Canadian Arabs, Racism And The Gulf War*, we learn
the ugly truth. The Canadian wartime tradition of victimizing innocent citizens stands untarnished.

There are some quarter million Canadians of Arab descent in
Canada; about four-fifths are Muslims. Many are second-, third-,
fourth-generation Canadians. During the war, some of them strongly
backed Saddam Hussein. Many more defended Iraq's attack on
Kuwait. And large numbers — 80 per cent by some estimates —
opposed the war against Saddam. Significantly, few seem to have
sided with the Arab nations in the anti-Saddam coalition.

I knew none of this, because the Arab-Canadian viewpoint, I now
understand, was largely missing from the public debate during the
war. Even though I vehemently disagreed with those who backed
Saddam and his invasion of Kuwait, it's surely remarkable that their
position was largely unheard during those months. To be sure, a
small number of pro-Saddam Canadian Arabs made some news. But
they paid a heavy penalty for their heresy. They received innumerable
hate calls, threats to their lives and to blow up their houses and
machine gun their kids, and obscene, racist, hate mail. At least one
pipe-bomb was discovered outside the home of one of these people.

But Canadians of Arab background needed no position on the war at all to be the victims of what Kashmeri calls "persecution, harassment and racism."

In a "flood" of incidents, school kids were abused and pushed around by their peers and sometimes humiliated by their teachers. One theology teacher told his class Iraqis should be flushed down the toilet, while some women actually had their *hejabs* — the distinctive Muslim scarf — ripped off their heads and spat on.

On top of such shameful behaviour came the antics of the Mounties and the CSIS, who turned up uninvited on between 500 and 1,000 Arab-Canadian doorsteps during this period. Reid Morden, then head of CSIS, plumbed new depths of inanity when he told a CAF delegation that his officers were visiting ordinary Arab-Canadians to improve their understanding of the Middle East.

CSIS's mandate is crystal clear: it's authorized to gather information only about those engaged in espionage, sabotage, subversion, political violence or "foreign-influenced activity." Yet CSIS agents as well as Mounties, never with the benefit of warrant, intruded repeatedly on the domestic privacy of perfectly innocent Canadian citizens — unless being of Arab descent was itself sufficient grounds for being suspected of disloyalty.

Innocent or not, however, no one wants to be accosted by the security forces. The interviews (interrogations?) that were conducted were invariably unnerving and upsetting to the participants, while the questions asked — usually about personal religious and political beliefs — were totally out of line. They surely violated the spirit of the Canadian Charter of Rights. Certainly they succeeded in intimidating many of those questioned, which helps explain why few of them felt secure enough to lodge complaints or even go public about their treatment.

It's hard to resist the conclusion that the security forces thought of Arab Canadians as the enemy within. Given the warped stereotype of Arabs that the western media has disseminated in the past decade, it may not be surprising that officials who get paid to root out spies and saboteurs should instinctively regard Arabs and Muslims as constituting a threat to Canadian security.

In the end, after all their snooping, the security boys came up utterly empty-handed: The record shows that not a single Arab-Canadian was charged with war-connected crimes. On the other hand, Canada has been allowed to maintain intact one of its oldest traditions: before the Gulf, in every war some innocent Canadians

— of Japanese, Italian, Ukraine descent, whatever — had been unjustly abused by their government. That dubious record stands untarnished.

∗   ∗   ∗

1993   HIT 'EM WHEN THEY'RE DOWN. This sacred principle of Tory government has already been applied to the unemployed, battered women's shelters, native communications, refugees and provincial governments.

Now it's about to be extended to truly global proportions: unless we can stop them, the next victims of unfettered Tory capitalism will be the poorest nations on Earth.

Everything, but everything, conspires against the Third World. Last year's UN Human Development Report showed that the richest developed countries, most notably the United States and Japan, provide far less aid than their affluence would dictate. Moreover, most of the aid that is available goes to the better-off among poor nations. What's worse, poor countries that spend a lot on their military are rewarded with twice as much aid per capita as those that spend more modestly.

Most Third World countries are also overwhelmingly dependent on exporting crops or minerals to the West. Yet prices for such commodities as coffee and cocoa, for example, have plunged in recent years, costing Africa alone some $50 billion between 1985 and 1990.

Next come the Structural Adjustment Programs (SAPs) that the World Bank imposes on poor countries desperate for cash. Funds are disbursed only if the recipient government agrees to accept free market dogmas that harm women, the poor and the environment, and if funds are cut for education and health, and if subsidies on basic food items are removed. As Third World economic specialist Susan George puts it, SAPs "destroy more children's lives than UNICEF can save."

Though the World Bank and the IMF claim their policies have helped the Third World reduce its horrendous debt load, the exact opposite is true. According to Percy Mistry, a British expert on African debt, at the end of 1982 Africa's total debt was $140 billion.

By 1990, African countries had more than paid off this staggering burden — $180 billion, in fact — at which point their debt stood at $270 billion! George estimates that the poorest countries on the globe transferred to the richest ones, between 1982 and 1990, the equivalent of six Marshall Plans.

Under the Conservative government, Canada has been a full partner in this past decade's multi-pronged screwing of poor countries. Not only has Canadian aid been miserly, too much of it has been linked to destructive SAPs, while three-quarters of it is fully or partially tied to the purchase of Canadian goods and services. Examining Western support for reducing poverty in the Third World, the UN Development Program says Canada has one of the worst records of any major aid donor.

As for Brian Mulroney's unconditional 1988 commitment to increase Canadian aid, more than $4 billion has been slashed from the CIDA budget over the past five years, while the Tories' December mini-budget announced further 10 per cent cuts again this year and next.

But now the government has decided to make a dismaying record even worse. With an election looming, the Tories can't bear the thought that CIDA still has a batch of money that's not being used directly to buy votes. And anyway, there's no political percentage in putting dough into Africa. But among Canadians of Eastern European backgrounds, now, there's votes.

So a scheme has been hatched to politicize CIDA, put it under the control of Barbara MacDougall at external affairs, reduce funds to the very poorest countries for development projects that might actually reduce Third World dependence on the West, and use dollars once earmarked for aid to help Canadian businesses set up profitable operations in Eastern Europe.

This is a major shift in Canadian policy, yet every step of it has happened in absolute secrecy, with not one iota of public consultation. Until, that is, the intrepid folks who run the Canadian Council of International Co-operation got wind of the plot last week and started to fight back. And with some surprising results.

The conspirators are unnerved that their secret is out and that their plans have inspired such vehement opposition. It may not be too late. With your help, it's still possible to stop this latest diabolical act of Tory inhumanity.

*　*　*

Following the American Leader

1985   THE 10TH ANNIVERSARY of the ending of the American war against Viet Nam is naturally provoking a torrent of both anguished and self-serving remembrances within the United States. But Canadians might take a moment to recollect that it was, in a very real sense, our war too.

Not, of course, that we fought. Nevertheless, for countless thousands of Canadians, opposition to America's brutal, senseless, and aggressive intervention in Viet Nam was a formative experience in our growing up. In virtually every city in Canada, a significant counter-culture grew and developed around the anti-war movement, including everything from assistance to American draft-dodgers to endless demonstrations and protests.

The anti-war movement represented both the worst and the best in the Canadian progressive tradition. Two aspects of it were unedifying. In the first place, in grand Canadian continentalist tradition, we typically reacted more passionately to American injustices than to our own right here at home.

Secondly, we fell then, as progressives and leftists seem irresistibly to do time after forgotten time, into the trap of transposing the badness of the bad guys into the goodness of the good guys. As was done by earlier generations to Stalin and Mao, so we did in spades to Ho Chi Minh and his Viet Cong. The authoritarianism and expansionism of Hanoi since 1975 shames each of us who was pleased to regard the North Vietnamese as begetters of a new socialist utopia.

On the other hand, the anti-war movement was a powerful and appropriate manifestation of Canadian nationalism at its most positive and honorable. It was, after all, a war with no redeeming features, as purely unjust as was imaginable. There was no remote justification for the atrocities Americans could be seen nightly on television perpetrating on this hapless, faraway land.

But all that, of course, was precisely why it had to be our war too. We were America's most reliable friend and ally. We were humiliated by being tarred with the same brush. The vast American take-over of so much of the Canadian economy under a succession of Liberal governments since 1945 meant that significant corporations in Canada were producing weapons to be used in Viet Nam. Somehow, our continentalist relation with the United States of America made us feel almost responsible for American behaviour, almost guilty about their cruel war.

In the end, Canadian reaction was instinctive. Canada was created, after all, because of our own perfectly rational fear of an American invasion. Call it anti-American or just call it sensible, but Canadians never quite trust a part of the American personality — the western hero, the gunslinger, the vigilantes, the ruthless Ayn Rand capitalist, the bully whose self-proclaimed doctrine of Manifest Destiny has justified countless military interventions in tiny, helpless countries on behalf of corporate interests.

As Americans are seeking the lessons of that tumultuous period, so should we. There is much that Brian Mulroney, above all, can learn from the Canadian experience during Viet Nam. Americans and Canadians disagree on many crucial issues. President Reagan considers, for example, that the war in Viet Nam was an honorable and just one. Mr. Reagan, many believe, is withholding a full-scale invasion of Nicaragua only because he fears American public opinion will not, after Viet Nam, tolerate a protracted foreign adventure that results in large numbers of American casualties: Grenada si, Nicaragua non.

The tighter the Prime Minister forges the bonds between Washington and Ottawa, the greater will be our sense of collusion in American policies. Viet Nam created a virtual civil war within the United States, and substantial friction within Canada between governing elites and the rest of us. The friction did not escalate here because many of our governors shared, however reticently, our opposition to the war.

Had we a government openly supportive of the Americans, Canada too might have faced a decade of nightmare, of war in our streets, of kids against parents, class against class, students against authority, young against old, governed against government. If Mr. Mulroney continues his fawning servility to a president chomping at the bit to launch the kind of immoral foreign adventures many Canadians would passionately oppose, we still might. That is the lesson of Viet Nam for Canada which a leader committed to conciliation and harmony must never forget.

* * *

1986   PROMISES, PROMISES. They are the stock in trade of politicians everywhere, from the most humble to the most exalted. Politicians live in a world where they are expected to make outlandish commitments and then figure out just how little they can get away with delivering. It happens in local elections, and, we'd be prudent to remember, it happens just as much at the international levels. And it happens among putative friends as well as between wary opponents.

Take, for example, Ronald Reagan's batty and dangerous little toy, Star Wars. The President is the only person in the world who truly believes that Star Wars will lead to a safer world — an accurate reflection of his intellectual capacity. Those who have jumped on the Star Wars bandwagon have more rational, if also more sinister, motives.

His advisors were immediate converts, since most of them are true anti-Communist fanatics who believe the proposed new weaponry will give the U.S. a qualitative advantage over the Soviets, perhaps even making a first strike against them possible.

The Pentagon was quick to fall in line, since increasing the store of Buck Rogers mega-death devices seems intrinsically a good thing to the American military, and a way each of the services hopes to get a leg up on the other in the eternal competition among them.

As for the gigantic and powerful corporate sector which actually produces all the hardware, the prospect of untold billions of dollars coming their way on top of the regular defence budget of one-quarter of a trillion dollars was not entirely unattractive.

But since the President alone believed in the peaceful uses of Star Wars, his advisers understood that some incentive was needed to persuade America's allies to support this wildly destructive and destabilizing Reagan initiative. They offered, in the best American fashion, material gain. The research budget alone for Star Wars was expected to be an initial $20 billion, and as much as $60–70 billion in the longer term.

You may remember that Canada was promised, along with the other NATO allies, a significant share of that irresistible loot if we came aboard. We'd please the Yanks and make big bucks doing so.

The Prime Minister was under great conflicting pressures from the business community and his right-wing caucus to support enthusiastically the Americans, and from opposition politicians and the vocal Canadian peace community to reject Star Wars entirely. After long agonizing, he attempted a Solomonic compromise. While the Canadian government would not directly get involved, Canadian corporations would be free to bid on Star Wars contracts.

Being the generous soul I am, I can only hope that not too many Canadian businesspeople stayed up late at night counting their unexpected windfall. Because it ain't going to happen. Although I have never seen the news in a single Canadian newspaper, the American Senate the other day decreed that all future Star Wars research contracts must be placed in the United States unless the Pentagon certifies that the work can't be done there.

The motives of those backing this unfriendly little move were clear. The politicians wanted to show their constituents that new work opportunities were staying at home. The big players in the defence industry were out in full force — you should pardon the expression. The Pentagon decided it was concerned about the security risks if work was farmed-out abroad. So tough luck to those who had taken America's promises at face value.

The Thatcher government naturally supported Star Wars and tried to get a guarantee for $2 billion of the research work in return for being the first to sign on; it got on board, but with no guarantees. West Germany believed billions were bound to come its way too. Canada just hoped for the best. In the event, Britain has won 5 contracts worth about $30 million, West Germany four for $20 million, Canada even less. Washington analysts believe all the Allies would be lucky if they shared $300 million.

Poor Mulroney. Every time he deals with Ronald Reagan he gets shafted just a little bit deeper. Is there a moral in this story, or is it just about how politicians deal with each other?

* * *

1988   THE BUDGET of Toronto Metro Council this year is $1.8
————————   billion. The six municipalities comprising Metropolitan Toronto will spend about another billion.

Metro constitutes about a quarter of the population of Ontario, whose budget is $38 billion. Metro probably receives its arithmetic proportion of those funds, or say $9 billion. Metro's population is also about one-tenth of the entire country, whose budget is $132 billion. Again, Metro's share is probably proportional, but let's conservatively say $10 billion.

So we can safely say that public funds devoted to the 2.2 million people who live in Metro Toronto are more than $20 billion.

Yet, Toronto has troubles galore: scarce low-rent accommodation, 60,000 people — half of them kids — relying on food banks, traffic and road problems, underfunded hospitals and universities, child-care shortages, low-paid job ghettos for visible minorities, especially women, violence against women; the list is long enough.

This column is not about Toronto. It is about tiny Nicaragua, which has been under attack by the United States and its proxies for much of this decade. Including international funds, the budget of Nicaragua for this year is about half a billion dollars, one-fortieth of Toronto's, of which some two-thirds goes to the war effort.

That's for a desperately poor country of more than 3 million people, half again as many as Toronto. Even before Ronald Reagan's war, the United Nations calculated that a third of the population could not meet elementary needs. But in the first four years of the Sandinista revolution, infant mortality was reduced from an appalling 120 to 70 deaths per 1,000 live births, polio was virtually eradicated, and illiteracy was reduced from 53 per cent to 12 per cent. As American aggression escalated, however, conventional development was substantially halted and the war dominated all aspects of life.

Some 45,000 Nicaraguans on both sides of the struggle have been killed, wounded or kidnapped in the past eight years; in perspective, that's the equivalent of 300,000 Canadians or 3 million Americans. (60,000 Americans were killed in Viet Nam, all of them of course soldiers.) The Nicaraguan military has actually suffered fewer casualties than the civilian population, reflecting a deliberate Contra policy of targeting civilians, especially health workers and rural teachers. Presumably that's why Prime Minister Mulroney praised President Reagan at the recent Washington summit so gushingly as "a man of peace."

The Nicaraguan economy is in a shambles, in part unquestionably from the Sandinistas' own mistakes, but mostly from the American war plus the American trade embargo plus the American blockade on loans from such institutions as the World Bank. Total indirect damage to the country through the end of 1987 is estimated at $3.6 billion — all of its budgets for seven entire years.

Revisiting the country last month after four years, as part of a Canadian mission for peace, I was immediately struck by the daily struggle to survive: the long lines, the shanties, the shortage of essential consumer items, the impossible prices, the overcrowded deteriorating buses, the power blackouts, the water and gas rationing.

And in a resettlement camp near the border with Honduras, attacked by the Contras three times in the past year — most recently only six weeks before our visit — we watched 17 kids in an old room being taught without one single notebook, textbook, pen or pencil. Nicaragua has regressed to commonplace Third World underdevelopment, compounded many times by the insupportable burdens of an unsought war.

Yet in Central America, it is not Nicaragua but Honduras that is the largest recipient of Canadian aid. Renowned for its corruption, dominated by its armed forces, transformed by $1.2 billion of American funds into an overwhelmingly militarized society, and with human rights abuses that seem mild only in contrast to the carnage in El Salvador and Guatemala, Honduras is structurally incapable of using development funds constructively.

On the other hand, direct Canadian bilateral aid to Nicaragua has actually declined since the Mulroney government took office, while Canadian aid of all kinds, including non-governmental, totalled only $40 million in the last five years.

It makes no sense — not economically, not in terms of social justice, not in terms of Canada's place in the world. A special all-party parliamentary committee, chaired by John Bosley, leaves today for Central America, with a mandate to assess Canada's potential role in regional peacekeeping efforts.

But peace and development must march hand in hand. Nicaraguans rightly believe Canadians to be both rich and sympathetic, and can't understand why our aid giving seems to be grudging. Our parliamentary committee would win widespread applause if it dealt generously with those reasonable expectations.

* * *

1989 IT WAS SWEDEN that played the all important power-broker role in bringing the United States and the Palestinian Liberation Organization together last year, one of the major foreign policy initiatives of this decade. Yet Sweden follows an independent, progressive foreign policy that, often as not, is antagonistic to that of the United States.

Sweden, for example, concentrates its aid in Central America almost exclusively on Nicaragua, while in Africa it long ago singled out the Southern African liberation movements for special attention. Yet at the same time, as the PLO initiative conclusively demonstrated, the very consistency and coherence of its policies makes Sweden a voice of consequence in Washington.

Surveys of Canadian public opinion suggest that Sweden seems to many Canadians the role model for our own international dealings: honest broker, mediator, bridge-builder. And former U.N. Ambassador Stephen Lewis and former British High Commissioner Roy McMurtry both publicly insist that the one thing they discovered in their international roles is how much influence Canada could wield in the world if we, too, more aggressively stood up and were counted on the important issues of the day. Yet, the distressing truth is that the Swedish prototype is the exact antitheses of our own.

Canadians would be surprised to learn just how uninfluential we have been in the world through the Trudeau decades and now in the Mulroney era. They would even be more dismayed to realize the basic amorality of so many of our international positions, and especially of the subordinate role played by concern for human rights, which so many Canadians wrongly take for granted is at the heart of our foreign policy. Indeed, the latest Mulroney Throne Speech itself complacently asserted that the government "will continue to take a strong stand in defence of human rights." The embarrassing truth is that we don't, as is methodically documented in an important new volume, *Human Rights In Canadian Foreign Policy*, edited by two University of Toronto political scientists, Robert Matthew and Cranford Pratt.

The book demonstrates the existence of a substantial "rhetoric gap" between government expressions of concern for human rights and actual government behaviour. "The prevailing pattern," one observer wrote at the end of the Trudeau era "from the Prime Minister down, has been one of timidity and often appalling indifference." Since Trudeau, Joe Clark's avowed "quiet diplomacy" has made us, compared to the outspoken Swedes, virtually impotent.

The various authors show that human rights have simply not been a weighty consideration in Canadian foreign policy. It's merely one item to be "factored in" along with other, higher priorities such as commercial self-interest, loyalty to our alliance partners and, above all, the views of Washington. In the end, all other considerations succumb to our relationship with the United States; as Francis Arbour notes, U.S. opinion of Canadian policy appears to be the only external pressure that constrains Canada from adopting a more independent and honorable foreign policy.

Numerous chapters illustrate how much more vigorous are Canada's criticisms of human rights violations when the villains are Eastern Bloc countries rather than deplorable American allies in Central America or Asia or the Middle East. And our subservience to American interests is depressingly recorded in Renata Pratt's powerful chapter on such international financial institutions (IFIs) as the IMF and the World Bank. Canada's illogical position is that these institutions should function non-politically, as if a government that systematically and grossly violates its citizens' rights can introduce the economic and social development the IFIs's funds are ostensibly to foster.

In fact, the United States long ago politicized the IFIs and flagrantly uses them to punish its enemies — Allende's Chile, Nicaragua — and reward its friends, however monstrous their regimes. What makes Canada's position so untenable is not just our failure to criticize these unashamed American manipulations but also our own willingness, in contradiction of our formal policy, to approve loans and credit to such dubious American allies as Guatemala, El Salvador and South Africa. Pratt's examples of these cases all spring, interestingly, from the late Trudeau era. But the bi-partisan nature of our hypocritical double standard is indicated by Michael Wilson's stated belief last year that "the introduction of human rights criteria would politicize the World Bank's decision-making with negative consequences for its activities."

Wrong again, Minister. This book establishes that it would, in fact, be realistic, effective, and by no means complicated to move human rights to a central position in every sphere of Canadian foreign policy. It requires, in fact, little more than the will.

* * *

1989   PRESIDENT BUSH will look back this holy season on his
first year in office with the great satisfaction of knowing
he's beaten the wimp rap at last. By his massive invasion of tiny
Panama, Bush has violated more international treaties than Santa
has reindeer, and is responsible for the deaths of dramatically more
Americans and Panamanians than General Noriega ever dreamed of.
He has, finally, become a real American man.

Certainly, Noriega is an unpalatable figure. The United States, of
course, has known this for the past 15 years. For almost all those
years, he was a staunch U.S. ally and well-paid CIA snitch, all the
while up to his neck in drug trafficking and every other manner of
despicable behaviour.

Noriega-U.S. relations are all carefully set out in two volumes every
Canadian will want under the Christmas tree: *Drugs, Law Enforce-
ment and Foreign Policy*, the official report of the U.S. Senate
Sub-Committee on Terrorism and Narcotics, and Ben Bradley Jr.'s
Guts and Glory: The Rise and Fall of Oliver North. Long after
Noriega's activities were common knowledge in Washington, Vice-
President Bush, Ollie North and other freedom-loving Reagan offi-
cials visited him seeking assistance for the Contras against the
Sandinistas. So give us a break that the invasion is about saving
Panama for democracy.

Noriega's place in history is secure. He is on par with such vicious
right-wing tyrants as Marcos of the Philippines, the shah of Iran,
Savimbi of Angola, Mobuto of Zaire, Pinochet of Chile, Somoza of
Nicaragua, Trujillo of the Dominican Republic, Rios Mott of Guatemala, and many other loyal American allies throughout the world.
In fact, the only difference between Noriega and all of them is that
they received U.S. military aid and thuggery training till the bitter
end, while Noriega forfeited his two years ago.

But you really can't discuss America's commitment to democracy
and freedom without El Salvador. Take the case of Cesar Vielman
Joya Martinez, a former soldier in the Salvador army now in the U.S.
exposing American government complicity in the Salvadoran death
squads. He's an expert on the subject: He was a death squad assassin
and in one year personally slit the throats of eight of his countrymen.

Joya Martinez worked with American advisers, two of whom
actually had desks only metres away from his own. "I do not
believe," he tells anyone who will listen, "the U.S. advisers could not
have known what we were doing. They funded everything we did."

The U.S. government gives the Salvador regime $1.5 million in military and economic aid each day, some $4 billion over the next decade. Joya Martinez illuminates how that money is being spent. American military advisers in El Salvador, in the words of *Washington Post* columnist Coleman McCarthy, "are counsellors in violence, educating El Salvador's poor in the arts of annihilating other Salvadoran poor." Successfully, too: 70,000 Salvadorans have been killed since the martyred archbishop, Oscar Romero, begged Washington 10 years ago to send no more military aid.

One dead American soldier justified the American invasion of Panama. What was Bush's response when six Jesuits were slaughtered by Salvadoran government death squads last month? Why, to increase U.S. military aid to the Arena government and to upgrade the equipment of the Salvadoran air force. Too bad George Bush never met Karen Ridd, the remarkable Winnipeg woman who was arrested last month by the dreaded Salvadoran treasury police, but who refused her release until her more vulnerable Colombian cellmate was also freed. Karen Ridd was a witness as the air force deliberately bombed and strafed densely populated sectors of San Salvador, massacring countless helpless civilians. Now those upgraded planes can do their work with enhanced efficiency.

Karen Ridd, and scores of other Canadians, have implored the Mulroney government to beg the White House to cease its senseless, murderous Central American policies. All to no avail. And, of course, now there's only sensitive "understanding" from the Tories of the American need to invade Panama. Brian Mulroney has chosen to make himself Washington's most reliable lapdog.

✳ ✳ ✳

1992 AND NOW, from the rocket scientists who brought you
——— the Canada–U.S. free trade agreement, something exactly the same: the North American free trade agreement. Yessir, yessir, ladies and gents, gather round; it's time to take it in the neck once again. See Brian Mulroney and Michael Wilson perform their renowned talking dummies act. See them sing *Yankee Doodle Dandy*. See them promise the moon. See them lie, lie, lie. Yessiree folks, like the man said, it's *déjà vu* all over again.

Actually, what's been so refreshing about our government's attitude so far is the absence of any pretense that NAFTA is any of the public's damn business at all. At least with the FTA they had the decency to swamp us with false promises and utopian expectations. The salvation of Canada, we were endlessly reassured, lay in that agreement, and if through some character defect you happened not to believe Conservative politicians, all of Corporate Canada leaped frantically into the fray behind them.

Did they tell us that free trade would be in our interests only if every conceivable circumstance worked perfectly on our behalf? Did they tell us that a high dollar and high interest rates would largely negate the FTA's alleged potential benefits? Did they tell us that they were about to bestow upon us a virtual depression that would completely undermine free trade? Did they tell us that the Prime Minister's sacred pledge of generous support to those who suffered from the deal was simply bunkum? Did they tell us that a substantial part of our manufacturing base would be shut down, never to reopen again? Did they tell us that a huge chunk of Canadian sovereignty would be lost forever? Did they tell us that Americans played hardball, both before and after deals were signed, and showed no mercy to little guys? Probably it slipped their minds.

But such a bout of temporary amnesia pales in comparison to what the Tories have forgotten to tell us about their latest, greatest deal. We know, if you'll pardon my Spanish, *nada*. For 18 months, the government has been negotiating this deal, and still the public knows only what we've been able to glean from leaked documents, unofficial sources, and gossip. But hey. You don't trust Brian Mulroney or something?

So what do we need to know? Here's the key: In all three countries, those who have most enthusiastically pushed the latest deal are the reigning governments and a handful of powerful corporations; remember it was the Reagan and Mulroney governments and a few multinationals with Canadian branch plants who initiated the first free trade deal.

And as with 1988, once again these same few powerful corporations will be the big beneficiaries. So, if you're the kind of person who has confidence in a pact put together by the Mulroney and Bush governments on behalf of Corporate North America, this deal's for you.

In fact, we have every right to predict that this deal will be bad for most people in all three countries. We know a large majority of

Canadians oppose it. We know a significant coalition of social, environmental and labour groups in the U.S. have mobilized against it. And we know that many courageous Mexicans are terrified about the impact of North American free trade on their country. Why courageous? Because taking on the government can be very bad for a Mexican's health.

Poor Mexico. Canadians who know the country only from demeaning movie stereotypes or as tourists should understand that it can no more negotiate as an equal with the U.S. than can Canada. This is a country with a per capita gross national product of $2,010, compared to the U.S.'s $20,910 and Canada's $19,000.

In many ways, it remains a Third World country, with rich and poor literally inhabiting two different worlds. One in four workers is unemployed or underemployed and many who do work make among the lowest wages in the world.

Scrupulously documented human rights abuse, including torture, is widespread. Finally, its corrupt and undemocratic government is in the hands of free market zealots, cheerfully working with the IMF to impose the same neo-conservative "structural adjustment programs" that have brought such added misery to so many other poor countries.

With his typical integrity, Michael Wilson assured us only days ago that no deal was imminent. Now, after a weekend in — where else? — Washington, an agreement is virtually complete. But before the Tories start trumpeting their triumph, they should have no illusion that this is the end of the process. On the contrary; it's only the beginning. Canadians will not accept a second deal from the gang that brought us the FTA.

∗   ∗   ∗

The American Way

1985   I HATE TO BE THE ONE to bring you the bad news, but
certain American capitalists are once again giving a bad
name to the entire private enterprise, dog-eat-dog, exploitation-of-
man-by-man system that has made our continent what it is today.

Just when our government is successfully implementing its daring
plan to base the entire future prosperity of this country on American
capitalism, some of the giants of U.S. free enterprise are letting the
side down. Frankly, I think it's a crummy way to treat Brian
Mulroney after he brought the boss home to Quebec to dinner and
all.

Here's the situation. President Reagan, committed to getting big
government off the backs of American initiative, is putting it straight
into the bank accounts of multi-billion dollar weapons contractors.
Countless corporations, both vast and small, rely on Ronald
Reagan's quarter-trillion-dollar military budget. But it's the giants
who are positively wallowing in the gravy.

Of America's 10 top weapons makers, six sold two-thirds of their
output to government in 1984, the other four, at least 40 per cent.
One of them, General Dynamics, made revenues last year of $7.8
billion, of which 94 per cent came from government contracts. You
also understand that General Dynamics, which made pre-tax profits
of $683.6 million last year, naturally, has paid no taxes since 1972.
This touching little capitalist success story has, of course, been
carried on in the sacred name of free enterprise.

There is also a Washington revolving door policy that operates
constantly within the military-industrial complex. Senior executives
move between government and military positions and corporate
boardrooms with a casualness that is almost charming in its open-

ness. Hell, we're all in it together to clobber the Russkies, aren't we?

Well, you can just imagine then how embarrassing it was for some of the good old boys the other day when faithful old General Electric was asked by the Pentagon to refund $168 million in excess profits it had collected on spare parts for jets. Or when Pratt and Whitney was asked for $40 million back. Or when General Dynamics, which makes nuclear-missile submarines, jet fighter planes and tanks, was accused of systematic waste, corruption, cover-up and shoddy work.

Oh, they had some fun, those fellas at General Dynamics. You've probably heard those great stories of the Pentagon paying $7,600 for a coffeemaker or $400 for a hammer — after all, you charge what the system can bear, that's how capitalism works, isn't it? And then there was the diamond earrings they gave to the wife of the head of a major navy program. And what about the $155 they billed Washington to kennel a VIP's dog?

And the charges of hundreds of thousands of dollars to the government to cover the costs of their own political contributions to Reagan's party. Oh, have I mentioned that since Reagan's 1980 victory the leading arms manufacturers have doubled their contributions to the Republicans?

Now look, I don't like nit-picking any more than you do. I know the name of the game is the profit motive. It's survival of the fittest, after all. Of course the industrial giants have no choice but to maintain secret multi-million dollar accounts for entertaining Pentagon muckey-mucks; that's the way you protect the bottom line, isn't it? And isn't that what it's all about?

But what about our poor Brian? Here he is handing over the entire kit and caboodle to Ronnie and his pals, in the name of unfettered private enterprise, and what does he get back? The president turns out to be the greatest single Keynesian since they invented economists. The American love affair between big business and big government is positively idyllic. The role of the state has never been more central. And some of Brian's favorite role models have been caught red-handed with their arms and legs in the rich, juicy till.

The prime minister has given his — and our — all to Reagan. It's time he got something back. It's time for political leadership. Brian should tell Ronnie that he'd better come up with some smarter capitalists, and pronto. After all, at least ours haven't been caught — yet.

✳   ✳   ✳

1985   I FIRST HEARD OF MARTIN LUTHER KING in 1957, a very
long 29 years ago. I was in Montgomery, Alabama with
my undergraduate pal Stephen Lewis, a couple of young Canadian
radicals inflamed by the plight of black Americans.

That was not surprising. To grow up a leftist in Canada in the
decade after the Second World War was to plunge into a host of
international causes: South Africa (even then); the Algerian revolution; and in general an opposition to the paranoid anti-Communist
world-view espoused by President Eisenhower's Secretary of State,
the insufferably sanctimonious John Foster Dulles.

Even today, decades later, I remember one specific reaction to a
speech Dulles had made in Holland. "I do not want to hear Dulles
say in Amsterdam," the great socialist muckraker Izzie Stone had
written with passion and indignation, "that man is created in the
image of God. I want to hear him say it in Atlanta, Georgia, when
one of those images, done in charcoal, has been strung up to a tree."

We shared the passion and the indignation. We grew up to Paul
Robeson singing of an ideal America in *The House I Live In*, to
Richard Wright's powerful novel *Native Son*, to Pete Seeger and the
Weavers and their songs of social justice and equality.

And then came Rosa Parks and Martin King. The year before we
arrived in Montgomery, Rosa Parks had been too exhausted to heed
a white bus conductor's order to move to the back of the bus, and so
the civil rights movement was born. King, only 28 years old, found
his natural mission in life: he became the leader of oppressed
America.

We failed to meet King — he was away writing a book about the
revolution he had helped launch — but we followed his career and
adventures more closely having witnessed his Old South at first hand.
It was so much more terrible than even we had imagined. In their
fear and hatred, whites made blacks into non-humans, and thereby
de-humanized themselves; that's why otherwise decent white people
could exploit them mercilessly and treat them like animals. Sure, the
U.S. Constitution said all men were created equal, and these plain
white folks plainly believed it. The little catch was that blacks were
simply not regarded as people.

So the South we saw, and from which Martin King arose was, in a
real sense, still the slave south of a century earlier, for which a great
and bloody and, it appeared, futile civil war had been fought.

But King was in many other ways a man set apart from the rest.

Many of the freedom-fighters of the 60s, both black and white, failed to draw any larger lessons from the black struggle. Racism was racism. Eliminate the racial barriers to equal opportunity, allow blacks to attend the same public schools as whites, knock down the structures of discrimination, and the dream would come true.

King knew better. In the first place, blacks are the only people to have arrived in America through pure coercion, so their cultural values and drives have always been different from every other immigrant group. Secondly, King grew to understand that black oppression was part of a larger economic and social struggle, that it was an inevitable consequence of monopoly capitalism, which explains both his controversial stand against the Viet Nam war and why he was in Memphis supporting striking garbage workers when he was gunned down. Long a target of the demented J. Edgar Hoover's FBI, only the most credulous believe King was assassinated by a single, isolated ne'er-do-well.

No wonder Ronald Reagan, who has been wrapping himself in the glory of the national holiday named after King, was not long ago defaming him as a fraud and probable Communist.

What hurts most is that the Reagan dream of America is proving more realistic than the King dream. One-third of all black Americans live below the poverty line. Over half of all black kids are born poor. Most don't finish high school. Many live eternally on welfare. Violence is endemic.

The new black middle class, the real beneficiaries of King's work, have substantially forgotten about the majority they have left behind. Black America is America's own internal Third World, but there is no Martin Luther King to lead a new crusade. The dream that moved the world at the Washington monument in the innocent days of 1963 has become the harsh reality of Ronald Reagan's Two Americas.

* * *

1985   SOME RELATIONSHIPS hit you in the eye. Let's put together two separate stories. First has been the revelation in various American magazines over recent weeks of a major ideological split in the U.S. black community on questions relating to future black development. A new group of neo-conservative black intellectuals has recently emerged seeking solutions to black problems that are based far more on self-reliance than on the traditional black approach of seeking government intervention.

This phenomenon has a certain ring of common sense to it, at least until we introduce the second story. For this story vividly illuminates the magnitude of the crisis within the black community, and makes the innocent-sounding Horatio Algerism of the black New Right appear in a rather less palatable light. It is a tale of poverty, illness and death which has — it is not melodramatic to assert — more in common with a third world country than with the glories of the American republic which President Reagan hypes so mawkishly.

One-third of black Americans live in poverty. Blacks are 3 times as likely as whites to be living below the poverty line, and suffer twice the unemployment. The average black family had an annual income in 1981 of $13,000, the average white family $10,000 more; and that was before the ravages of the Reagan counter-revolution had begun to be felt. Black life expectancy is 69.9 years, the level reached by white Americans 30 years ago, while the black infant mortality rate is double that of whites.

These distressing data come from a new report released by the U.S. Department of Health, containing the findings of a year's study by 18 scientists on the health of black Americans. Their overriding conclusion: racial minorities in the U.S. are scandalously failing to benefit in anything like an equitable manner from the unprecedented advance in recent scientific and medical knowledge. Indeed, if the black death rate had approximated the white, 60,000 fewer blacks would have died in 1981.

And the real cause was poverty.

Technically, the causes were much more commonplace: heart disease and cancer were two of the three major killers of blacks. Says the report: "Black Americans make fewer office visits to physicians than do whites, and are less likely to be seen by . . . specialists. Blacks have more difficulty in entering the medical care system than whites and express greater dissatisfaction with services." In other words, because there is no system of universal health care such as is taken for granted in Canada and in every other western nation, most blacks can't afford proper medical care.

Enter again our little troupe of black academics, sitting comfortably in their splendid ivory towers. They, after all, have made it, and are invoking the great American tradition of rising from one's class. The contrary ethos, the socialist concept of rising together with one's class, pervades a moderately successful political party in Canada.

But in the U.S. such "anti-individualism" becomes almost anti-American. One of the new black conservatives, Glenn Loury, writes in the *New Republic* that the solution for black poverty is to inculcate a "pick yourself up by the bootstraps mentality." I suppose there's no point in asking Loury how you can afford good medical or hospital treatment through this approach, since he is "not ashamed to say I voted for Reagan," a president who passionately opposes the introduction of medicare into the United States.

To be sure, thoughtful blacks are understandably frustrated by the apparently unending disintegration of black community and family life in the United States. Ghetto life in America has truly become Hobbesian: short, nasty, violent and brutish. But the answer is not to condemn the liberal policies of the 1960s and 1970s. The need for massive government intervention to deal with systemic unemployment through sweeping economic reforms and massive job re-training programs is as vital as the need for universal medicare.

The truth is not that the interventionist schemes of the past were wrongly conceived; it is that they were executed either poorly or half-heartedly. The perennial American disgrace — the condition of its visible minorities — will not be solved by the mean simple-mindedness of the new right, whatever the colour of its exponents.

* * *

1989   ONLY AN OLD CURMUDGEON would deny Ronald Reagan his due. He has been a wildly successful president, accomplishing a remarkable amount of his agenda.

He entered office eight years ago determined to block advancement for black Americans, to halt the sluggish march towards equality for women, to make America walk tall again by beating up tiny poverty-stricken nations, to allow insatiable greed and ruthless personal ambition to reap lavish rewards, to fire up the economy through trillions of dollars in defence expenditures, to invite industry to desecrate further the environment, and to legitimate a morality in which any means justified his particular ends.

Notwithstanding his unparalleled laziness, ignorance and immersion in fantasy, in all these areas his administration triumphed, a splendid example of what conservatism means in the modern world.

The new values were never in question: Soon after Reagan's first inauguration, the United States cast the only vote against the World Health Organization's code of ethics on feeding Third World babies with instant formulas prepared with contaminated water.

The Reaganites practised what they preached. As good conservatives, they despised government and venerated individual initiative. When appointed to high office in Washington, they consequently felt little compunction in stealing the government blind. His has been the most corrupt, unethical administration in America for 60 years.

The world was Reagan's set. History may, perversely, remember him as the president who helped end the superpower cold war. But in the here-and-now, death was the Gipper's co-pilot. Morning in America meant that the United States could interfere around the globe at whim, recklessly flouting both American and international law, disdaining such (apparently) liberal constraints as honesty, legality, democracy and resolutions of Congress. The multi-faceted immorality of the Iran-contra scandal was one direct consequence.

Under him was assembled a team of bellicose conservatives like CIA director Bill Casey, Oliver North, and an entire semi-secret team of ex-CIA agents, ex-Pentagon officials, fascist Cuban exiles, professional killers and international drug traffickers. They ran a succession of secret wars and open attacks on very small nations for which both they and American soldiers paid an appalling price.

The Reaganites set out promptly to destroy Nicaragua (population 3 million), in the process causing unspeakable horror as well to the hapless citizens of Honduras, Salvador and Guatemala. He then sent the Marines to Beirut to show that Americans could go where they choose; when 241 died in a widely predicted terrorist attack on their barracks, the survivors were withdrawn. Two years later, a CIA plot to assassinate a Muslim leader allegedly linked to the attack went astray, missing its target but killing and wounding 280 Lebanese bystanders.

Two days after the Marine massacre, in retaliation, Reagan ordered 7,000 U.S. troops to invade Grenada, a country about three-quarters the size of P.E.I., or about one soldier for each 14 inhabitants. Once again CIA intelligence was faulty, and 19 American kids were killed, 115 injured, some by what's euphemistically called "friendly fire." For this remarkable showing, 8,612 U.S. army medals were awarded, some to soldiers who never left the States.

In besieged Angola (population 8 million), Bill Casey teamed up with the South African government he so admired in successfully making that poor country, like Nicaragua, an economic basket-case, while tens of thousands of Angolans and Nicaraguans perished.

For despised Libya (population 3 million), Reagan sent American bombers to attack its two largest cities, naturally killing or injuring many civilians. Six months ago, an American destroyer in the Gulf attacked without provocation a commercial Iran Air flight, killing 290 people; no American apology or reparations have ever been made.

At home, too, conservatism worked its magic. Poverty bloomed; 14 million more Americans live below the poverty line today than in 1981. Almost one child in four lives in poverty.

The enforcement of civil rights for blacks in voting, housing, employment and education almost ground to a halt. Serious reactionaries were appointed to courts at every level, to entrench the rights of the privileged for decades to come. The President vetoed a Clean Water Act that had been passed overwhelmingly by both houses of Congress.

The old Gipper never lost his faith in Gipperish. Even last week, in his last budget, Reagan recommended increasing the defence budget by $5 billion to almost one-third of a trillion dollars — and cutting the same amount from child nutrition programs and medical insurance for the aged and poor.

His country loved him. What more can be said?

✳   ✳   ✳

1989 I DON'T MEAN TO SPOIL YOUR NEW YEAR quite so early, but with George Bush's inauguration upon us, you better know some ugly truths from the beginning.

Last September, during the U.S. election campaign, seven American ethnic leaders resigned from Bush's election team, accused of links with known anti-Semitic, racist, neo-fascist and even pro-Nazi organizations. Bush's spokesman dismissed the charges as "politically inspired garbage" which the Bush campaign had "looked into . . .

and was unable to substantiate." The story, alas, quickly died.

Yet, all the charges have been fully and publicly documented, and merely expose the surface of a shameful situation that has foully polluted the American political system since the end of World War II. Howard Goldenthal, a dedicated Toronto investigative journalist who tracks the extreme right, has introduced me to new studies that reveal, in frightening detail, the full magnitude of the scandal.

One is *Blowback*, a powerful and chilling new book by American writer Christopher Simpson, based on extensive previously unreleased documentation obtained under the American Freedom of Information Act. Providing 12 pages of archival sources and fully 64 pages of source references, Simpson meticulously demonstrates how, in the immediate post-war period, the U.S. government's various intelligence agencies, including the CIA, cynically and knowingly brought thousands of Nazi scientists, SS officers and intelligence experts, as well as countless East European Nazi collaborators, to the United States to help fight the new enemy, the Soviet Union.

Among the book's endlessly horrifying revelations, Simpson documents how the nature and extent of the post-war threat posed by the Soviet Union was grossly misrepresented by former Nazis and Nazi collaborators sitting comfortably in America on U.S. intelligence agencies' payrolls. Indeed, many of the perceptions of the Soviet Union concocted by those twisted sources have remained the conventional wisdom of Americans until only recently.

"We knew what we were doing," according to one senior CIA officer: "any bastard as long as he was anti-Communist."

"He's on our side," CIA director Allan Dulles said of Hitler's senior military intelligence officer on the Eastern Front, "and that's all that matters."

Klaus Barbie, the notorious butcher of Lyons, worked for U.S. intelligence in Germany and was then assisted in fleeing to Argentina. Incredibly enough, even senior officers of Adolf Eichmann's Holocaust bureau were financed and protected by the CIA. Mass murderers, Gestapo agents, sadistic torturers: all were clandestinely welcomed to "our side" in the holy name of anti-Communism.

Many East European Nazi collaborators, leaders of fascist groups and governments in Eastern Europe, and leaders of pro-fascist East European emigré organizations soon became politically active in the States. They quickly developed particularly close ties to the Republican party and gained remarkable access to the most powerful intelligence chiefs, politicians, business associations and media moguls in America. Their cooked-up anti-Communist propaganda was systematically (and illegally) disseminated throughout the U.S. by the CIA during the 1950s, significantly hardening public opinion towards the Cold War.

Not all organizations in the U.S. representing "Captive Nations" — those that came under Soviet domination — were fascist sympathizers. But many were, and over the years they came together in several umbrella coalitions. Among the most prominent was the ultra-nationalist, reactionary Anti-Bolshevik Bloc of Nations, the ABN, which included European Nazi collaborators and other whom Simpson documents as "wartime genocidalists and quislings."

Yet the ABN enjoyed substantial support. Radical right-wing politicians like Senator Joe McCarthy gave it open support, as did the publisher of the highly influential *Time* magazine. In 1960, a key organizer of the ABN's annual Captive Nations parade in New York was Austin App, an American of German descent who became a close collaborator of Canada's own Ernst Zundel, and whose books are often considered the foundation of the "Holocaust as hoax" school of anti-history. Open apologists for Nazi genocide sat on the rostrum.

Yet 84 U.S. senators and congressmen endorsed that parade, William Buckley and Sydney Hook promoted it (Hook was a self-described anti-Communist socialist, and a Jew), and scores of ethnic leaders and otherwise prudent politicians marched in it — all in the name of patriotic Americanism and anti-Communism. Some were Jews, reflecting the bizarre, ongoing collaboration between Jewish neo-conservatives and ultra right-wingers who blame the world's ills on the Jewish-Communist conspiracy.

Some of these remaining emigré fanatics, together with home-grown American neo-fascists and racists, now thrive in George Bush's Republican party. And a kinder, gentle new year to you, too.

* * *

1991   IT WOULD BE REASSURING but dead wrong to write off
———   David Duke's stunning performance in last week's governor's race in Louisiana as a mere fluke or a local aberration. Last year, running for the U.S. Senate, Duke won 60 per cent of the white

Louisiana vote. This time, with his sordid life an open book, fully 55 per cent of white voters still backed him. They knew what they were doing, all right. The American dream had failed them, and they voted Duke to show they weren't going to take it any more.

Once, under FDR, Truman, Kennedy, Johnson, Americans voted more or less along natural class lines, workers against bosses, Democrats against Republicans. It has been the genius of the Republican party for the past 20 years to turn that coalition on its head and to persuade white Americans — poor, blue collar, middle class — that in fact their real self-interest actually lay in an alliance with Big Business against liberal governments.

It's all spelled out in an important new book by Tom and Mary Edsall called *Chain Reaction: The Impact of Race, Rights and Taxes on American Politics.*

The Edsalls demonstrate how Republican strategists have cynically and brilliantly exploited the bitter resentment of white Americans for whom the American dream has clearly become an impossible dream. The deadly enemy of frustrated and angry Middle America was no longer big business and the filthy rich but big government and the filthy poor.

For the corporate world, of course, the nemesis is always "Big Government," that is, one that intervenes against their interests. But in a strategy crafted under Richard Nixon and systematically refined under Reagan and Bush, for ordinary white Americans the enemy became undeserving blacks who allegedly were ripping off the wasteful social programs initiated by Democratic administrations.

These Americans needed only a little help from conservatives to be convinced that the root cause of their frustrations and disappointments was special treatment by governments of unworthy minorities. But their hostility was directed not at real special privileges for the rich and powerful but at alleged preferential treatment for the poor and blacks.

So when American conservatives rail against high taxes, they mean public money lavished on black people. The notorious Willie Horton commercials used by Bush in the 1988 election told insecure white Americans that bleeding-heart, card-carrying liberal Democrats were soft on vicious, terrifying black rapists.

In America, when you attack welfare cheats, wasted taxes, affirmative action, excessive government, "the liberal social welfare system which encourages the rising illegitimate birthrate," everyone understand the code: it's racism, pure and simple, and it's been the rhetoric of Reagan and Bush for years. Except that all these words were David Duke's in the past month.

Respectable Americans have made it possible for this dangerous, depraved outsider to join the mainstream of American politics.

In Louisiana, the anti-Duke campaign carefully relied far more on the dire economic consequences if he won than on his racism or his anti-Semitism, knowing that many white Americans don't find either so shameful. After all, southern white racists were an integral part of the Democratic coalition for a century, while bigots and racists of the most violent and extreme variety have been at home in the Republican party for decades.

This lurid aspect of American Republicanism was painstakingly documented in two 1988 publications, Christopher Simpson's *Blowback*, and Russ Bellant's *Old Nazis, the New Right, and the Reagan Administration: The Role of Domestic Fascist Networks in the Republican Party and Their Effect on U.S. Cold War Politics*.

They demonstrated, in chilling detail, how the Republicans have consistently embraced the most virulently right-wing enemies of democracy so long as their anti-Communist credentials were unsullied.

Many East European Nazi collaborators, for example, achieved positions of remarkable prominence and influence in the Republican party. In 1988, a reluctant George Bush was forced publicly to eject from his campaign team seven ethnic leaders because of their proved links with known anti-Semitic, racist, neo-fascist and even pro-Nazi organizations.

But until publicly exposed, these fanatics — along with home-grown American neo-fascists just like David Duke — thrived at all levels of the party. Anti-Communist organizations with whom Reagan and Bush worked closely included the likes of the American First Committee whose head, Art Jones, wore both Nazi uniforms and KKK robes and who participated in a Klan-Nazi unity meeting sponsored by Aryan Nations in 1985.

Now Republican racism is coming home to roost. David Duke will likely challenge Bush in the presidential primaries, as will Patrick Buchanan, a senior Reagan staffer, media darling and pugnacious right-wing Republican whose "anti-Semitic diatribes" are described at length in Alan Dershowitz's new book *Chutzpah*.

But here's what I'm dying to know. Take Judge Clarence Thomas, who made his home in the Republican party, or Norman Podhoretz, the dean of Jewish neo-conservatives who says all Jews must do the same. When all three Republican primary candidates peddle the same diseased message using the same code words, how will they decide which one to vote for?

*　*　*

1991　I DON'T KNOW ABOUT YOU, but it didn't take Stormin' Norman Schwarzkopf to persuade me that America's Number 1. Anyone who has followed the exposés that have rocked the Republican administrations of Richard Nixon and Reagan-Bush has never doubted it. Glen Kealey's accusations against the Mulroney government and the RCMP are kid's stuff compared to five different political scandals of monumental proportions that have sullied Number 1 in the past 20 years.

Watergate, of course, was the grandaddy of them all. But Watergate was also a model in this ominous way: it was far more sinister than was ever acknowledged. For it was not a mere matter of the dirty tricks that Nixon's team played on the Democrats, nor of their elaborate cover-up. It was a repudiation of the rule of law, of consitutional rights, in short, of every democratic principle conservative Americans love speechifying about.

While Nixon preached law and order, he was prepared to see a police state in America. In tapes made public for the first time last June, his chief of staff, H.R. Haldeman, is heard recommending to Nixon in 1971 that "hard-hats and legionnaires" and Teamster union "thugs" be used to assault anti-Viet Nam war protesters. Nixon replies: "They've (Teamsters) got guys who'll go on and knock their heads off." Haldeman: "Sure. Murderers . . . They're gonna beat the shit out of some of these people."

From there to the secret government that clandestinely, undemocratically, ran much of U.S. foreign policy under Reagan and Bush was no great leap. The Iran-Contra scandal was not the work of a few rogue fanatics like Oliver North. It was the deliberate plot of the head of the CIA, the head of the National Security Council, and umpteen other senior, unelected officials acting under the instructions of a White House that flagrantly violated the clear wishes of the elected Congress.

Then came the savings and loan exposure, the largest single financial scandal in all of United States history — and that's saying something. Thanks to the key Reaganite principle of socialism for the few, the wiliest con artists in America grew rich beyond avarice while creating nothing and risking nothing. Bailing out the S&L industry will cost ordinary U.S. taxpayers more than half a trillion — right: trillion — bucks.

Next we visit the largest single banking scandal in all the history of the cosmos — the Bank of Credit and Commerce International caper, where drug runners, dictators, terrorists and the CIA all kept secret accounts. Though this is not exclusively an American affair, the revelations include some insights into U.S. spying on friendly countries.

According to the *Manchester Guardian*, BCCI was used to pay nearly 500 people who spied for the CIA in Britain for money. These included "124 people employed in government or engaged in politics; 53 in commerce, industry and banking; 75 in academic institutions; 24 scientists; 124 in communications; and 90 in the media." Gosh, I wonder who's on the payroll in Canada.

And finally, perhaps the single most despicable affair of all. Now get this: in order to keep Jimmy Carter from winning re-election, Ronald Reagan's 1980 campaign team almost certainly made a deliberate deal with Ayatollah Khomeini's regime in Iran not to release 52 American hostages before election day. In return, a victorious new Reagan government would reward the fanatics in Iran with arms sent via Israel.

These accusations give entirely new meaning to traditional concepts of cynical political opportunism. But the motivation remained the same as in Watergate and Iran-Contra: the belief of a small group of privileged, ultra-conservative Republicans that laws and democratic principles did not apply to them.

Two congressional committees have just been struck to investigate these allegations. According to Gary Sick, the most influential of the accusers, 15 different sources confirmed for him that William Casey, Reagan's 1980 campaign chair whom he later made CIA head, held a series of meetings in Paris in October, 1980, with high-level Israelis and Iranians who agreed the American hostages wouldn't be released before the U.S. election and that Israel would in return send arms and spare parts to Iran on behalf of the United States.

And so it happened. No hostages were ever released to Jimmy Carter. Once Reagan won the election, the Iranians suddenly reopened negotiations offering major new concessions. On Jan. 21, 1981, literally five minutes after Ronald Reagan was sworn in, all the hostages were dramatically released. Immediately, thereafter, Sick's informants told him, "hundreds of millions of dollars" of Israeli arms began to flow to Iran. Coincidences? You judge.

Nixon was re-elected. Reagan was re-elected. Bush was elected. I guess if you're Number 1, you can just about get away with murder.

*   *   *

1991   EVERYWHERE I GO, business people talk with some enthusiasm of moving their families to the U.S. along with their companies. Many of their kids are already studying at American universities, with the expectation they may well not return.

I don't want to rain on anyone's parade, but these folks should do a little more research on what they may be letting themselves in for. Sure Canada's going through a rough patch these days. But the fact is the U.S., too, is in big trouble, and even for its most privileged citizens the quality of American life leaves something to be desired.

In a real sense, America has marched backwards in recent decades, particularly since Ronald Reagan and George Bush were elected. "Middle-income families," summarized the bipartisan National Commission on Children this summer, "report greater difficulty making ends meet. For perhaps the first time since the Great Depression, American children will no longer routinely pass their parents' standard of living." After years of neo-conservatism, the U.S. is in decline. The American economy is in deep difficulty; its education system's a mess, its health-care system a travesty; poverty, hunger and homelessness increase by the hour; the environmental crisis accelerates; violence has taken on epidemic proportions, and class and racial divisions have been sharpened in a truly ominous manner.

But don't take my word for it. According to Larry Hunter, chief economist for the U.S. Chamber of Commerce, "The bad news is that we are in a long-term economic decline. The economy is not growing fast enough to get us back to recent growth peaks. That means we have suffered a permanent reduction in our standard of living since 1988."

During the 1980s, courtesy of Reaganite social and fiscal policies, the very rich are now filthy rich, their taxes actually having been reduced by 6 per cent during the 1980s. The poor have been devastated by crime, drugs, hunger and lack of health care — and a 16 per cent tax hike. And the income of the middle class has stagnated or even fallen. In fact, according to the 1991 *Green Book*, issued by the House Ways and Means Committee, "When comparing the U.S. to other countries . . . on an after-tax money income basis, the U.S. is the most unequal of the 10 modern (industrial) nations studied." The U.S. Census Bureau has just reported that the number of Americans living below the poverty line — a preposterous $13,359 before taxes for a family of four — rose in 1990 by 2.1 million to 33.6 million souls. That's 13.5 per cent of all Americans, one out of every seven, a total far exceeding the entire population of Canada. Twenty per cent of all American kids and fully one-third of all black Americans are considered poor. A quarter of all kids under 12 are hungry or at risk of being hungry, while 3 million American citizens are homeless.

Of course, the obscenely rich still live the life of Riley with their private schools, their exclusive neighborhoods and clubs, their moderately secure jobs and income. But would you want to hide behind guarded gates in their gilded ghettos?

Looking at recent data on poverty, one academic expert predicted that "We can expect to see more homeless people on the street, more street crime, more gang violence, more domestic violence, more family instability, increasing drug addiction, and increasing physical and mental health problems." For those who aren't dirt-poor, he added, "the rise in poverty means higher taxes to pay for law enforcement and social services, and an atmosphere of heightened racial and ethnic conflict. When middle class suburbanites go to their town jobs, they'll have to step around the homeless on the streets."

In the week of the Killeen, Texas, massacre, it's not surprising to learn that a March report by the U.S. Senate Judiciary Committee called the U.S. "the most violent and self-destructive nation on earth." Since 1960, the country's population has grown by 41 per cent; violent crime has risen 516 per cent. More teenage boys are killed by guns than by all other causes combined.

At the same time, rapes in the U.S. reached unprecedented peaks in 1990, with a rape reported on average every six minutes; heaven only knows how many hundreds of thousands are never reported. According to committee chair Senator Joseph Biden, "The U.S. leads the world in the number and rate of rapes."

Move to the land of the free market and the home where you'd better be brave? Not me. In many ways America remains the most exhilarating society in the world. But now the whole country's like New York: a great place to visit, but who'd want to live there? Me? I'm staying put.

* * *

Bombs Bursting in Air

1986 "WE LEFT THE HOUSE," Mirian wrote, "because they
burned it. And they killed my grandparents on me . . .
They were chasing us. The soldiers and police raped 12 year old girls
whenever they felt like it . . . They killed my mother and threw my
one-month-old brother in the river. Before they killed my mother,
they raped her and chopped her breasts. In front of me and my
brothers they killed our animals."

Mirian is a displaced person in El Salvador. More precisely, Mirian
is a 12-year-old child, who has already witnessed, and suffered from,
more cruelty and horror in his short lifetime than most Canadians
want to believe exists in the entire world.

Mirian is one of the helpless children who are caught up, along
with tens of thousands of adults, in the miserable violence of Central
America. As a nun said, the kids are 12 going on eternity.

For years, the oligarchies of Guatemala and El Salvador especially
— the unholy alliance of landowners, politicians, military, established church and American embassy — have been waging war
against the Indians and the poor and anyone who dares to criticize
them.

In the fraudulent name of anti-Communism, a racist, classist
offensive goes on even now in a campaign carefully calculated to
instill fear and intimidate potential dissenters. But if the United States
cared to stop it, this barbarous violence would soon be drastically
reduced.

It is possible to know all this abstractly, harder to feel it in your
guts. Now an exhibition called "Disrupted Lives: Children's Drawings from Central America," will bring all your emotions to the fore.
Indeed, long before you finish absorbing the message in all 63
drawings and their accompanying few words, your heart will be
wrenched and you will be shaken to your very toes.

Death, murder, bombings, slaughter, rape, hunger, flight, illness, poverty, burning: it is all there, the anguish unrelieved. What is the effect of this unthinkable assault on the psyches of these uncomprehending kids? According to Linda Dale, the excellent curator of the exhibition who collected these drawings from refugee centres in Honduras and Costa Rica as well as centres within Salvador itself, even those who were physically unscathed are scarred for life.

Some are catatonic. Some scream all night. Others have repressed every conscious memory. Still others speak as if it all happened to someone else.

Their drawings, clearly the work of children, speak eloquent volumes. Renée, a 12-year-old, perfectly describes her own vivid drawing: "A fig tree and a cashew tree, a coconut tree, a dead cow and the people go running. The houses are burning and the trees are catching fire. The soldiers are killing people and the people are running. The airplanes behind, killing people with bombs. The helicopter machine gunning and the soldiers coming behind shooting. The planes in front and the soldiers behind." It's all in this astonishing drawing.

The exhibition is sponsored by two Canadian development agencies, Inter Pares and CUSO, which believe development also means raising the consciousness of Canadians about events abroad and our role in them. It is travelling for two years across Canada, and a fascinating pattern has begun to emerge in those cities through which it has passed — Halifax, Windsor, Toronto.

Teachers have begun taking classes to see, and then discuss, the drawings. And the kids have begun getting angry. Nice Canadian kids have been appalled that such unspeakably awful things were happening to other kids somewhere else in the world who were exactly like them — only suffering for no reason at all.

Adult viewers irresistibly find themselves understanding these could be the drawings and voices of their own kids.

I hope they all are wondering why Ronald Reagan is letting — or helping — all this happen, and what it means for Canadians that President Reagan and our Prime Minister are the best of friends.

The exhibition is now in Calgary; soon it will appear in Winnipeg, Nanaimo, Moncton. It should not be missed. Kids the same age as Renée and Mirian should be encouraged to go. They should feel not only the agony but the spirit. They will see the drawing by young Selvin Rouda, a Salvadorean refugee living in Costa Rica, and read his remarkable words. "Peace," Selvin writes, "My drawing is about peace, because in El Salvador there is no peace. Many countries only know war. The peasant man says we want peace . . . Peace is a kind of friendship. Long live peace!"

✳   ✳   ✳

1986   I FEAR NICARAGUANS are never going to appreciate their
———   great debt to what Ronald Reagan miserably calls "that rag in Beirut." That "rag" was an obscure Syrian-backed magazine that blew the whistle on American attempts to trade arms for hostages in Iran. From that humble beginning, the entire Reagan administration has begun to unravel, and with it, thank heavens, the life-and-death threat it has posed to poor, innocent and completely helpless people in many parts of the globe.

For the caper that led Lt.Col. Oliver North to swindle the Iranians and funnel the inflated profits to the Nicaraguan contras was no mere aberration in American foreign policy. On the contrary, it was at the very heart of the "Reagan doctrine." It is easy to dismiss "Ollie" North as a cowboy clown closer to Stan Laurel and Ollie Hardy than to serious international policy. But to do so would be a major mistake.

It's now openly acknowledged what progressive observers of Latin America have charged for some time: that North managed a broad network of arms supplies to the contras for the past two years working in conjunction with private sources belonging to semi-fascist American anti-communist organizations; that Reagan knew about and approved the operation despite a congressional ban on U.S. military aid to the contras; and that officials in the State Department, Pentagon, CIA and National Security Council also knew.

Ironically, the deception around Nicaragua was inconsistent with the quite open "Reagan Doctrine" of never-ending war against alleged pro-Soviet regimes in the Third World that was described in both the *New York Times* and *Washington Post* earlier this year.

Behind the so-called doctrine stands the fanatical hatred of something called communism that is shared by the president and his chief advisors. Recognizing their helplessness to take on the "evil empire" itself, which is what they fantasize about doing, these deranged neo-conservatives decided they would satisfy their lust for commu-

132

nist blood in more manageable territories: Angola, Grenada, Nicaragua, Chad, Ethiopia — wherever there were local conflicts that could be painted as surrogates for American-Soviet rivalry. These miserable small-scale wars are known in the jargon as low-intensity conflicts, and they represent what passes for a coherent foreign policy under Ronald Reagan.

The CIA was put in charge of this new policy, which openly justified American intervention just about anywhere in the world it had the might to get away with. But for Reagan, this was no institutional matter. This was personal. This was a matter of personal courage and individual heroics. This was a case for Rambo-ism, and in Ollie North, the president found his real-life Rambo.

It has been said many times that Ronald Reagan's view of the world almost literally reflects the world of Hollywood in which he worked. Life is a big movie, with heros and bad guys, tough talk and good deeds, hard fighting and happy endings. The Reagan doctrine was the shrewd way his advisors were able to manipulate his simple-minded American capitalist verities into practice, and North was the Marine man of action who made it all seem possible.

Ronald Reagan is a sincere man with a genuine vision of the American way; that's the secret of much of his persuasiveness over the years. He believes America was built by the Lone Ranger, Davey Crockett and the Marines. In a sense of course, he's right. The Marines, as every Canadian child learned when I was growing up, messed around from the halls of Montezuma to the shores of Tripoli, which happens to be from Mexico to Libya. Later, some of us learned a little about economic imperialism and military adventurism, and the Marine Hymn fell into a different context.

In Marine Officer Ollie North, Reagan found his mythic American, and unleashed him. Even after the jig was up, after North's illicit role in channeling Iranian money to the contras was exposed, the President publicly called him a "national hero." No wonder North believed he could get away with all his destructive activities all over the world. What was he doing other than carrying out the Reagan Doctrine?

Sensible people must now hope this tragic period in American history has ended, and that the appropriate lessons are learned. But what a cost in third world lives has been paid.

* * *

1990　　AMERICA'S INTERVENTION in the Gulf crisis, George
Bush explained the other day, was undertaken on
behalf of a new world "where the rule of law supplants the rule of
the jungle (and) nations recognize the shared responsibility for
freedom and justice." This will be surprising news right around the
world.

Liberia. In this West African nation, the brutal reign of President
Samuel Doe led to a vicious civil war that cost Doe his life and has
left the wretched country reeling. Doe was Washington's boy from
the time he violently seized power in 1980, ruling in ways reminiscent
of Idi Amin's Uganda. But Doe protected American interests: the
Voice of America's major transmitter, the Navy's key navigation
system, the U.S. embassy's intelligence-gathering capacities.

That's why the Reagan-Bush administration gave Liberia more
than $500 million between 1980 and 1985, more per capita than any
other country in Africa. In 1985, after Doe conducted one of the
more farcical elections on record, the exercise was praised by the
assistant U.S. secretary of state for African affairs as being "a
democratic experience that Liberia and its friends can use as a
benchmark for future elections."

Last year, just as the civil war was being launched, the new assistant
secretary announced that Liberia was "on the right track." This
summer, with the corrupt and dictatorial Doe on the run, the same
State Department official abruptly discovered that the Doe regime
"was corrupt, it was repressive."

South Africa. Nelson Mandela's dramatic release form prison this
year resurrected a story that Africanists have believed for the past
quarter-century: that Mandela was turned into the South African
police 27 years ago by a CIA agent based in the U.S. embassy in
Pretoria. According to an American newspaper report this year that
neither the White House nor the CIA would confirm or deny, the
Pretoria CIA station chief bragged openly about Mandela's arrest
only hours after it happened in 1962. Convinced that it was a
Communist front, the CIA planted a paid informant in the ANC's top
ranks. An American official was reported as saying at the time: "We
gave them every detail, what he would be wearing, the time of day,
just where he would be. They picked him up. It is one of our greatest
coups."

Indonesia. In 1965, the Indonesian army conducted a massacre of
alleged Communists in which between a quarter and a half a million

civilians were slaughtered. The CIA later described the operation as "one of the worst mass murders of the 20th century."

This spring, a former U.S. congressional investigator named Kathy Kadane revealed the results of an exhaustive investigation she had undertaken of the U.S. role in the slaughter, based on lengthy taped interviews with a number of Americans who had been directly involved. Kadane accused the U.S. embassy and CIA agents in Indonesia of handing over to the army, after the massacres had begun, a hit list the Americans had systematically drawn up of some 5,000 alleged leftists, who were promptly hunted down and murdered.

One former embassy official told Kadane that "I probably have a lot of blood on my hands, but that's not all bad. There's a time when you have to strike hard at a decisive moment." Another admitted to her that "No one cared, so long as they were Communists, that they were being butchered. No one was getting very worked up about it."

El Salvador. George Bush, similarly, doesn't get worked up about the hundreds of Salvadoran soldiers who are being trained every year at the Fort Benning, Ga., U.S. Army School of the Americas. Salvador boasts Latin America's cruelest and most corrupt military; why they are being trained in the U.S. at all is not easy to fathom. Moreover, they return eager to embrace the prevailing local standards. In the words of one trade unionist who suffered at their hands, "They come back and become a gang of Salvadoran Noriegas."

Being an American, it has been observed, means never having to say you're sorry. No U.S. president has ever acknowledged, let alone apologized for, the actions documented above. Hell, none has ever apologized for Viet Nam. George Bush, vice-president during the aggression against Nicaragua and the president who invaded Panama, will surely forgive us if we take his new-found commitment to the rule of law with a tanker of salt.

＊　＊　＊

1993   GEORGE BUSH'S SECRETARY OF STATE is leaving office advocating a war-crimes tribunal to try certain Serbians for crimes against humanity. Lawrence Eagleburger has named one man who has killed more than 50 women and children, another who leads a gang accused of 3,000 civilian deaths, and Serbian President

Slobodan Milosevic himself for atrocities committed by his subordinates. Who can disagree?

Yet at the very same moment, Eagleburger's boss has pardoned six prominent Republicans who played key roles in the Iran-Contra scandal. By arming the Ayatollah's Iran in its long war against Saddam Hussein's Iraq while Washington was arming Saddam himself, and by arming the Contras in their vicious war against Nicaragua, these men were directly responsible for countless deaths and untold suffering. So they were pardoned.

Heaven knows our era has not lacked for crimes against humanity. A list of the most notorious would likely include the Viet Nam war, the pitiless Pakistani massacre of Bengalis in 1971, the operations of the Shah of Iran's secret police, the brutal Pinochet years in Chile, the secret U.S. bombing of Cambodia that created the conditions for the Khmer Rouge's killing fields, the bloody 1974 Turkish invasion of Cyprus, the betrayal of the Kurds in 1974–75, the Indonesian slaughter of some 100,000 East Timorese, the war against the government of Angola, the policies of the white governments of Rhodesia (now Zimbabwe) and South Africa.

What we do know, however, is that all of them had in common Henry Kissinger. As Richard Nixon's national security adviser and secretary of state in those years, Kissinger was either responsible for or, at the very least, endorsed every single one of them. And Larry Eagleburger worked under him throughout.

All this information comes not from any weird pinko source but from the recent bestselling biography *Henry Kissinger* by Walter Isaacson of *Time* magazine. Isaacson found the subject to be a two-faced, deceitful, callous, paranoid, duplicitous, devious, lying, conspiratorial, amoral megalomaniac who caused untold human misery largely to satisfy his own monstrous ego.

Yet in the end what is as appalling as Kissinger's own evil deeds is his celebrity and lionization. He has gotten away, literally, with murder. Isaacson shows that in return for access, even the most prominent of Washington's pundits and columnists routinely peddled Kissinger's self-aggrandizing lies and twisted analyses as if they were gospel. Even now that the truth is known, even after his shameless public support for the Beijing dictatorship during Tiananmen while he was making a mint opening Chinese doors for American corporations, Kissinger remains a media darling.

He counts among his dinner partners the likes of Tom Brokaw, Ted Koppel and Barbara Walters, plus senior VIPs from CBS, ABC, *News-*

week, CNN and the *New York Times* — and the head of the AFL-CIO! Corporations that fork out big bucks to get him on their boards or to act for him, such as our own Conrad Black, are expected to crow lustily about their great coup.

Then there is the Argentinean Nobel Peace Prize winner who once accused Kissinger to his face of "genocide and collective massacre."

Yet the man remains an American icon, even as does Ronald Reagan. One of George Bush's other last acts last week, besides a final, manly kick of some Iraqi ass, was to present Reagan with the Presidential Medal of Freedom for his contribution to "world peace."

No doubt. But when you add up the grisly carnage for which Reagan was directly responsible through his vicious wars against Nicaragua, Grenada, Libya and Angola and the loathsome governments he promoted in El Salvador, Guatemala, Zaire, Liberia, Panama, South Africa, Iran, Iraq and Somalia, the record is on a moral par with the butchers and rapists of Bosnia.

What do Reagan and Kissinger's admirers feel when they grasp the two men's blood-drenched hands? Are certain crimes against humanity less equal than others? By all means let's have that war-crimes tribunal — but for all those guilty of such atrocities.

Distant Causes

1987   BY STANDING UP to Margaret Thatcher, Brian Mulroney has just taken another major step in his leadership in the struggle against apartheid. Now the question is whether
he can stand up to his own party and civil service and take the next
logical, and crucial, step.

Of all Mulroney's actions as Prime Minister, none has shown more
principle or has been less driven by political motives than his
consistent attempt to put the screws on the white regime in South
Africa. His government has already introduced a first round of
sanctions against South Africa, and Mulroney has repeatedly promised to go much further if the Pretoria regime failed to show a
readiness to begin negotiating itself out of existence. As he has now
admitted, there are no such signs to be seen.

At the Vancouver Commonwealth meeting, Mulroney hoped to
find unanimity, but found Margaret Thatcher instead. Mrs. Thatcher
and her aides showed not the slightest hesitation in introducing a
kind of gutter, knife-in-the-back politics unprecedented in Commonwealth history and directed solely at humiliating Brian Mulroney.
For the British Tories, close cooperation with white South Africa is
a matter of both racial preference and economic interest, although
they glibly invoke all the correct anti-apartheid rhetoric.

Lesser politicians might well have been intimidated by the
Thatcherite intimidation. Brian Mulroney refused to back down one
inch. The Commonwealth consensus has utterly rejected the line —
peddled in happy collusion by both the British and South African
governments — that sanctions will have no impact on the white
minority.

But having held the Commonwealth to its proper course, surely

Brian Mulroney has, in honour, no recourse but to escalate Canadian sanctions on South Africa drastically and immediately. And that involves another titanic battle. Having refused to bow to Maggie Thatcher, the PM must now take on his own caucus and, more remarkably, his own bureaucracy.

The latter represents a case of "Yes Minister" run amok, but this time it's not amusing. The civil servants in the Ministry of External Affairs have interests quite contradictory to those of the Prime Minister of Canada. They would be much more comfortable following the approaches of Washington and London, notwithstanding the de facto support for apartheid by both Ronald Reagan and Thatcher.

In fact, shockingly enough, it's been officials in External, not Tory politicians, who have been telling reporters that polls are showing a decreasing Canadian interest in South Africa. It's not bad enough our government are slavish followers of polls; now our civil service is getting into the act too.

If public interest in Canada is waning, it's because the South African government has become brilliantly effective in controlling its own news coverage. It does so in two ways. First, it has dramatically censored the amount of hard news that's coming out of the country, which has led to less dramatic news coverage, which has led to less media interest in South Africa around the world, which has in turn reduced public interest. Exactly as the white government intended.

Secondly, the Botha government has undertaken a multi-million dollar campaign of disinformation that speaks to those ugly, seldom admitted yet deep-rooted racist tendencies that seem to be found throughout western societies, as the South Africans understand only too shrewdly. It is this deliberate attempt to undermine the anti-apartheid crusade that has, for example, produced all that specious propaganda about sanctions working only to hurt black South Africans.

Further evidence of the campaign was seen in Vancouver at the Parallel Conference that was run under the sponsorship fo the Canadian Council for International Cooperation. Those in attendance watched a new video that is being widely distributed by South African propaganda services, a perfectly nasty and deceitful piece of work that slickly and cunningly exploits anti-black sentiments and ties anti-apartheid organizations to an international terrorist network featuring your worst villains from around the world.

The Tory caucus has been filled with such propaganda. Many of its members are only too happy to buy it holus bolus. In their hearts, they're with Thatcher, not Mulroney, and the PM knows it only too well. He also knows, however, that history is on his side, and that on this single issue Brian Mulroney can make his mark in the history books on the side of justice and human equality. The time to act is now.

✳ ✳ ✳

1988   A FRIEND OF MINE is in hospital and may be dying. I know many of you could make the same distressing statement, except that my friend, Albie Sachs, is a South African living in exile in Mozambique, and an African National Congress activist whose car blew up last week when he opened it. He lost an eye and an arm and may or may not survive.

But this is not isolated event. Albie was the victim of the long arm of South African state terrorism.

In the last two weeks, there have been four other comparable incidents in southern Africa and Europe. The ANC representative in Belgium escaped being killed in a bomb blast outside his office. Four people were murdered in a most grisly manner in a raid on Botswana. Dulcie September, the ANC representative in Paris, had 22 bullets pumped into her by what the French police describe as a "professional killer." In Maseru, Lesotho, an ANC guerrilla was shot to death even though he was under police guard in a local hospital. And now Albie.

For years, South Africa has cavalierly murdered its opponents both inside and outside the country and gotten clean away with it. There are more Canadians than anyone realizes with African or liberation movement experience who have had close friends assassinated over the years.

At the same time, South Africa has, at will, undertaken armed invasions against every one of its neighbor states, killing and maiming. Some 30 ANC officials in exile have been victims of sporadic assassination attempts over the years. And of course, South Africa has long sponsored violent internal destabilization against Angola and Mozambique.

But there seems to be a new pattern at work now. At home, brutal repression is the order of the day. The media has virtually been shut down. Foreign reporting is tightly controlled. Eighteen anti-apartheid organizations have been banned. Vigilantes have been unleashed to terrorize and exterminate those involved in seeking peace between competing anti-government movements.

This systematic campaign to break the opposition forces is apparently being carried out by the State Security Council, a clandestine body chaired by President Botha and responsible only to him. The cabinet, the Nationalist Party and parliament have all been usurped by what some consider a de facto internal coup d'état. The SSC is running the show.

Not satisfied with merely dominating all of southern Africa, the president and his council evidently have decided to teach the world another lesson: that South Africa can trace and attack its enemies anywhere on earth with impunity. It seems certain that South African hit squads have been dispatched as part of a secret, dirty war to wipe out anyone, anywhere, whom the regime chooses to target.

Dulcie September sought protection from the French police, but in vain. ANC officials have now warned authorities in over half a dozen western countries of their fears of South African death squads. Here in Canada, ANC representative Yousuf Saloogie is seeking police protection. The pattern of the last weeks strongly indicates the RCMP must treat Mr. Saloogie's request both seriously and urgently.

There is a Canadian political dimension to this issue. In October 1985, the prime minister stirred a jaded United Nations General Assembly with an eloquent attack on apartheid and an unequivocal commitment that Canada would escalate economic and diplomatic sanctions unless South Africa quickly demonstrated its intention to reform itself.

Since that time, 30,000 South Africans have been detained in the country, half of them kids under 18. Three thousand South Africans have died in so-called "political violence." One hundred and five people died in police custody in 1987; not a single policeman has been found responsible.

Countless thousands have been murdered in the front-line states either by invading South African soldiers or local surrogates. And now we face this new international campaign of terror to eliminate deliberately selected opponents of the regime around the world.

South Africa is getting away, quite literally, with murder, murder on a massive scale. Yet from the western democracies it hears little more than cheap anti-apartheid rhetoric with little concrete action to back it up.

Believe that even dour President Botha allows himself a thin, smug smirk each time he hears Brian Mulroney or Joe Clark passionately condemn the evils of apartheid, then explain why this is still not the perfect moment for Canada to tighten its sanctions.

Albie Sachs and his friends always insisted that Canada's stance — whatever it is — sends an unmistakable message to all the forces at work in southern Africa. What more will it take to get our government to send the right message?

∗ ∗ ∗

1988   IN ORDER TO MAINTAIN its continuing control in South Africa, the Botha government believes it is essential to maintain current economic and diplomatic support from abroad. To this end, it has launched an international campaign of propaganda and misinformation in which, you may be surprised to learn, only the United States and Britain are higher priority targets than Canada.

Riding gallantly to the South African cause last year came Toronto journalist Peter Worthington, with a 25-minute video cassette called *The ANC Method: Violence.*

Worthington has long been an outspoken foe of African nationalist movements in southern Africa, and a champion of such figures as Jonas Savimbi, head of the Angolan guerilla group called UNITA which is funded by South Africa, the Reagan administration and the CIA.

Worthington's video is an effective piece of special pleading, following substantially the main themes of the Botha propaganda effort. While Worthington tells us that he hates apartheid, he insists that the system is in fact being dismantled from within, yet "the media of the world" are ignoring this profound change.

The real villains, we are told, are not the white racists who hold power but the ANC, the African National Congress, which is responsible for the ugly violence that blacks are perpetrating on other blacks inside South Africa; the tape is chock-a-bloc with grisly scenes of necklacing and other disgusting and intolerable acts. It has no footage of whites brutalizing blacks, nor of the fierce treatment the South African army has visited upon its African neighbors in recent years.

The video is also highly cunning in lumping the ANC in with a bevy of unpopular and often despicable terrorist organizations, such as the Palestine Liberation Organization, the Irish Republican Army, the Red Brigades, and the German Baader-Meinhoff gang.

Shots of ANC president Oliver Tambo are squeezed between those of Lybia's Moammar Khadhafi and PLO chairman Yasser Arafat, while the assassination of Lord Mountbatten, the massacre at Rome airport, necklacing, hijacking, the murder on the Achille Lauro and violence in Northern Ireland are all promiscuously linked together.

A key device in Worthington's video for adding credibility to these dubious linkages is the use of apparent experts, especially one Craig Williamson, who comments unflatteringly on the ANC on seven separate occasions and who is described four separate times as "former member ANC/SA Communist party." The viewer irresistibly infers that Williamson is a disaffected ANC man who decided to spill the beans about his former colleagues.

In fact, as Peter Worthington knew perfectly well, Craig Williamson was a spy for the South African Security Police.

Williamson was recruited into the security services in 1968, at the age of 19, and for the next dozen years, Agent RS 167 led, in the words of the *Sunday Times* of London, "a life of deception betraying all those with whom he had claimed to sympathize." First he infiltrated the ranks of South Africa's liberal student organizations. In 1977, promoted to captain, Williamson feigned danger resulting from his anti-government activities and left the country. He quickly found employment in Geneva with the International University Exchange Fund (IUEF), of which he eventually became deputy director. This was an enormous coup for South African security.

The IUEF was a curious organization that, among other things, supplied funds to leading anti-apartheid groups all through southern Africa and in Europe, offered scholarships to southern African refugees, and had close contacts with just about anyone who was anyone among the world's anti-apartheid organizations.

The IUEF received support from various sources in Western Europe — and Canada. In the three years Williamson worked with it, the Canadian International Development Agency gave the IUEF almost $1.5 million, the United Church chipped in $33,000, and CUSO contributed as well.

Over the years, as part of Operation Daisy, Williamson systematically passed on to his control in South Africa, Brig. Johan Coetzee, head of the South African police, literally thousands of pieces of information on people within South Africa who were quietly co-operating with IUEF in everything from assistance to the liberation movements to refugee and welfare work. As a result, he compromised the safety of every one of them, which was, of course, his job.

In January, 1980, fearing his cover was about to be blown, Williamson confessed all to the IUEF director and then flew home to South Africa for a hero's welcome. He was lauded in parliament by the minister of police, Louis Le Grange, for his "outstanding service to his country," celebrated by the Afrikkan-language press, and publicly saluted by Coetzee as "my best agent."

Williamson himself never hid his light under a bushel. He gave a major press conference where he proudly asserted that his public emergence had created "a lot of very worried people in South Africa ... They have reason to be nervous." His family reacted to the news with pride: "They are South Africans."

Williamson happened to touch the lives of dozens of Canadians, most of them in development agencies, and of figures well known to Canadians.

Some insiders are persuaded it was Williamson who tipped off South African security that Steven Biko, with IUEF assistance, was about to skip the country. Within a month, as millions of us now know, Biko was arrested, beaten and died.

Williamson remained with the security police after his return home, rising first to major, then commandant or lieutenant-colonel, apparently being groomed to succeed Coetzee. But he resigned in 1985 to become a private consultant on "security matters" as well as to companies intent on sanctions-busting.

In May, 1987, he entered the South African whites-only general election as a Nationalist party candidate, boasting of his prowess "as a bomb-maker and informer." Publicly described as South Africa's "superspy," Williamson bragged of the "militants" he had helped send to jail. But some critics in the local press denounced him as a "professional deceiver," and he failed to take his constituency.

Now what's important about all this information is that it's entirely public. And Peter Worthington knew it. "I should have said that he was an agent of the government," Worthington told me, "but I didn't doubt his information and I considered the source less important than the material." Readers must decide for themselves whether this is a satisfactory response from a life-long journalist.

It's also noteworthy that the video was distributed for Worthington in Canada by C-FAR (Citizens for Foreign Aid Reform), headed by

Paul Fromm. C-FAR sent 3,000 to 4,000 copies to their own mailing list, and sent another 400 gratis to media outlets across the country and to all MPs. They sent me my copy after I sent them $10 (although the South African embassy in Ottawa also sends copies on request).

C-FAR is tied in with any number of far-right causes such as opposition to non-white immigration to Canada. Like Worthington, they support Savimbi and UNITA and loathe the ANC. Paul Fromm has been closely connected to the World Anti-Communist League, another umbrella group for right-wing extremists of the most notorious kind.

C-FAR's office manager, Daryl Reside, was once appointed editor of *Aryan*, the organ of the now defunct neo-Nazi group the Western Guard, led by John Ross Taylor. Taylor loved Hitler, and the magazine was filled with articles claiming the Holocaust was a hoax, "Communism was founded and funded by the Jews," and that the Talmud allows Jews to "betray, murder, rob and rape Christians without violating the Jewish religion." *Aryan* also reprinted the *Western Guard*'s petition to the Queen and Parliament that "the ancient law of England, 1290, (be enforced) THAT ALL JEWS BE EXPELLED FROM CANADA."

Fromm and Reside are directors of the Canadian Association for Free Expression (CAFE), whose conference in Vancouver last February featured Ernst Zundel's son, Pierre; Doug Collins, a B.C. journalist who testified for the defence at the Zundel trial; and Ron Gostick, whose Canadian League of Rights has been described by Manuel Prutschi of the Canadian Jewish Congress as "perhaps Canada's primary anti-Semitic organization." CAFE bitterly protested the convictions of Ernst Zundel, while C-FAR published and promoted excerpts from the trial speeches of Doug Christie, Zundel's defence counsel.

(Zundel last week was convicted, and sentenced to nine months, for "wilfully spreading false news" about the Holocaust. This week he was released on $10,500 bail pending an appeal.)

Worthington told me that he had approached C-FAR to distribute the video, even though he had had little prior connection with the organization. But he has been a guest speaker at a C-FAR public forum on Angola. While he is on their mailing list, he doesn't read their material "closely." In fact, except for its positions on South Africa and Canadian foreign aid policy, "I don't know of any of its other activities."

That's why my information about Ron Gostick and *Aryan* magazine and Daryl Reside (whom Worthington told me is Paul Fromm's spouse) "doesn't bother me because I'm not associated with any of it."

It's all a little disquieting. First a life-long journalist decides it was irrelevant to come clean about the background of his key witness in eviscerating the African National Congress.

Secondly, he denies knowledge of some of the more unpalatable dimensions of the organization he approached to distribute the work, although such information is easily come by.

Thirdly, he appears to feel he is not tainted by these distasteful activities of theirs since his involvement with C-FAR excludes them.

Here's something to wonder about: If a left-wing publicist in a parallel situation responded as Peter Worthington has done, can't you just imagine the scornful column Worthington would now be writing?

* * *

1989 ANTI-APARTHEID ACTIVISTS everywhere have been shaken by the shocking stories swirling around Winnie Mandela. A perspective is essential here.

First, it must be acknowledged that Mandela has clearly been involved in at least some completely unacceptable and indefensible activities, for which she must be judged by the same high standards we use to judge any other person. This has been the approach of both the exiled African National Congress and leaders of the black movement inside South Africa, and their prompt public criticism of her has significantly enhanced their credibility worldwide.

But if Mandela must be judged as any other person, she can hardly be understood as such. For she is not any other person. Even in South Africa, where the totalitarian apartheid system distorts the collective and individual personalities of peoples of all races, her experiences have been singularly soul-destroying and dehumanizing. She has borne far, far more than any human being can be expected to and survive psychologically intact.

It began with her marriage to Nelson Mandela in 1959. From then until now, fully 30 years, she has lived a life characterized by cruel harassment, relentless intimidation and unending persecution at the hands of a vicious white power structure.

The marriage was no marriage. Even before Nelson was sentenced to life imprisonment in 1964, he was barely home. Soon Winnie too became, willy nilly, a leader of her people. She gave birth twice, the first pregnancy coinciding with her first imprisonment. In 1962, she was banned — made a virtual non-person — for two years. In 1965, she got five more years. In 1969–70, she spent 491 days in prison, most of them in solitary confinement. In 1970, the banning order was renewed for another five years together with house arrest each night and on weekends.

In 1974, she was imprisoned for six months for violating her banning order by lunching with her two children and another banned person. In 1975, after 13 years of banning, there were 10 months of "freedom," but then came five more months of prison. In 1977, she was banned again for five years, and in 1982 for yet another five years. In 1986, Winnie Mandela was released at last. For the first time in a quarter of a century, she was as free as a black person ever gets in South Africa.

In her 1985 autobiography, Mandela makes the story more vivid. In prison, she washed out of a toilet bucket. "During menstruation we only got toilet paper or the white guards would say 'Go use your big fat hands.' " As a banned person, she could not be with more than one person at a time. She often would not know what had become of her children after the police summarily hauled her from their home, leaving them screaming in fear. Nelson, of course, she saw only intermittently and under the tightest scrutiny.

Intense, intimate surveillance was unending. So was loneliness. "The empty long days drag on," she wrote, "the solitude is deadly." And after Nelson received his life sentence: "That was hell. Solitude, loneliness, is worse than fear."

"No human being," she herself understood, "can go on taking those humiliations without reaction."

So when she was finally able to return to her people to resume her oppressive burdens as the "mother of the nation" — was she not still Nelson's surrogate, after all? — who can wonder if she had cracked a bit, if she refused to accept the authority and discipline of the movement's leadership? And who can be surprised if the ever-vigilant white intelligence apparatus didn't quickly perceive their opportunity and move to infiltrate her controversial bodyguard, as the ANC plausibly believes? Certainly it is clear that the regime is cynically exploiting the distress she has caused in brazenly calculating ways.

Suddenly we have white police arresting Winnie's bully boys (and likely murderers), making cops seem, for the first time ever, almost like the good guys instead of the vicious oppressors they are. Suddenly white authority emerges as the champion of tyrannized Africans against Winnie and her Mandela Football Club. The entire white power structure has schemed and plotted to squeeze this one for all it's worth.

They won't get away with it. Winnie Mandela, her usefulness to her cause perhaps ended, has probably been destroyed by the pernicious system she spent her life fighting. But in the overall struggle, these awful events are, in fact, a mere blip. The just struggle will continue until the day is won, and history will record not that Winnie Mandela embarrassed the movement for three trying years, but that she was one of its martyrs for three heroic decades.

∗   ∗   ∗

1989   GIVEN MY SOCIALIST COMPASSION, I certainly don't begrudge Joe Clark quietly slipping away from Ottawa's oppressive heat for Australia next week. I'm just kinda sorry he's going to embarrass himself and humiliate his country while he's there.

Clark's off to chair a meeting of the special Commonwealth Committee of Foreign Ministers on Southern Africa, which will be considering an independent Commonwealth-commissioned report on sanctions against South Africa. Poor Joe. Such lousy timing. Canadian actions against South Africa have been proving, well, not 100 per cent effective. Last year, there was a 68 per cent increase in South African imports into Canada over 1987, and we've just learned that those imports more than doubled in value in the first four months of this year compared with the same period in 1988.

It was inevitable. The simple truth is that we still trade with South Africa, the government wants to go on trading with South Africa, and it's time we stopped dredging up Prime Minister Brian Mulroney's 1985 United Nations commitment that we will stop trading with South Africa. It's dead as a dodo.

In fact, our government has been moving in exactly the opposite direction. We have now quietly aligned ourselves with Margaret Thatcher in a perverse policy of giving the new South African leader, F.W. deKlerk, a chance to prove that he's really a serious reformer, and never mind the demonstrable evidence that he is no such thing. In fact, we can expect Canada and Britain not only to refuse to use new sanctions to increase pressure on South Africa, but to offer to soften existing sanctions in return for some kind of movement towards reform.

This scenario helps explain Canada's extraordinary behaviour in the past year. At the last Commonwealth foreign ministers meeting in Toronto a year ago, a secret interim report from the sanctions study group was discussed. Besides a reception featuring the world's most scrumptious jumbo shrimps, Joe Clark's contribution to the meeting was, apparently, to block seven of the report's 10 recommendations for tightening economic sanctions against South Africa.

This spring, Clark vetoed the publication of the final report of the independent study group and External Affairs officials have been busily badmouthing it since. Now, there's a real fear Clark will try to stall the public release of the document until the actual Commonwealth conference in Malaysia in October, instead of agreeing to circulate it immediately to help mobilize public sentiment.

No wonder Clark's antagonistic to the study: Even though it's resolutely moderate and thoughtful, its conclusions utterly undermine the British-Canadian approach to South Africa. It demonstrates that sanctions do work, that sanctions are necessary for real change in South Africa, that sanctions now in place helped persuade South Africa to surrender its formal control of Namibia. And it advocates that the full Commonwealth conference in October approve a new program of steadily escalating sanctions against South Africa. Otherwise, believe it or not, sanctions by the Scandinavian countries and even the United States will remain tighter than present Commonwealth measures.

There is remarkable flux in southern Africa at the moment. Angola, Namibia and Mozambique may actually be seeing the end of decades of catastrophic war, while South Africa itself is in unprecedented crisis. Real optimism, however, is surely premature. No one must forget for a moment the stakes involved here, nor the lengths white South Africa will go to protect its stunning privileges. That's why unrelenting pressure must be applied.

According to a University of Natal research group, more than

4,000 South Africans died in politically inspired violence between September, 1984, when unrest broke out in the black townships of the Transvaal, and the end of 1988. According to a 1989 study commissioned by the Commonwealth secretariat, South African destabilization of its six neighboring black-ruled countries has inflicted more than a million deaths and cost some $35 billion since 1980; the authors called their findings "conservative."

A new UNICEF study published last April, tells us that more than a million people have been killed and 11 million displaced by South Africa's wars against Angola and Mozambique since 1980. The report also reveals a "shocking" situation in Namibia under South African rule, where the mortality rate is among the worst in the entire world; of every 1,000 children, 300 die before the age of 5. Yet Canadian External Affairs officials have taken to peddling the straight South African line on evolving developments in Namibia.

It's literally true that all over the world anti-apartheid activists have been looking to Canada for leadership. I fear they're going to be bitterly disappointed. Bon voyage, Joe. Canberra may prove hotter than you expect.

* * *

1989 DID I EVER TELL YOU that I fell madly in love in Nicaragua last year? The moment I laid eyes on Cesar Jerez I was smitten. He looked precisely the way one always believed a Jesuit and a university president ought to look but rarely does. He emanated wisdom and integrity, combined with an irreverent wit and a mischievous twinkle in his eye. A Guatemalan, he spoke English with enviable epigrammatic elegance. At the end of our meeting, I was ready to follow him anywhere.

He was interested in me too, but mostly, I'm forced to concede, because I was a Canadian rather than for any of my personal qualities. For a "critical supporter" of the Sandinista revolution such as he, Canadians were a pretty attractive commodity. Now Father Jerez has, in fact, followed me back to Canada. This very night we're sharing a platform at Harbourfront at a public meeting on the peace process in Central America. I'm a nervous wreck already.

Let me reveal something else about myself, both ideological and personal. I normally hate big power aggressors more than I love their victims. History suggests this to be a prudent position for a left-winger; radical apologists for totalitarianism in the name of the socialist revolution have always enraged me.

So I condemned angrily the Soviet invasion of Afghanistan, though with no confidence whatever in the government the fanatical fundamentalist Mujahadeen rebels will provide. I was a fervent foe of the U.S. invasion of Viet Nam, but I thought many on my side were blind and foolish to idealize Uncle Ho Chi Minh so unreservedly; unlike them, I was not shattered by the way the Communists ran the country when they finally took over. Castro's Cuba provides another depressing example of the same syndrome.

That's why my opposition to the U.S. attempt to destroy the Sandinista government was more categorical than my support for the Sandinistas themselves. And that's why I was so influenced by the balanced judgments of the exquisite Father Jerez as I sat captivated in his office at the independent University of Central America in Managua.

Jerez knew well how life was lived throughout the rest of Central America as well as South America, Europe and North America. From his perspective he had become, to repeat his key phrase, "a critical supporter of the revolution." Heaven knows he was critical. The Sandinistas' initial treatment of the east coast Indians was deplorable. Agrarian reform was handled poorly. Serious human rights abuses have accompanied the waging of the war against the American-backed contras. Many of the economic measures attempted, such as huge mega-projects, were wrong-headed.

But admitted government mistakes had not wrecked the country's precarious economy, Jerez said. That was the direct responsibility of the American war exacerbated by the American embargo. The U.S. was suffocating Nicaragua's economy. Two-thirds to three-quarters of the entire budget — already pathetically picayune — went to the war effort, while virtually all progressive forms of nation-building had ground to a halt. Low-intensity conflict — America's adorable euphemism for the wars it was supporting against poor Third World countries — didn't seem low intensity when you were at the receiving end.

The real Sandinista contribution, he went on, was in the courage, the dignity and the determination with which they had led their people against the American aggression. "We're poor, but we have our dignity. The revolution has given the poor here more dignity than in any other Central American nation. People may complain a lot, but if they were summoned tomorrow by the Sandinistas to defend their country against the Americans, they'd respond en masse." This wonderful man is likely to advise Canadians that this is an historical juncture for Central America, that his message is one of real hope, and that there is a singular opportunity for Canada to play a unique and meaningful role in the peace process. We must encourage the new American administration to its own *glasnost* in Central America, to see the crisis there in non-cold war terms. We must encourage them to open a serious dialogue with Nicaragua. Our government, he might note tactfully, could make a far greater contribution to Nicaraguan reconstruction than it has to date.

Cesar Jerez is a man who radiates love, caring and good humour. It will be in that spirit that he speaks to Canadians. The question for the Mulroney government will then be: Does love mean never having to say you're sorry to the White House?

✳   ✳   ✳

1990   LEADERS OF CANADA'S JEWISH COMMUNITY are doing a
————   profound disservice to Canadian Jewry and the state of Israel. By either blessing, or justifying, or remaining silent about every reprehensible activity of both the Israeli government and Israeli extremists, they undermine their own credibility in the eyes of many thoughtful Canadians, Jews included. Their behaviour is not only immoral; it is counter-productive.

Never mind the routine beatings, torture, killings and harassment of Palestinians by Jews. Take the recent move of 150 Israeli fundamentalists, surreptitiously subsidized by the Shamir government, into the old Christian quarter of Jerusalem. The mayor of Jerusalem, a Jew, calls it "stupid and ignorant." The American Israel Public Affairs Committee, the principal pro-Israel lobby in the U.S., warns that American Jews may now cut back their financial support of Israel. The director of the Anti-Defamation League of the B'nai Brith in the U.S. calls the settlement "provocative and insensitive," while the president of the American Jewish Congress is "appalled" by the move.

Then, there's Canada. The Canadian Jewish Congress issues a statement reaffirming its belief that Jews have a right to live in any part of Israel. The Canada-Israel Committee affirms this same right but with the mealy-mouthed qualification that "the manner in which recent events have unfolded is disquieting."

And worst of all: The Canadian B'nai Brith. A B'nai Brith delegation of 20 Jewish leaders from across Canada, in Israel when the Jerusalem issue explodes, are ready, aye, ready, to perform as mindless cheerleaders. "We support," a spokesperson say, "what the duly elected government of Israel does" — a peculiarly witless and uninformed principle.

And to demonstrate the boundless nature of their irresponsibility, the delegation then visits and pays homage at a Jewish settlement in the occupied West Bank that had been founded by Rabbi Moshe Levinger. Levinger, a fanatical leader of Israel's Jewish settler movement and a bigot who calls Arabs "dogs," was just convicted of killing an unarmed, unthreatening Palestinian shopkeeper.

Is there no limit to what Canadian Jewish leaders will tolerate from Israel? Wrong question. Is there any level of iniquity they'll fail to celebrate? Is there a more monstrous Israeli figure than Ari Sharon, chauvinist, authoritarian, ultra-hawk, architect of the 1982 invasion of Lebanon — who failed, an Israeli commission of enquiry found, to prevent the bloody massacre by Israel's Lebanese allies of more than 700 helpless Palestinians in the Shatillan and Sabra refugee camps?

Not ghastly enough, it seems, for the Canadian Friends of the Jerusalem College of Technology, whose board has chosen to invite Sharon to speak at a Toronto fund-raising event. What kind of message does this invitation send to Canadians, I asked their official spokesperson. "We're not politically naïve or stupid," he replied. "The board weighed all the considerations before deciding. There were lots of considerations involved here."

So the question remains: Is there any act of "the duly elected government of Israel" that will shame the leaders of Canadian Jewry into saying, with Jewish leaders in American and in Israel itself, "Enough is enough. You are despoiling every great historic tradition of Judaism"?

When Israel renewed diplomatic relations with Ethiopia earlier this year, it was revealed they would also be sending military advisers and arms, including cluster bombs, to Menghistu's demented, murderous regime. Was there a peep of concern, let alone dissent, from the

Canadian Jewish establishment for this heinous act? Has there been even an eyebrow raised at the intimate 15-year collaboration between Israel and South Africa, actively promoted by the leaders of both major Israeli parties, involving not only commercial trade but weapons development, military co-operations and joint nuclear research, very possibly including the joint testing of a nuclear bomb?

"Because of their historic experience," writes Irving Abella in *A Coat Of Many Colors*, his new history of Canadian Jewry, "Jews have tended to be sensitive to oppression and to threats to religious and political freedom." Except, it appears, in Israel.

Yet, those of us who dare speak out for traditional Jewish values are rewarded with menacing and abusive midnight phone calls. Why pick on us? Why not harass instead those 780 American-Jewish leaders who, according to a recent poll by the Israel-Diaspora Institute, are overwhelmingly opposed to the most fundamental Israeli policies of recent years?

* * *

1991   HECTOR OQUELI COLINDES, a leading member of the Salvadoran socialist opposition, was murdered last week, apparently by a Salvadoran government death squad. I had lunch with Oqueli in Toronto last June, together with Don Lee and Terry Meagher, Canadian trade unionists working for social justice in Central America.

For Meagher, Oqueli's murder was a terrible first, but Lee's almost an old hand at mourning Central American colleagues; he knew many of the 10 people blown away in San Salvador last year when a trade union headquarters was blown up.

Grieving, I'm afraid, is an inescapable component of being involved in one of the many Canadian-Central American solidarity groups. It's virtually inevitable that you'll quickly meet some Central American trade unionist or human rights activist who'll soon be murdered by military death squads tied closely to the brutal governments of Salvador, Guatemala, or Honduras.

My friends Tim Draimin, Michael Czerny and Laurel Whitney, who have worked on Central America for the Toronto-based Jesuit

Centre for Social Faith and Justice, all knew Oqueli. They also knew well some of the six Jesuit priests who, it's now officially acknowledged, were murdered recently by Salvadoran soldiers. In Tegucigalpa two years ago, Whitney and I met with Dr. Ramon Custodia, president of the Honduras Human Rights Committee, whose closest associate had been murdered only weeks before; he, and we, fully expected he'd be next, and we frankly breathed a sigh of relief when the evening finally ended.

It's the same for those involved in anti-apartheid movements over the years; you don't ever get used to the murders of friends and allies, but you learn that it's a tragic part of the struggle. Recently, the lethal activities of South African death squads were finally exposed. I spent my last day in Mozambique three years ago tootling around Maputo visiting local artists with Albie Sachs in his Volkswagen Beetle. A year later, a South African death squad booby-trapped Sach's Bug outside his home. He was luckier than most of their targets: miraculously, he escaped certain death. You may remember the ghastly photo of him splayed all over the road, virtually dismembered.

My old friend John Saul, a Toronto Africanist who's been at the heart of the anti-apartheid struggle for 25 years, has lost eight to 10 good friends in that period and perhaps dozens of others whom he had known less well; Ruth First, the South African activist who fled to Mozambique, was blown up by a letter-bomb she opened moments before the farewell reception she had organized in Maputo for Saul's return to Canada.

These experiences not only help explain our passionate commitment to these causes. They equally explain why we're so bitter about those nations that have actively supported the governments responsible for these outrages.

Many Canadians will bristle when I accuse two countries in particular, the United States and Israel, of having reprehensible records here, precisely because both are self-proclaimed democracies and both are proud Canadian allies. Yet both have for years been up to their eyeballs in shameful, clandestine complicity with the governments, the armed forces, the security services and the intelligence agencies of both South Africa and the brutal fascist governments of Central America.

Like it or not, the evidence for these assertions — for those not so blinded by their biases that they simply refuse to see — is abundant and unanswerable; I'm surrounded by reams of it as I write, and it's not just propaganda. Israel has provided arms, training and intelligence advice to almost every pariah regime in the world. The U.S. government doesn't actually see South Africa as a pariah at all but as a loyal, if awkward, anti-Soviet ally in Africa and the Indian Ocean. As for Central America, the American record for direct involvement in the most heinous possible crimes against humanity is infinitely worse and more widespread than even many U.S. critics quite grasp. In fact, the U.S. is beyond question the chief enemy of freedom and justice in Latin America.

Will some accuse me of being blindly anti-American? Disloyal to Israel? Unfair in attacking the Mulroney government's failure to speak out against its American and Israeli allies? I'm only sorry they can't ask Hector Oqueli these questions any more.

✳ ✳ ✳

1991   AFRICA? WHERE'S AFRICA?

Canada's going to hell in a handbasket. The federal government lacks all legitimacy. One and a half million citizens are jobless. Half of all Quebeckers favour outright sovereignty.

Who cares about Africa when our own crises absorb all our attention and energies? Hardly anyone. This isn't only a Canadian reality, however; the entire world seems to have succumbed to an epidemic of Africa fatigue. After all, there's eastern Europe and what was once the Soviet Union and the eternal problems of the Middle East and, and, and.

So Africa, for centuries the most exploited continent on earth and today humankind's most outstanding failure, has been marginalized. During the 1980s, a new United Nations report states, "the average African continued to get poorer and to suffer a persistent fall in an already meagre standard of living."

About half the continent's 650 million people live in absolute poverty. Thirty million are staring famine in the eye, and untold thousands have already died. More than 100,000 qualified Africans have left for the West, a calamitous brain drain. Without billions of new dollars from the West, the UN report makes clear, Africa will continue in "stagnation and despair."

Compared to resolving our own crises, however, solving those of Africa is really a piece of cake, especially if you listen to the World

156

Bank and the International Monetary Fund and the American government.

All it needs — yep, you guessed it — is a pile of market-oriented reforms, usually described as Structural Adjustment Programs (SAPs), that will clean up the entire mess in no time. Simply remove subsidies on food, slash spending on health, education and social services, lay off public sector workers — all this, mind you, for the poorest of the poorest countries on earth — and all will be hunky-dory.

This very sick joke was imposed on poor countries a decade ago by the bank and IMF. That it was a recipe for absolute disaster was universally predicted by all those the Bank and its allies routinely ignore or dismiss. Five years ago the UN adopted an ambitious program for African economic recovery. With SAPs still the order of the day, it proved to be an abysmal, utter failure, although those who go around chanting "market, market," as if it were some kind of magical mantra, insist that those countries that introduced the most market-oriented reforms had the greatest successes. Right: the operation was a success, but the patient died.

What success means to the market mafia is that Africa continues its age-old role of enriching the capitalist world. Remember the Marshall Plan that saved Europe? It brought 2 per cent of America's Gross Domestic Product into Europe in the years after World War II. But in recent years, Africa, the world's greatest basket case, has actually been *sending* 4 per cent of its GDP to the opulent West.

Africa's present debt burden of $270 billion is actually one-third greater than when the economic recovery program began in 1986. Through debt repayment, unbelievably enough, the IMF itself has taken $4 billion out of Africa since 1986. In fact during these years, some $60 billion in capital has fled the continent.

Then there's the falling commodity prices, which, since 1986, have cost Africa yet another $50 billion in lost export earnings as prices plummeted. Here the World Bank can take the credit. Its charter document for African development in the 1980s, the Berg Report, urged an export-oriented growth strategy as the solution to Africa's economic woes. Improved terms of trade in commodity crops and minerals would both assist Africa's balance of payments and also finance its industrialization.

This was a guaranteed prescription for disaster. The inevitable oversupply of commodities led to a massive decline in their prices. Yet, even now the Bank *et al.* continue to urge on Africa ever-greater production of cocoa, coffee and cotton.

I said "urge." I meant "insist." What was absolutely apparent this month at the UN was that the New World Order is alive and well and ravaging Africa. With George Bush as President of the world, American ideologues and their confederates simply dictate what individual countries, indeed entire continents, must do.

In the past decade, their market dogmas have set Africa back generations. Imports have declined, investment levels have fallen, development programs have been severely disrupted. Yet, even half-decent African governments, desperate for immediate funds, have little alternative but to accept the absurd policies responsible for such destruction.

Who cares about Africa? A handful of dedicated Canadians who aren't yet ready to sacrifice an entire continent on the altar of discredited neo-conservative nostrums.

$$* \quad * \quad *$$

1991 I FIRST STEPPED FOOT ON AFRICAN SOIL in 1964. Most of the continent had barely emerged from colonial rule, and the sweet promise of a dazzling future was palpable everywhere. Charismatic leaders were taking charge, a ferment of freedom and hope was in the air.

A sense existed that, like the Jews, Africans knew better than anyone about racism and inequality and man's exploitation of man and woman, having been victimized by them for centuries, and now that Africa was taking control of its own destiny it would seek to forge a new, superior kind of civilization.

Looking back, it seems incredible that such a romantic, innocent dream was possible as recently as 27 years ago. That brief moment was the high point of African optimism in this century, for the great promise died even as it began. Africa had learned the lessons of white civilization only too well: soon great leaders turned into unimaginable tyrants, mass parties into terrorizing thugs, artificial nations into warring factions.

Quite unexpectedly, African armies quickly flexed their muscles, everywhere over-throwing civilian governments and turning most of the continent into a vast, inept, corrupt, military dictatorship. Western governments and the world's arms merchants soon happily discovered that poverty and squalor did not preclude billions of dollars in arms sales.

As for Africans controlling their own destinies, nothing was further from reality. The former imperial masters or their agents everywhere remained ruthlessly in charge of all major economic and financial decisions. Those leaders or governments that dared defiance soon paid severe penalties — sometimes the ultimate one.

Where its perceived economic or geo-political interests were at stake, the U.S. intervened forcefully. Many fragile African entities became helpless surrogates in spurious Cold War machinations. And at the same time, of course, the entire southern third of the continent was kept in tumult and desolation by the destabilizing strategies of the mighty apartheid government in South Africa, with its intimate if unpublicized links to the western powers.

In recent years, as the African nightmare ground on, world interest drifted away. Africa has just emerged from yet another lost decade. Hardly anyone cares.

The great, all-powerful western financial institutions such as the World Bank and IMF — extensions of American global interests, really — continue to insist that market-based economic and social reforms are the path to recovery, even though the UN Economic Commission for Africa has thoroughly discredited these findings. But to no avail.

Neo-conservatism remains the latest white man's burden that Africa must bear, even though its promise of short-term pain for long-term gain remains a leap of faith at the expense of the most wretched of the earth. Certainly, the Canadian government and CIDA have enthusiastically joined this highly suspect western bandwagon; not only has Canadian aid been cut substantially, it is being made conditional on Third World countries adopting policies that both increase human misery and are economically calamitous for them.

The UN this month has been debating Africa's economic future. I was asked to attend the session by Inter Pares, a small, excellent Ottawa-based development agency on whose volunteer board I sit. Together with several other Canadian colleagues, we represented Canadian development agencies that have not given up on Africa and that don't accept the market as the panacea for Africa's desperate plight.

I have always felt great admiration for those Canadians who have devoted their lives to this pursuit. And through them, here at the UN, I learned that Africa itself has in recent years begun throwing up its own non-governmental organizations (NGO's as they're known), democratic movements, citizens' organizations, grassroots efforts that include farmers, environmentalists, development animators and, maybe the most important of all, women — all those the World Bank and most western governments habitually ignore.

These Africans reject the neo-quackery of western capitalism just as they repudiate the corruption of their own governments, and they are determined to lay the groundwork for new, progressive development strategies for the future. There are no pat solutions to Africa's crisis. But simple common sense demonstrates that the present western-imposed policies are a disastrous failure, and that there must be a better way.

The struggle of the men and women of these NGOs will be laboriously uphill, but they are the hope for Africa's future. They also signal the direction in which future Canadian efforts must lie.

I was proud to learn that Canadian NGOs already have such close working relationships with their African counterparts. Canadians like them are the real reason for Canada's remarkable, and often undeserved, reputation around the world.

* * *

1992   SEVERAL HIGH-PROFILE FOREIGNERS have recently visited Canada. Last week it was Chief Mangosuthu Buthelezi, head of the South African Inkatha Freedom party and one of the great villains of our era. Nelson Mandela's African National Congress are no angels, heaven knows, but there are many reports by independent observers documenting Inkatha's special responsibility for the horror that has enveloped South Africa in the past two years. Buthelezi conspires against the ANC with the most despicable and racist elements in the white community, and inspires, according to independent pollsters, only minute support in his country.

Yet there they stand together in the photo, smiling amiably, the murderous Buthelezi and our own Brian Mulroney. For all I know, the Prime Minister lambasted Buthelezi in private, but not one word of censure did he issue publicly. And in South Africa itself, the photo has sent a disheartening message to those seeking justice who have considered Canada a trusted friend.

That was bad enough. But the symbolism became even more oppressive when it was learned that the PM had refused to meet earlier this month with Rigoberta Menchu, the recipient of this year's Nobel Peace Prize. Menchu is a Mayan from Guatemala, a woman who has seen enough of the dark side of human nature to break her spirit completely. Yet there is neither bitterness nor pessimism about her, only determination and sincerity.

Menchu's visit was sponsored by the Catholic Organization for Development and Peace; mainly she met with that world of Canadians who devote their lives to human rights activism — trade unionists, feminists, progressive church groups, development agencies and the like.

It's unlikely her path would have crossed another recent guest to our land, a certain Pat Buchanan who was speaking as part of a series sponsored by the *Globe and Mail* and *EnRoute*. Their target audience was mainly businessmen, many of whom, we can safely guess, never heard the name Rigoberta Menchu. Talk about a country of solitudes.

So these Canadians were treated to Pat Buchanan, pugnacious anti-feminist, anti-Semite, anti-black, anti-immigrant, anti-gay, anti-liberal champion — a proud contribution by the *Globe* and *EnRoute* to the enlightenment of Canadian business.

As adviser to Richard Nixon and Ronald Reagan, Buchanan was a hawk among hawks, always pressing for the most belligerent possible responses to what he perceived as threats to American interests anywhere on the globe. If that meant enthusiastic backing for and active co-operation with some of the most loathsome and sadistic regimes on Earth, if that meant actually training foreign soldiers who returned home to commit acts of such bestiality and cruelty as to beggar the imagination, that was the price Pat Buchanan and his ilk have always been ready to pay. Ask Rigoberta Menchu.

In the years after the CIA in 1954 overthrew one of the first democratically elected presidents in Guatemalan history, the United States supported a series of governments, each crueller than its predecessor, transforming the small country into a living nightmare, especially for its large native population.

Hundreds of thousands of mainly Mayan peasants have been tortured and slaughtered by military death squads, among them Menchu's family. Her mother was tortured and left to die. Her father was burned to death while peacefully occupying the Spanish embassy in Guatemala. One of her brothers, when 16, was tortured for three weeks, so that, in her words, "When they were done with him, he didn't look like a person anymore." Then he was burned alive before his family in their village square.

But our Prime Minister, happy to have a photo op with the evil likes of Buthelezi, was too busy to see Menchu. Maybe he just doesn't like Guatemalans. Late last week, three prominent Guatemalan opposition members were denied visas to enter Canada, even though they had been invited to appear before a Commons subcommittee.

The week ended fittingly: B'nai Brith, that great Jewish human rights organization, sponsored a lunch for — no, not Rigoberta Menchu, but — you guessed it — Mangosuthu Buthelezi. What a country we have become.

✳   ✳   ✳

Native Wrongs

1990   ONE OF THE REWARDS OF THIS COLUMN is sharing with
faithful readers the latest tale of courageous, independent action by your government and mine. Like drawing to your
attention, this spring, the government's current assessment of Canada's security situation. "The most serious direct threat to Canada,"
we were warned by the defence department, "is a Soviet nuclear
attack on Canada." So while Michael Wilson's budget ravaged all
kinds of urgent social programs, defence's share was increased by 5
per cent to $12 billion — a tidy 11 per cent of every dollar Ottawa
spends.

Today, I reveal another glorious example of proactive government
at work. Recall that, in May, Canada lost a heart-breaking chance
to complete the destruction of the Innu people of Labrador when
NATO decided that Western civilization could survive without a new
jet fighter training centre.

From the present military base in Goose Bay, pilots from several
NATO counties make only 7,000 low-level jet sorties a year screaming
over Innu territory. The new centre, for which our government
lobbied ferociously, called for almost 40,000 flights, which could
have ended the Innu's woes definitively.

Our department of defence was disconsolate at the bad news. The
minister, a certain Bill McKnight apparently, publicly grieved the lost
opportunity for Canada to make a really positive contribution to
NATO and its objectives.

Low-level flights, you'll understand, are inherently offensive. Their
job is to penetrate the enemy's territory without being detected by its
air-defence systems and then drop weapons — including nuclear
weapons — on key strategic targets. So you can see why Bill

McKnight was so dejected that Canada can't do even more for international peace and security.

But here's the good news. Is our defence team buying the peacenik line about the Cold War kind of winding down a bit, or the pinko accusation that continuing these practice flights might be seen as provocative and destabilizing? Did the bleeding hearts expect the present flights to have been grounded already? On the contrary, you silly people.

Only recently the defence department reassuringly reminded us that under the Multinational Memorandum of Understanding governing current Goose Bay NATO operations, low-level flights theoretically could in the next few years more than double to as many as 18,000 a year.

The defence department pooh-poohs this possibility. The Innu, given the track record, are not nearly so confident. After all, a few quiet words from our government to our NATO allies could prevent this escalation, but no such words have been uttered. That's hardly surprising, given Joe Clark's continued hard-boiled recognition that "Soviet military capabilities" mean NATO still needs "a strong military mandate."

But even if he's not a complete dupe, Clark's always been a mealy-mouthed Red Tory, as you know. Now he's going around claiming that we need a "New direction for NATO" based more on security through European co-operation than on military might. "It makes little sense," Clark asserts, "to retain nuclear weapons whose only targets can be our new friends in Poland, Czechoslovakia and East Germany."

Some Western military analysts even believe that since most Warsaw Pact countries are now led by strong anti-Communists burdened with wrecked economies, desperate for Western assistance, and determined to force Moscow to withdraw its troops from their soil, the likelihood of a Red invasion of Western Europe is somewhat lessened.

Even the magisterial International Institute for Strategic Studies in London has been taken in, its annual strategic survey claiming that the U.S.S.R is no longer a superpower, that the Warsaw Pact is moribund, and that NATO's very existence is in question since it is "without a clear threat to oppose."

Indeed, the chair of NATO's Military Committee himself, Norwegian Gen. Vigleik Eide, now insists that "the threat from a united Warsaw Pact no longer exists." So what do you do with a gargantuan military machine and no enemy to mobilize against, when the real issue has become not whither NATO but whether NATO?

Why, you redouble your efforts against the real enemy of Our Way of Life, the Innu. It was always one of the great NATO humiliations that its initial invasion of the Innu had been only partly successful. But it's not too late to finish the job, dear reader, so don't lose faith. With NATO and the Mulroney government standing tall together, subversive aboriginals don't have a prayer.

* * *

1990 THE ONLY SURPRISE anyone should feel observing the show-down at the Oka corral is that it took so long to happen. Literally, wherever in this country you find native Canadians, you find simmering anger, seething bitterness, and an unrelenting sense of betrayal.

Urban Canadians witness the consequences in the street Indians who have responded to their plight with despair and degradation, neatly reinforcing ignorant and bigoted white stereotypes of native peoples. At the opposite extreme stand the Mohawk Warriors, whose Rambo-like image sustains the other, contradictory, white fear of the so-called savage Indian whose history has been so recklessly distorted by decades of fraudulent Hollywood films.

But for most natives, life is both less romantic than the militant Warriors and less passive than the despondent street Indians. Surviving with a modicum of cheer and self-respect is a full-time job, since in virtually every area of existence simple survival itself is a laborious chore. Take the prosaic but elementary pursuit of good health.

About two years ago, Ontario NDP leader Bob Rae led an NDP task force on an intensive investigation of native health in Northern Ontario — not sexy politics, maybe, but exactly what the NDP exists for. For 18 months they travelled through dozens of communities across the vast breadth of Northern Ontario, receiving over 250 submissions and discussing native health with everyone from ambulance attendants to patients' advocacy groups.

What they found was a microcosm of native life in Canada: Our First Nations also constitute our Third World. In the blunt worlds of their excellent report, *First Come, Last Served*, "Ontario's native Indians are living in conditions unthinkable in any other part of the province." And "the Liberal provincial government is doing almost nothing about it." Even the most rudimentary services like running water and proper sewage and garbage disposal — the *sine qua non* of decent health, as every public health authority knows — were often absent. Small wonder that kids on northern reserves die twice as frequently at birth as other Canadians, or that life expectancy is 10 years less.

What a tragic irony. Over the millennia, native peoples had developed a lifestyle and health habits that enabled them to survive one of the most brutal environments on Earth. Then the whites came along to uplift them to our own lofty level of civilization. We conferred upon them smallpox, tuberculosis, venereal disease, booze, and a reservation and education system that consciously aimed at destroying their very identities. In a matter of only decades, native physical and psychological well-being collapsed.

Today, the situation has deteriorated even further. Even in southern Ontario, the standard of health care services most of us have taken for granted has now declined significantly — overcrowded hospitals, long delays in surgery, nursing shortages. So imagine what it must be like for northern natives. Presentations to the NDP task force movingly described the deplorable lack of services: communities with no doctors, with inadequately equipped hospitals, nursing shortages, minimal chronic care for the elderly, non-existent mental health care, and, of course, shameful sanitation facilities.

The NDP offered no simplistic solutions to these scandalous conditions. But its key recommendations have been backed by health professionals throughout the north. Beside a major investment in proper public health facilities, it called for "major reallocation of health care dollars into locally controlled, preventive, culturally appropriate, community-based health care . . . That means doubling the budgets for the next few years in community and preventive programs and developing ways to move decision-making out of bureaucracies to local committees." In this creative way, the NDP linked the means to better native health to larger native demands for self-government and land claim rights.

So far, I'm afraid, the Peterson government has moved on these recommendations only with a few more dollars for services, some rhetoric about native control of their own health care, but mostly the customary indifference.

The Liberal government is hugely philanthropic in allowing tax concessions for the richest of this province's rich, yet bestows only a mean pittance on the neediest of the needy. It's not right. The Premier expects to sail through this provincial election enjoying fine weather and rosy polls. Let's spoil his plans just a little; let's not allow him to forget the human issues that really matter.

*   *   *

1990   YOU'VE GOT TO SAY THIS for the Mulroney government:
————   Its instinct for clobbering the most vulnerable of this world remains unerring. In last year's budget, the chief victim was the Third World. This year they've mercilessly battered our own home-grown Third World.

It's hard to believe that even Tories are unaware of the wretched plight of native Canadians. Our best newspapers have editorialized forcefully about this enduring national scandal. Television news has prominently carried the horror stories generated by the investigations of the justice systems in Manitoba and Nova Scotia. CBC-TV's powerful drama, *Where The Spirit Lives*, vividly exposed a long, ugly chapter of recent Canadian history when official government policy was to obliterate native culture and self-worth.

Geoffrey York's important new book, *The Dispossessed: Life And Death In Native Canada*, documents the relentless injustice, overt racism, ruthless exploitation and endless violations of practices that have endured for centuries. CBC Radio's *Morningside* played an eloquent, angry, passionate speech by native leader George Erasmus last year in which he bitterly laid bare Canadians' smug double standards: "We criticize the racism in South Africa. Why can't we deal here with the problems we criticize them for . . . ? We have no reason to criticize anybody else. We have no examples to show the world."

Independent scientists and other experts have publicly exposed as a disgraceful fraud a $6 million "environmental impact study" by the Department of National Defence justifying a proposed NATO flight training base in Labrador. The Canadian Human Rights Commission calls the treatment of our native people "a national tragedy" that must be put at the very top of our national agenda.

Over the years, native Canadians have attempted to respond to their ghastly plight through a variety of self-help measures: Local self-government, land claim negotiations, militant campaigns of civil disobedience, independent business initiatives — and the creation of a native communications network.

Talk about French and English solitudes: These native media — newspapers, radio and TV — are virtually unknown outside aboriginal communities, where they have been highly successful.

Indeed, they constituted one of the few instruments by which the almost irreversible forced march to native cultural genocide might yet be stopped in its tracks. They've served as a unique lifeline by which native Canadians speak to each other across this vast land mass, sustain their own languages, reflect with pride their own culture, and interpret the wider world through native eyes.

I chanced to meet many representatives of these new media when they made presentations to the task force on broadcasting that I co-chaired a few years back. They were without exception singularly impressive and sophisticated men and women, and our report enthusiastically endorsed their broadcasting ventures.

Of course, all such self-help initiatives routinely face serious under-funding as a fixed reality, even though the sums involved are often quite small yet offer tremendous value for the money. So guess what was cut in last week's budget? Consistent with the mean, survival-of-the-fittest, kick-'em-when-they're-down Darwinism that's inherent in neo-conservatism, our Third World — Canada's shame — was dealt its latest devastating blow. In a budget where not one penny more in taxes was exacted from corporate Canada, native Canadians, through funds slashed from the Department of Indian Affairs, will generously contribute $100 million in the next two years to the government's phony debt reduction exercise.

But even worse, the native media program in particular, which falls not under Indian affairs but Secretary of State, has been substantially gutted. The Native Communications Program has been completely wiped out, taking every one of the 12 native newspapers it funded down with it. The Northern Native Broadcast Access Program, a radio and TV production fund for 13 native broadcasting societies, was cut by a critical 15 per cent. In fact, unbelievably, native people will absorb 40 per cent of all cuts made to Secretary of State this year.

Natives will hardly be shocked. Another broken promise? Another assault on native dignity and cultural development? What else is new? So let's keep our outrage under control the next time George Erasmus warns us that dire consequences must ultimately result as native patience finally, inevitably, is worn away to nothing, and that responsible leaders like himself "are not going to be able to control what is going to come next."

∗ ∗ ∗

1990   FOR BETTER OR WORSE, the New Democratic Party is not a party like the other two. You don't, mostly, join the NDP expecting political power, you join for its principles and philosophy and not to pursue power for its own sake. This isn't meant to be the usual tedious NDP self-righteousness. It's simply a fact.

That's why, for example, one of the legendary dates in Canadian socialist history is September 10, 1939, when CCF leader J.S. Woodsworth stood alone in the House of Commons and voted against declaring war on Germany. Woodsworth loathed the Nazis, but his life-long commitment to pacifism took precedence, and his party, which overwhelmingly disagreed with him, never respected him more.

That's why October 19, 1970, is a second mythic day for socialists, when 16 NDP MPs stood in Parliament to cast the lone votes against the imposition of the War Measures Act. It was Pierre Trudeau's most sinister deed as prime minister, yet 90 per cent of Canadians were with him. New Democrats' pride in their party soared as public support plummeted.

And now we add June 12, 1990, the day that an aboriginal NDP member of the Manitoba parliament, Elijah Harper, stood alone in Canada for the rights of native peoples.

It was no easy position for Harper to take. The mood of the country had moved powerfully to say yes to the Meech Lake accord as a way of saying yes to Quebec. Harper could not. His destiny was to articulate the bitter disappointment all native peoples felt after last week's first ministers meeting, to proclaim to the country that his people will not again accept being dismissed and ignored, that they're not prepared any longer to play the white man's absurd, irrelevant constitutional games.

And if Harper's courageous stand prevented the Manitoba Legislature from endorsing Meech in time to save it, Brian Mulroney must be held personally responsible for his cynical, reckless decision to call the first ministers together only at the last possible moment.

How is it that so many progressive Canadians found themselves in the same Meech camp as such specimens as Mulroney, Vander Zalm, Getty, Devine, and Buchanan, and against the likes of Elijah Harper. Let's have plain talk here: A majority of those good old boys around the table, if not implacably hostile to aboriginal rights, couldn't give a tinker's damn about them.

The basis for the unnatural alliance was Quebec. Period. Quebec demanded Meech as the price for remaining within Canada, and everyone bowed to Quebec's needs. So Quebec stays — for the moment. But why did Quebec's interests take precedence over those of native Canadians, whose treatment and condition constitute nothing less than the greatest unremitting scandal in our history? Why weren't their needs at least as important as Quebec's? Why, for heaven's sake, was it beyond the will and wit of those smug white men to satisfy the demands of both Quebec and natives?

Because, as usual, ultimately nobody cared two hoots for aboriginal peoples. After all, since 1982 four constitutional conferences devoted exclusively to aboriginal issues made precious little progress. Then the overriding priority became "bringing Quebec into the Constitution." Now the next five years will be given over, of all things, to Senate reform.

Why? Because most of these premiers are totally unsympathetic to the plight of Canada's native people, while Quebec sees new agreements as potential infringements of their distinct society status. I understand that preoccupation of Quebec's leaders, but do three centuries of injustice to natives count for nothing? Yet Robert Bourassa can make not a single concession that won't be denounced in Quebec as a sell-out. So one more time: To hell with native Canadians.

Well, I'm with Elijah Harper. I've always tried to be sensitive to Quebec's aspirations and sensibilities, and a Canada without Quebec seems inconceivable to me still. But enough is enough. One of the most destructive consequences of our endless constitutional haggling is that all the other glaring woes of our country have been completely ignored. At the head of that list stands the predicament of our first peoples. It's far past time to say yes to them. A sensible world would not force us to choose between Quebec and native Canadians. We can accommodate both. But if we don't, I'm with them.

* * *

1991   THE HEIGHTS AND DEPTHS of our largest metropolis:
————   This Thursday night, the Music Hall Theatre on Toronto's Danforth Ave. will witness an exceptional concert by and for native Canadians. Admission is $14.92 in advance, $19.92 at the door, as befits "A Columbus Day Benefit for the Innu Nation, the Lubicon Nation and *Beedaudjimowin.*"

Beedaudjimowin is a 9-month-old, Toronto-based quarterly publication that calls itself "A Voice for First Nations." It dedicates itself to "promoting the uniqueness of First Nations people from the perspective of the First Nations — our history, our philosophy, our culture, our relationship to the environment." This week's concert does precisely that.

Some of Canada's most exciting native artists will be performing, including the band Seventh Fire; Syren, a musical group; actor Kenneth Charlette; and folksinger Shingoose. And so will some of this country's most remarkable leaders, Peter Penashue of the Innu Nations and Chief Bernard Ominayak of the Lubicon Cree.

If these native artists aren't familiar to most non-native readers, the Innu and Lubicon surely are. At a time when native concerns have suddenly been discovered by even the most unsympathetic of white politicians, it's useful to remember the Hobbesian reality of life for most native peoples in this country.

Ask the Innu of Labrador. Thanks to policies first of the Trudeau, then of the Mulroney governments, these hunting, trapping and fishing people have been virtually under invasion by NATO forces for the last dozen years. Having few other targets to attack, NATO members turned their war planes against the mighty Innu, flying thousands of low-level test flights often as low as the tree-tops. The Innu say the sound "makes your heart pound and your ears ring," and in fact the flights, besides causing sheer demoralizing terror to all beneath them, have nearly destroyed the Innu's environment and very means of survival.

As for Alberta's Lubicon, theirs is a saga of almost unimaginable betrayal, deceit and racism at the hands of both Liberal and Conservative federal governments, plus the Alberta Tory governments of Peter Lougheed and Don Getty. This tiny Indian band has been fighting for half a century for a small land claim in northern Alberta that everyone agrees was promised in 1940 but has never been delivered.

As with the Innu, the modern world has invaded Lubicon land in the form of oil, gas and timber developments which, naturally, take precedence over mere human rights and earnest assurances. They have been reduced to little more than their own determination and integrity and the support, this week, of the good citizens of Toronto.

This is Toronto at its best. But at the same time, from the city's sewers resurfaces one Paul Fromm, for years the mouthpiece of a pure, all-white, non-Jewish Canada. During remarks by a native Canadian at a Toronto meeting of the Mayor's Race Relations Committee last week, Fromm cried out the words "Scalp them," and was turfed out of the meeting.

But can that be the end of the story? It so happens this man is an English teacher at Mississauga's Applewood Heights Secondary School. How is that possible? Fromm's record is hardly a secret.

Paul Fromm vigorously champions anti-Semites Ernst Zundel and James Keegstra; is an associate of Ron Gostick, one of Canada's leading anti-Semitic propagandists; embraces apartheid and belligerently opposes all non-white immigration to Canada; organized a meeting for Phillipe Rushton, the academic proponent of racist ideas, where security was organized by Don Andrews, a Swastika-brandishing Canadian neo-Nazi; defends John Ross Taylor, a lifelong, Hitler-loving Nazi supporter; and co-sponsored a meeting with the Heritage Front, an organization that glorifies violence in order to preserve "Our Great White Race!"

And as role models for his ideal society, Fromm surrounds himself with gangs of neo-Nazi skinheads with black leather jackets bearing white supremacist badges.

Recently, a New Brunswick court ruled that Malcolm Ross, an avowed anti-Semite and school teacher, could not remain in the classroom even though he was not directly peddling his poison to his students. Compared to Fromm's unrelenting malevolence, Ross is merely a crank. Fromm, after all, doesn't merely target Jews; his odious propaganda is an affront to much of the population of this country.

How can any of the multitude of Canadians he reviles, or how can any decent person, for that matter, tolerate this man in a classroom? Would you let your kids in a school with him? How can the Peel School Board keep him on its payroll one minute longer?

Thursday's concert will be a sensation. But it's only a small step on a long, tough road toward a decent community.

*   *   *

Women's Equality: The Never-Ending Story

1985   WOULD YOU NOT HAVE GIVEN ANYTHING to be a fly on the wall the other evening when the Albany Club was invaded? A bastion of WASP conservatism in Toronto, the joint didn't even accept women as members a mere six years ago.

Yet there they were, some 80 of the country's most prominent women in politics and the media, for a private party to honour Ellen Fairclough, Canada's first woman cabinet minister (appointed by John Diefenbaker), on her 80th birthday.

The evening was the first major initiative of a remarkable group of 12 women, the Committee for '94.

Self-described feminists all, they include Liberals, New Democrats, a Tory and some of unknown political affiliation. Perhaps the most well-known are two of Canada's finest writers, Christina McCall and Michele Landsberg. But all are Canadians of accomplishment.

After months of intense, invigorating discussions, the group was able to agree on an over-all goal — to see that half of all members of Parliament are women by 1994 — and the concerns they hoped these women would espouse: equal pay for work of equal value, publicly funded child care, reproductive freedom of choice and old age pensions above the poverty line.

The Fairclough dinner was a conscious attempt to spoof the "old boys' network." Besides the location, the affair was strictly black tie, and many of the women really did wear tuxedos.

The main speakers were chosen with scrupulous political impartiality — former Trudeau health minister Monique Bégin, Tory Employment Minister Flora MacDonald and Nova Scotia NDP leader Alexa McDonough. Rosemary Brown, who once contested the leadership of the national NDP, flew in from Vancouver. MacDonald introduced Fairclough, and McDonough was the keynote speaker on the future of feminism.

Which is precisely where the tensions and contradictions of the venture became apparent. Only months ago, during the Nova Scotia provincial election, Flora MacDonald twice flew to Halifax to campaign for the Conservatives in the seat held by, yes, one Alexa McDonough. On these occasions, evidently, partisan considerations outweighed shared feminist goals in MacDonald's mind. (McDonough, in the event, won a resounding victory.)

Why not? Should New Democrats in Kingston have voted for MacDonald? Many socialists, after all, argue that women's exploitation is inevitable in the present social system. Few progressives of either gender would wish to see more Margaret Thatchers or Jean Kirkpatricks in positions of power.

Does a progressive woman not have more in common with a progressive male than a conservative female? How far did group member Maude Barlow get as adviser on women's issues to former prime minister Pierre Trudeau, and what realistically can Libby Burnham, the committee's Conservative, expect to gain by working within an increasingly right-wing Conservative party?

I put these questions to fully half the committee members. All agreed that on certain issues, probably many issues, ideology and partisanship would divide them. That did not disturb them. Every one of them has several strings on her bow, other areas in which she is active (beside having, in most cases, children and a career to tend to).

But they all believe that increasing the participation of women in politics at all levels is a common goal worth some scarce time.

Had not women of all parties forced the addition to the Charter of Rights of Section 15 on equality rights? Would a House of Commons half full of women of whatever party have snickered derisively when NDP MP Margaret Mitchell raised the issue of wife abuse?

What the committee reflects is that a real revolution has taken place in the past decade, a revolution in the consciousness of many women. Especially for the generation of women under, say, 50, their femaleness is a trait neither to be ignored nor belittled.

In both the United States and Canada, female politicians in all parties have found themselves, willy nilly, becoming the focus of the expectations of other women and, often as not, emerging as spokespersons for women's causes.

The revolution, however, has barely touched the lives of those women who are most exploited, most abused, most in need. There are a hundred areas in which politicians must act with urgency.

If the committee's efforts are another step on the road to the real equality of women, even a partisan old leftie has little choice but to applaud.

✳ ✳ ✳

1988   SOME CANADIAN COURTS are being curiously lenient to a peculiarly vicious kind of criminal.

Look how thoughtful Sault Ste. Marie, Ontario, District Court Judge Vannini was last week, for example, to poor Bruce Glassford. Bruce beat a woman up and raped her, and was convicted of sexual assault causing bodily harm. But the good judge's heart went out to Bruce. He saw no evidence, after all, that the woman suffered any lasting emotional or psychological harm: "The assault was very traumatic but of short duration." Bruce was only 22, came from "a good family," and had surely learned his lesson since he had developed an ulcer. The judge's sentence: 90 days, to be served entirely on weekends.

But Judge Vannini is by no means alone in his compassion and concern for poor males who commit sexual assault. Well, maybe not "poor." According to some stunning research gathered by the Metro Toronto Action Committee on Violence against Women and Children, the more middle class the criminal the more likely is the judge to play social worker — to him.

As a result, right across Canada men convicted of sexual assault and abuse may well draw remarkably light sentences if they don't fit the stereotype of some crazed thug.

So the Nova Scotian convicted of sexual assault received a suspended sentence since he was a prominent businessman, involved in the community, and "had suffered a great deal already" just being charged with the offence. Or the man convicted of sexually assaulting the 11-year-old daughter of a friend: "When a citizen of 40 years has led an exemplary life," the caring judge found, "where he has been concerned with military and family duties, he deserves to have the court put this into the scale of justice on his behalf." Penalty: a suspended sentence.

Or the man who got a year for sexually assaulting his daughter and step-daughter over a 12-year period. Not only had he been "a productive member of society" with a good reputation, the judge found there'd been no lasting impact on the children.

In fact some judges are blithely confident the victims rarely suffer lasting traumas from their ordeals. So the woman who was urinated on and beaten with a bathroom plunger suffered "no lasting psychological damage." And the victim who passed out during the rape "was not hurt in any way and has not suffered any psychological damage." And the 14-year-old girl assaulted by a cop suffered "no permanent effects."

And, and, and. This column, this page, this newspaper can be filled with stories of this kind, all of them true. Their impact is obvious. They trivialize sexual assaults on women. They send a message that assaulting women is no big deal. They reinforce the predisposition of those 32 per cent of male freshmen at Toronto's York University in 1985 who believed that when a woman said no, she really hoped the man would force himself on her. Indeed, these stories make perfectly clear that many judges believe the victims have, in one way or another, been "asking for it."

Section 15 of the Charter of Rights and Freedoms states that we are all equal under the law, regardless of gender. Tell it to the judge. Tell it to some of these white, middle-aged privileged males who have no grasp of the real meaning of violence, who would laugh you out of their courtrooms if you asserted that sexual assault reflected the traditional power relationship between males and females in our society, who simply ignore the unspeakable violation of a women that is inherent in every sexual assault — even one of "short duration."

Every study ever done shows that such assaults are infinitely more common than is often understood. Every study ever done shows that the psychological consequences of such an assault are invariably profound and enduring.

The latest yuppie conventional wisdom is that the feminist revolution is on its last legs, most of its goals having been realized. The truth is exactly the opposite. The battle for women's equality, in a dozen different areas, is only just beginning. Nor is victory assured. The way our courts often treat women victims of sexual assault is only a particularly brutal example of how far from justice and equality we really are.

＊　＊　＊

1988 ANTI-CHOICE ACTIVISTS WERE ECSTATIC when Mother Teresa agreed to speak at last week's National Rally for Life in Ottawa. Who could more eloquently represent them than the saintly Nobel Prize-winning nun who had selflessly dedicated her life to the wretched of the Calcutta slums?

What surprised many, however, was the unexpectedly extreme positions that Mother Teresa publicly took in Ottawa. Already some had dared wonder why, with neighboring Bangladesh facing unspeakable horrors from recent floods, she would consider one anti-choice meeting across the world in central Canada such a priority. Apparently this issue is all-important to her.

Known for her compassion and mercy, Mother Teresa demonstrated few charitable feelings for those how don't share her views on abortion. Women who had abortions and doctors who perform abortions, she stated, are murderers and should be imprisoned; she did not say how harsh their punishment should be. There seems little doubt she meant this remarkable proposition literally. According to Statscan, 60,956 Canadian women had abortions in Canadian hospitals in 1985, at least 15,000 others in clinics or in the United States. It's impossible to know the number of doctors involved — at the very least many hundreds, perhaps a few thousand.

In the United States in 1983, there were, by conservative estimates 1,515,000 abortions; in Britain 80,600; in India itself, in recognized hospitals alone, 518,000, and we can be confident of millions more completely beyond the ken of statisticians. Mother Teresa would condemn all these women and girls, and many millions more around the world, to prison.

Moreover, unlike the overwhelming number of Canadians, she opposes abortion even in life-threatening situations. The mother must be prepared, if necessary, to sacrifice herself to save the unborn child: "As Jesus died to save us, so the mother should be ready to die for her child." Why the woman's life is less sacred than the unborn child's will not be self-evident to many Canadians. Any why is it always the woman, never the man, of whom great sacrifices are invariably demanded?

What will we do with the unwanted babies that in Mother Teresa's world could not legally be aborted? Adoption, she tells us. And "If you do not want the child," she told her audience, "I want it. Give it to me." This too she seems to have meant literally.

So, yes, let's send all the world's unwanted kids to Calcutta to mingle with the hundreds of thousands already sleeping on the pavement there. The Indian government, however, might not appreciate her generous offer. According to UNICEF, one-quarter to one-third of the world's poverty lies within India, which is rapidly challenging China as the world's most populous nation, and where 16 per cent of all babies — compared to 1 per cent in Canada — fail to survive to their fifth birthday.

The Indian government's own desperate goal is to deal with its soaring population by achieving an average birth rate of two children per family by the year 2,000, an achievement that will depend in substantial part on family planning. Mother Teresa, however, rigidly opposes all forms of artificial birth control.

Mother Teresa's personal dedication is undoubted. Yet the effects of her beliefs would be disastrous for poor women around the world. Well-off women have fewer children, and in any event will always find some means for safe medical abortion, while poor girls and women will be forced to deal with ghastly back-alley butchers, with entirely predictable consequences.

The Ottawa rally was meant to be non-partisan, but that didn't deter John Nunziata, the Rat-Packing Liberal, from deliberately insinuating himself at Mother Teresa's side during her post-speech news conference, when she again insisted that all woman who have abortions should be jailed. Nunziata had better hope he never finds himself responsible for the Canadian prison system.

The Ottawa demonstration may have been non-partisan but it was explicitly political. Many in attendance intend to force upon all politicians their conviction that the only consequential issue in the coming election is legal protection for the rights of the unborn. With luck, they will discredit themselves by being as unsympathetic to women's rights, and as far out of touch with mainstream Canadian opinion, as Mother Teresa proved to be.

They are also wrong. The real issue of this campaign should be the women of the Third World, who function both as beasts of burden and producers of children; the 280,000 children who die needlessly every week from simple infection and undernutrition; and the countless millions of unwanted street kids who are homeless, hungry, beaten and exploited, and who all the loving Mother Teresas in the world cannot begin to save.

* * *

1989   FOR ALL THE OUTPOURING OF GRIEF for the women slaughtered by Marc Lepine, I fear little has changed in our society save in the ravaged lives of those directly affected.

Those already alarmed by the reality of violence to women care more passionately and more urgently than ever. Those who were either indifferent to or responsible for the problem remain unconcerned or unrepentant. So for me, the tragedy of the Montreal massacre is compounded by the fear that no lessons will be learned from Lepine's rampage by those who have refused so far to learn.

In fact, in many circles there's already an abusive backlash developing against those who argue that Lepine's act was against women at all. How dare we lay such an indiscriminate guilt trip on all men? How dare we take the random, capricious act of one deranged man and exploit it for the purpose of radical feminist politics?

Talk about blaming the victim: This takes the cake. Imagine had the victims all been Jews; imagine the very suggestion that anti-Semitism was not at the root. Imagine arguing that such a tragedy could be divorced from its larger social context or be analyzed in a social vacuum. Yet there are a dismaying number of people, some, alas, women as well as many, many men, whose own psychological fears seem to blind them to realities staring them brutally in the face.

For some of us, the movement for women's equality is among the great, constructive social revolutions of our time; indeed, I can't conceive considering oneself to be progressive, let alone a socialist, without embracing feminism. Conversely, the women's revolution — though it's really barely begun its work — is one of those tumultuous upheavals that threaten those whose needs include a certain order, an assured status, to cope with the feelings of inadequacy an unequal society generates.

Erich Fromm, the brilliant psychoanalyst, once identified this pathology as an "escape from freedom." When societal change seems excessive and out of control, frightened, insecure people retreat to the reassurances of charismatic leaders offering simplistic, authoritarian panaceas. At the same time, their unhealthy need to find some scapegoat, some group they can feel superior to, escalates ominously. This is precisely the origins of contemporary neo-conservatism, embodied by Ronald Reagan and Margaret Thatcher. And not least among the threatening changes is the women's movement. As Marc Lepine himself understood, it was his fear of competing with the new breed of woman that was tearing away at his twisted sense of failed manliness.

Lepine's phobia was come by honestly. His father, who believed "women are not men's equal and are servants to men," according to his mother, brutally beat the entire family. So when Marc Lepine got even, he marched in his twisted father's footsteps.

But Lepine and his father were hardly alone. The dread of women's equality in our society is as pervasive as the violence against them. Think of those god-fearing Christians behind Operation Rescue who viciously harass pregnant women who dare to take control of their own destinies. Or those nice REAL Women who are scared to death of women who demand real equality. Or those fancy male lawyers who in court torment female victims of physical abuse. Or that legion of distinguished male judges who trivialize assault cases against women.

Of the mountain of monstrous data on violence against women, one fact grips me most: An astonishing one in four Canadian women is likely to be sexually assaulted during her life. That's why so many females in Canada live with a terror we males rarely even sense exists. Marc Lepine became the nightmare that haunts so many women. The dismaying reaction to his mad act means the nightmare is far from over.

* * *

1990   FIRST MOURN, then work for change. That was the inspired response adopted by many Canadians to the Lepine massacre, but one year later, it's painfully evident that the attainment of anything remotely like equality for women is as distant a goal as ever.

Those who then insisted that Lepine's was the act of an isolated madman will, presumably, remain unmoved even by his own explicit suicide note. Echoing the self-pitying whine of so many ostensibly "normal" men, he snivels that "the Feminists . . . want to keep their advantages as women . . . while trying to grab those of men." So he decides to kill, he announces in absolutely classical blame-the-victim terms, "the feminists who have ruined my life."

Those who care to know, know. There is no detail of women's exploitation or women's harassment and brutalization that is hidden. Excellent books and studies pour out, each reinforcing the other. For the latest sordid documentation of poverty and powerlessness among women, see *Women and Labor Market Poverty* by Gunderson and Muszynski, or the National Council on Welfare's *Women and Poverty Revisited*. The findings are unambiguous: More than 1.5 million Canadian women over 16 live in demeaning poverty for reasons quite beyond their control — labour market inequities, child-care responsibilities, marriage breakdown, widowhood.

Meanwhile, violence against women continues unabated, as Canadian as the maple leaf itself. As the Ontario Association of Interval and Transition houses simply puts it, women are never safe, either on the streets or in their homes — in fact, above all not in their homes. At least one of every four women eventually becomes a victim of sexual abuse, and many — yes, many — are sadistically tortured. Yet, as Barrett and Marshall observe in *Criminal Neglect: Why Sex Offenders Go Free*, "the myth continues that sexual assaults are isolated occurrences, that 'nice' men don't do it, that 'nice' women aren't assaulted, and that the victim often provokes her own violation." It's all untrue, yet it conveniently comforts so many of us, including, not least, the guilty. Who's responsible for this shameful scandal in our society? Better to ask: Who's not?

All those who, in whatever way, act to devalue women, to make them things, objects, commodities. All those who insist on using the language of inequality, calling adult females "girls" and female heads of organizations "chairmen." All those exploitative companies and their ad agencies who use blatantly sexist advertising, and the media and regulators who permit it. All those businesses that profit by systematically paying women less. All those who have any complicity whatever in the porn-and-violence video and film business.

All those cops who trivialize allegations by women of sexual assault. All those contemptible judges whose biases make them more sympathetic to the rapist than his victim. All those fancy criminal lawyers, beneath contempt, who re-victimize in court victims of physical abuse. All those smart-ass men who think it's a macho caper to harass and intimidate women. All those inadequate, anxious men who need to take out their self-doubts and frustrations on girls and women, who need someone inferior whom they think they have a natural right to beat the stuffing out of. All those Tories in Ottawa, the self-styled feminist variety especially, for the abject surrender to the gun-nut lobby that opposes even half-hearted gun-control measures.

All those employers who try to blackmail female employees into sexual favors, and all those bullying male workers who get their pathetic jock jollies by harassing female "sisters." All those dangerously misogynistic "men's rights" groups. All those cretinous university students who still harass women, and all those university administrators who don't turf them out.

All those opportunistic women who've built careers attacking feminists. All those insecure, frightened, conservative women who malign active feminists instead of their common enemy. All those pious folk who champion unborn fetuses while they persecute and terrorize grown-up females choosing abortions.

It's disheartening beyond words how many of our politicians have abdicated all leadership in the job of breaking the vicious cycle of women's inequality. In all of Canada, only the new Ontario government has shown a real determination to treat the matter with the proper urgency. Ontario can, and must, show the world that the exploitation and brutalization of women will simply no longer be tolerated. No cause deserves greater priority.

* * *

1991   TWO YEARS AFTER MARC LEPINE slaughtered 14 women because they were "a bunch of feminists," it's become almost fashionable for men to disapprove of violence against women. It's not that I'm cynical, exactly, about the sudden mass conversion of thousands of men to the cause. Let's say I'm just a tad skeptical.

Of course, the more Canadians of both genders who speak out against the scourge of anti-female harassment and violence the better.

Notwithstanding all the attention this crisis has been receiving, our world has yet to become one iota safer for a single Canadian female.

Women are being murdered and maimed by their partners or ex-partners just the same as ever; just check your paper any day of the week. The Ontario medical profession's McPhedran Task Force has exposed the prevalence of sexual exploitation by male physicians of female patients. And one female trade unionist told the recent Ontario Federation of Labour convention that "there isn't a woman in the workplace in this province who hasn't been harassed or patronized." Yet a recent Angus Reid poll found that no fewer than three-fifths of all women who said they'd been sexually harassed in their workplace failed to report it, often fearing that their co-workers would assume they were over-reacting if they complained.

Still, painful as it is, women are finally speaking out publicly. At the OFL convention, woman after woman came forward to relate personal incidents of intolerable harassment at work, as much by fellow trade unionists as by management.

This is progress, but it's far from enough. Men, too, must stand up and be counted. After all, here's a crisis in which, overwhelmingly, men are the perpetrators and women the victims; it's not much more complicated than that.

So hoorah for the organizers of the white-ribbon campaign to encourage men to speak out against violence against women. In encouraging men to wear a white ribbon last week symbolizing their protest, they've met with unexpectedly widespread support. Which is precisely what makes me uneasy. In a strange way, it's too easy, too pat, for men to tie on a white ribbon and think they're making a real difference.

Now I don't mean here the tiny handful of largely middle-class men who've been real leaders on this issue. Or an increasingly vocal band of male trade unionists who have come to understand that real men don't prove they're tough guys by beating up on women. It is true, sadly, that some prominent labour leaders make fine speeches condemning violence against women yet personally practise what Judy Rebick, president of the National Action Committee on the Status of Women, calls "male power-tripping over women." Still, on the whole the labour movement has moved miles ahead of most governments and businesses in meeting the crisis head-on.

The Canadian Auto Workers is one union that at least tries to practise what it preaches, and its official policy is a "zero tolerance level of sexist treatment of women." The OFL has also unanimously endorsed zero tolerance of harassment in the workplace. So have other unions.

But as one labour leader candidly acknowledged, it's easier to speak out at a large meeting than to challenge another guy's sexist behaviour eyeball to eyeball.

That hard truth is why I'm not yet celebrating some of the unexpected endorsements of the white-ribbon campaign. Actions speak louder than ornaments. So while I'm glad, for example, that many police forces wore their ribbons, real progress will begin when cops start treating wife-beating as a serious crime.

I'm glad the School of Family Studies at Ryerson Polytechnical Institute sponsored a series last week to commemorate the Montreal massacre, and I'm proud to have participated. But I'd be even happier if it had been organized by Ryerson's notoriously sexist engineering department. I'm glad Trevor Eyton supported the white-ribbon campaign, but I'd be even happier if he got his corporate pals at the *Sun* newspapers to scrap their Sunshine girls. I'm glad some business leaders agreed to wear their ribbons, but it would be infinitely more constructive if the male business culture put an end to its puerile, sniggering sexism, its lewd jokes and its smart-ass cracks.

I'm glad Tory MPs sported white ribbons, but I'd take it more seriously if the Prime Minister hadn't slashed budgets for shelters for abused women or if he had ejected from his caucus the cretin who called Sheila Copps a slut.

Facile words and empty gestures are easy. In the meantime, power-tripping men still crush and batter women as if it were their natural right. We've got a long way to go, boys.

* * *

1992 QUESTION: What does Canada's own Preston Manning have in common with Pope John Paul, Ronald Reagan and George Bush, and the majority of the U.S. Supreme Court?

Answer: They're all privileged, older, white men who have in the last month insisted on THEIR right to control the bodies and destinies of women around the globe. THEY, not she, will choose what a woman is allowed to do with an unwanted pregnancy.

The Reform Party's Preston Manning would deny women the right to choose an abortion even in cases of rape or incest. This is a taste of the New Morality that Canadian women can expect from more Reform members of Parliament.

The Pope returned to his native Poland where he likened abortion to the Nazi Holocaust. Poland was a uniquely inappropriate place to draw this parallel since 3 million of Poland's 3.3 million Jews were systematically murdered by the Nazis and their collaborators. To compare the genocidal annihilation of 3 million people with the acts of individual women who choose not to bring their pregnancies to term trivializes the Holocaust and maliciously insults those women.

Ronald Reagan and George Bush trampled women's rights repeatedly in the past decade, not least in denying them reproductive choice. First, the Reagan administration literally demanded that the 4,000 federally funded health clinics in the U.S. refrain from even murmuring the word abortion or else forgo further federal funds. Even if a doctor believes an abortion is medically necessary or if a young girl is raped by her father, the 1988 regulation explicitly compels clinic staff to answer all abortion inquiries with the words, "The project does not consider abortion an appropriate method of family planning." Naturally such clinics cater to poorer women, better-off ones being able to afford private medical advice including all the abortion counselling money can buy. The immediate impact of this cruel, class-based policy is that poorer women end up waiting longer and longer for their abortions, and many eventually resort to dangerous, illegal procedures.

But Reagan-Bush didn't stop with U.S. women; the empire encompasses the world, after all. They also cut off U.S. funds for family planning to any organization in the Third World that provides any abortion service of any kind — whether counselling, education or actual referral.

Never mind the links between poverty and overpopulation, or the world-wide proliferation of programs, many of them foreign-funded, that provide family planning advice to millions of women. American conservative ideology forbids governments from interfering in the marketplace, but insists that they regulate the most intimate aspect of a woman's life.

In the last month, the male majority on the U.S. Supreme Court first upheld the ban on discussing abortions in American clinics, then refused to hear a challenge against the government's policy toward Third World clinics. Even *Time* magazine described the court's ruling as making "little medical or intellectual or moral sense."

Look at the evidence. Earlier this year, Statistics Canada issued a report called *Therapeutic Abortions, Canada, 1970–1988*. Its findings were dramatic. Because legalized abortion has meant earlier and safer procedures, many fewer Canadian women are dying as a result of abortions and many fewer are experiencing abortion-related complications. In other words, the later, often illegal abortions to which many poor American women will now resort will pose far greater medical risks than would earlier procedures.

Similarly, a study last year by the Worldwatch Institute, *The Global Politics of Abortion*, demonstrated that restrictions on legal abortions merely increase the rate of illegal abortions, and therefore deaths, especially in Third World countries. In fact the report estimated that an incredible 200,000 women die around the world each year from illegal abortions!

Yet in countries where abortion is part of family planning programs, the rate of abortions has dropped rapidly. The study concluded that the best way to reduce both abortions and related deaths is precisely to make abortion a legitimate component of family planning instead of a crime.

Finally, here's the unexpected findings of a report published last year by a team of research scientists in the journal *Science*: the vast majority of women who have legal abortions, especially in the first trimester, suffer no psychological ill-effects from ending their unwanted pregnancy. In fact 76 per cent of women reported feelings of relief and happiness after the abortion, while only 17 per cent felt remorse or guilt, feelings which soon diminished for most of them.

Still, for our own Preston Manning, it must be kind of heady to find himself in the company of all those powerful men whose intolerant prejudices, like his own, make them the foes of human rights, common sense and plain facts.

* * *

1992   HERE'S A SMALL RAY OF SUNSHINE to brighten these gloomy times: it's increasingly rare these days that I find myself in meetings comprised only of men. Ever so slowly, and often only in token ways, serious, aware people are coming to realize that all-male boards and committees and all-male anythings no longer make any sense in this world.

Yet there we were last weekend, some two dozen men from across Ontario, women conspicuous by their total absence, busily following up on last December's wildly successful White Ribbon campaign.

Launched modestly enough by a small group of intrepid men to commemorate the anniversary of the Montreal massacre, the campaign spread like wildfire. White ribbons were tied on from coast to coast to coast — around 100,000, it's being estimated — to the point where it became de rigeur even for such unexpected lapels as those of federal ministers to be sporting them.

The message of this entirely unanticipated achievement seemed clear enough: however skeptical one could be about the commitment of some of the bearers to ending male violence against girls and women, here was a crusade whose time may have come. The moment is not being squandered.

As of one week ago, the White Ribbon Foundation of Canada is a reality, an all-male organization that will use an annual December white ribbon week for the purpose of mobilizing year-round activities with one overriding goal: to create a climate of zero tolerance in every nook and cranny of Canadian life for the abuse or harassment of women by men. And though we'll keep in close contact with appropriate women's groups, because it's men, overwhelmingly, who abuse women and girls, it's men who must play a central role here.

We're immediately reaching out to eastern and western Canada to make this a truly national effort (though we won't presume to speak for Quebec). So from now on, every week is white ribbon week in Canada.

But the job won't be easy. No one, of course, actually says it's okay for guys to beat women. But for all the white ribbons that were ever worn, all kinds of men still batter women and get away with it, while all kinds of others refuse to face up to the issue at all.

Lots and lots of men — some of them, tragically, judges — still say that women who have been sexually assaulted may well have been asking for it. All kinds of men get stubbornly defensive on the subject since, after all, not all men do such terrible things — you know, how come you're picking on me, I've never hit anyone.

Then there's the so-called men's rights advocates, in reality the male equivalents of REAL Women, little men driven both by simple terror at the prospect of women's equality and by simple gratification at the publicity they reap. Or the faddish followers of Iron John and the mystical, male-bonding rubbish associated with such new diversionary cults. Or those apologists who insist they just can't sell their beer or newspapers without using images and stereotypes that degrade women.

Our neighborhood teenage boys — punks, as I'm afraid they seem to me — engage in loud, belligerent shouting matches about their alleged latest conquests, ominously filling the air with profanity and a sense of intimidation. The culture of certain sports seem to lend itself to the notion that beating up women is an appropriate pastime for jocks. And few are the health clubs or squash courts in which men don't titillate each other with shabby off-colour stories that routinely demean or denigrate women. Real macho guys, it appears, still need female victims to prove their manhood. Some guys. Some manhood.

Curiously, men's violence against women is one of life's truly egalitarian pursuits. It's a respecter or neither class nor ethnicity, vocation nor colour, religion nor status. In some subcultures it is merely more or less blatant than others. But almost everywhere, whistle-blowing is the hardest thing in the world to do. As one gutsy trade unionist said after the last Ontario Federation of labour convention, it's easier for a man to stand up before 1,400 people to denounce harassment of women in the abstract than to challenge another guy's specific actions or remarks in a bar or at work. Our job is to make it harder not to speak up.

The new White Ribbon Foundation has two complementary aims, one far more ambitious than the other. The first is simple (or ought to be): it's to eliminate male violence against women. The second is far more elusive: it's to change the socialization process that creates men who beat women. In the words of the foundation's driving force and its first national director, Michael Kaufman, "Harassers, rapists, batterers and murderers of women aren't simply deranged. They're men in pain who have bought the message that they've got to dominate to be men." And since men are the chief abusers of other males as well as females — some 90 per cent of abusers of kids, both female and male, are men — if we ever succeed in changing the systemic causes of male violence, we'll have civilized our entire society.

Such qualitative changes will come only slowly, at best. But the need for behavioral change by men on a massive scale must begin immediately. That's why the foundation intends to encourage across the country the creation of a series of sectoral groups — sports, unions, the media, Rotary Clubs and the like, the police, native people, business, anything at all you can think of — with the aim by no means merely to get more men to wear white ribbons next December, but to devise creative strategies to get more men to treat women appropriately today.

For decades, men beating up women has been one of this society's dirtiest little secrets. Now a group of men have come together to break the silence and to take responsibility for ending this horrendous scandal.

This is truly one of the great Canadian causes of our time, and whatever you think of the Constitution and whatever party you belong to and whatever your cure for the recession might be, you're welcome to join with us in the urgent task of putting an end to the epidemic of male violence against women.

Wouldn't it be something if we actually made a difference?

* * *

Values

1985   SOMEONE HAS MADE a terrible, terrible blunder in the Ernst Zundel affair. Through his trial, he has been transformed from an underground crank into a prominent individual whose hideous and twisted notions receive prominent daily media coverage. Most people dismiss his rantings with the contempt they deserve. Yet I greatly fear the very magnitude of the attention he has received has afforded him and the witnesses who supported him some legitimacy in the eyes of innocent Canadians. And the media, apparently, are obligated to report these grotesque perversions of history because notoriety equals newsworthiness. As a result, we read in our press — it actually rated a headline in one paper — that female prisoners in Auschwitz were really a happy smiling lot, addressed by their guards as Miss or Mrs. The witness? A Nazi soldier stationed at the Auschwitz death camp. Another witness announced that Auschwitz Jews enjoyed good food, a theatre, a banquet hall, an olympic-sized pool, and a dancehall.

And Zundel himself assures us that Dachau, rather than being a slaughtering centre where tens of thousands were gassed in showers and then cremated in vast ovens, was really a pleasant compound with tree-lined streets, chapels, and large kitchens. Publicizing these lies desecrates the memory of those who perished and mocks the ordeal of those who survived.

But look at the ironies. At the very same moment the trial gives Zundel credence, Canadians are riveted by the story of how Charlie Grant saved Jewish lives. Embarrassed by reminders that the Mackenzie King government would allow virtually no Jews into Canada at the height of their extermination. Scandalized that more Nazi war criminals have not been exposed. Outraged that the evil Dr. Mengele might once have slipped into this country.

Dr. Mengele. Responsible for 400,000 deaths. And Ernst Zundel. On the very same page of your newspaper these past weeks, you were able to read, in one story, assertions by Zundel's witnesses that Zionists had concocted most of the horror stories about the Hitler regime. And in the next column the testimonies of 29 survivors of Auschwitz who appeared before a panel in Jerusalem to describe their own experiences with the "Angel of Death."

But we know only too vividly their stories from Hell. Thousands of them have been published. And the Zundel trial itself was shown a one-hour documentary, called Nazi Concentration Camps, which was compiled from 80,000 feet of film taken by American troops at the end of the war.

Some of Zundel's defenders argue it is not anti-Semitic merely to want to re-examine the accepted version of the Holocaust in a cool and dispassionate manner. It is a disingenuous protest. In the face of the marshalled evidence of history, their perverse position can be seen only as sophisticated bigotry.

What we have, then, is a handful of anti-Semites and neo-fascists who, for their own pathological reasons, worship at the vile shrine of Adolph Hitler and his barbarous regime. Zundel was involved in a booklet titled *The Hitler We Loved and Why*, published by White Power Publications. "We love him still," it states. Zundel talks incessantly about "the Aryan race" on one side, and treacherous Zionists on the other. It is the language of the Third Reich.

The indignity of paying attention to such people is not just against Jews. It is against blacks and Chinese and Indians and all peoples shut out of the warped concept of Aryanism. We call most of them visible minorities. Zundel calls them inferior races.

And finally, and perhaps most of all, it is an indignity against all Canadians, all who remember why we fought World War II, all who are determined never to let Zundel's kind touch power again.

Zundel, like most of his fanatical ilk, lives in a shadowy world on the margins of decent society. We must not again make the error of allowing them into the limelight where their evil vision can poison our souls. They must be left under the boulders where they belong. To be sure, complex issues of liberty and censorship are involved. But surely we can, and must, find a more effective way to undermine the purveyors of hate than by disseminating their message for them.

* * *

1988 IN THE END, BEN JOHNSON was an even more perfect symbol of the modern Olympics than was expected. Whether or not he was unwittingly administered steroids, as we all pray was the case, Big Ben came to represent not only the glory of individual athletic achievement but simultaneously the corruption of the Olympic soul.

The commercialization of the Olympics is now total. Everything connected with them is for sale — not least the athletes. Fame and fortune have become the real prizes of victory, to which a medal is merely the necessary prelude. The modern Olympic spirit is embodied in this new set of marketplace values.

It was all there in microcosm at the first press conference in Seoul to announce Ben's disqualification by the crushed Canadian Olympic spokespersons, each with a large Coke cup sitting conspicuously in front of them. The Coke sparked unedifying memories of our own Calgary Winter Olympics, when 96 corporations paid $87 million to have exclusive right to the esteemed Olympic logo. Before the vulgar orgy was through, those famous interlocking rings had been plastered on everything in sight: ashtrays, adhesive tapes, beer cans, cars, Barbie dolls and western boots. In return for coughing up $14.5 million (U.S.), for example, VISA was given a monopoly on all Olympic sites.

All of this reflected the explicit recognition by the International Olympic Committee that the Olympics had become big business, with, presumably, the same pragmatic — read amoral — approach to the world as business itself. Sponsorship was seen as "the new darling of marketing techniques," and a Swiss firm was actually hired to launch an aggressive marketing campaign to sell the logo across the world.

When the Johnson affair was revealed, one IOC official called it "a blow to the Olympic ideal." What that ideal is nowadays is somewhat blurry, but it appears to treat athletes as commodities barely a level above ashtrays. The concept of the amateur, for example, that we've heard much about this past week, has in fact been eliminated from the Olympic charter, as I learned with astonishment. Under the apparently infinitely flexible concept of "eligibility," we now have Chris Evert representing the U.S. in tennis, notwithstanding the $60 million she's earned playing pro tennis over the years.

Athletes can now earn unlimited lucre and remain well within the new guidelines by depositing their earnings in a trust fund, taking only expenses as approved by the national body of their sport. Alex Baumann, the Sudbury gold medal swimmer, was a millionaire when he retired last year at the ripe old age of 23.

Expenses, after all, are in the eye of the beholder. Big Ben's, as most of us have discovered with some surprise, have included a huge $750,000 home and a $250,000 Ferrari Testarossa. Steven Findlay of the Canadian Track and Field Association has said he is "quite happy with Ben's standard of living."

But if you're living the lifestyle of a successful pro athlete, what separates the Olympics from professional sport? I wanted to ask Findlay that question, but he's still in Seoul and I was told flatly that no one left at the head office of the CTFA in Ottawa could deal with that issue.

Everybody now knows that Big Ben has personally become a Big Business. Like all other successful athletes, he has a couple of marketing agents, who presumably have grown rich along with him thanks to Toshiba, Purolator Courier, Loblaws, American Express and countless other companies literally all over the world. And say goodbye to the legend of Shoeless Joe Jackson: Every running shoe manufacturer on earth is into big fat sponsorships. The gold medal was expected to be worth $10–15 million to Ben by the time the 1992 Games roll around. Some $500,000 was anticipated just in bonuses from existing clients. Running at international track meets would have been worth around $30,000 a shot, though he and Carl Lewis were each offered $500,000 for a re-match in Tokyo next week. "A half-million dollars to sprint?" one European athlete said; "I might dope myself for that too."

Ben Johnson a villain? Nuts. Free will or not, surely he's the tragic victim of an irresistibly corrupting system. He's only a runner, after all. The siren song of stardom is not easily withstood, and why should it be? The rewards of success are immeasurable, and the pressures to succeed, on all concerned, appropriately immense. Brian Mulroney was remarkably quick to write *finis* to Big Ben's career. What's so ironic is that the values of the marketplace that his government worships are precisely the values that did in poor Ben.

* * *

1989   THIS SUMMER HAS WITNESSED a historic transformation of public opinion on one of the great issues of our time. The Western world has fallen madly, passionately, in love with trade unions and strikes. So long, of course, as they're in the Soviet Union or its satellites, and not in Canada or the U.S.

Yes, dear friends, not since their infatuation with Polish Solidarity have the world's capitalists, and their countless government and media spokespersons, so gleefully embraced working class militancy. Traditionally, of course, Western trade unions and their leaders are about as popular as used car salesmen or politicians. Yet, by some magical alchemy, actions that would be censured as reckless and subversive at home are elevated into heroic deeds when their target is the Kremlin.

Now we're not talking here, remember, merely of some miners demanding more bread and butter. One of the U.S.S.R.'s largest industries was virtually paralyzed. The strikers demanded actual control over the mines. Appalling, shameful working conditions need to be radically improved. Billions will be required to meet these demands, yet the Soviet economy is already hopelessly in crisis. And the miners' example has led to the eruption of new strikes all across the country.

This is truly perestroika in practice. And we, lovers of justice all, we cheer the strikers on. When they're over there.

But in our own backyard? Look at today's classic strike in Virginia by American miners against the Pittston Coal Group. They, it seems, are less noble than their Soviet brethren. In 1972, a Pittston mine killed 126 people; Pittston settled out of court for $1 million, say about $8,000 a life. In 1983, seven miners died at Pittston's McLure pit; the company was fined $47,500 for breaching the safety code — this time maybe $6,800 per life. But as for the Mineworkers Union, last month it was fined $3 million for blocking the roads leading to the Pittston Virginia mine during their legal strike.

When the union contract expired last year, Pittston hired a "security firm" to aid it in the fight it was clearly after; this was the notorious Vance Security Asset Protection Team, whose recruits routinely include right-wing mercenaries with a history of provoking picket-line violence. The company also immediately cut off all benefits to disabled miners, widows and retirees. But the union kept working and negotiating for almost a year, then finally, in frustration, walked out four months ago.

Aside from some American trade unionists, the strike is largely unknown, while the company arranges a fat line of credit from friendly banks, hires one of American's many law firms specializing in union-busting, and spies on the strikers with its private police force. In good entrepreneurial fashion, union-busting has itself become a big business in the U.S., with entire consulting firms dedicated to protecting the right of workers to be freely exploited.

How come we care so much about Soviet workers and so little when our own power elite beat the hell out of striking unionists over here? How come in the U.S., Ronald Reagan's ruthless, dangerous sacking of all those air controllers was celebrated as demonstrating firm and decisive leadership? How come American unions can't get to first base in winning anything close to a livable minimum wage or decent health and safety laws? How come there are so many states that attract new industry — increasingly from Canada — with the proud boast that their non-unionized work force is both cheap and "cooperative"?

Canadians should refrain from self-righteousness. One of the best-kept and dirtiest secrets of Canadian history remains the amount of sheer viciousness routinely used over the decades by business, government and the police against the labour movement. Even now, strikers are brutally clobbered everywhere from Gainers in Alberta to your friendly local letter carriers in Toronto. These, untypically, became high-profile scandals; dozens more, often involving women and immigrant workers at the very bottom of the economic scale, never do. Now free trade provides the latest excuse for escalating the campaign against unions and for dramatically lower wages.

In the Soviet Union, Mikhail Gorbachev's reforms call for the workers to run the mines and dispose of any profits. Gorbachev in fact accepted the full radical package of demands of the striking Siberian and Ukrainian miners. "The workers are taking matters into their own hands," he said. "This inspires me."

It doesn't inspire our government; Michael Wilson threatens that its entire regressive, inflationary new tax scheme will be undermined if workers seek higher wages to keep up. Too bad they're not fighting for workers' rights in Siberia, so Mike Wilson could be their great champion.

✳   ✳   ✳

1989　　I HAVE BECOME INSUFFERABLE. Oh, I know, some
———————　would argue mightily with the tense. And maybe I have,
over the years, been a tad difficult from time to time. But this is
different. A life-long, knee-jerk liberal preaching the virtues of
tolerance and respect, I've become an out-and-out bigot.

The subject matter, of course, is smoking. I have some expertise
here, having been hooked for 21 suicidal years until that proud
moment 12 years, 7 months and 14 days ago when I went cold turkey
forever. Since then, I have grown by quantum leaps into a wearisome
anti-smoking vigilante. I, the quintessential champion of victims,
have become the classic blame-the-victim bully. It's time to atone. I
need a cause to get me off the backs of my fast-dwindling band of
nicotine-fingered friends.

That's why I was so thrilled to see the Canadian Medical Association knocking the stuffing out of Shoppers Drug Mart recently. CMA
president Dr. John O'Brien-Bell wrote an "infuriated" open letter to
Shoppers, accusing it of "hypocrisy" in co-sponsoring a TV program
on the hazards of drug abuse, including smoking, while continuing
to sell cigarettes in all its 615 stores. Ironically, O'Brien-Bell notes
harshly, Shoppers co-sponsored this program with Health and Welfare Canada, yet Shoppers' sibling company Imperial Tobacco Ltd.
(both, you see, owned by Imasco Ltd.) has challenged in court the
authority of Health and Welfare to prohibit tobacco advertising.
"Stop the hypocrisy," O'Brien-Bell concludes. "Announce today that
Shoppers Drug Mart will stop selling tobacco products . . . it will
cost you hundreds of thousands of dollars in lost profits, but it will
earn you priceless respect . . . The pharmacy is expected to dispense
life- and health-saving products. It should not be a seller of disease,
disability and death."

The best defence, somebody apparently taught Herbert Binder,
Shoppers' president, is a cheeky offence. Binder's letter responding
to the CMA constituted a veritable commercial for the crusade his
chain is apparently waging against all drug abuse, including smoking. As for actually ending the sale of cigarettes, however, Binder
notes that there are over 150,000 outlets in Canada selling tobacco,
which is "a legal product sold as a convenience to consumers who
elect to smoke." It's a dirty job, but somebody's gotta do it, right?

Wrong. What a powerful message would be sent to all Canadians,
especially kids, if Canada's largest, highest profile drug chain
declared that smoking is so socially unacceptable that its drug stores

were refusing henceforth to be drug pushers — and hang the expense.

But expenses, of course, do matter. Binder insists that "the fact Shoppers is a subsidiary of Imasco does not influence our decision" in these matters. No doubt, Sir. But Imasco is, after all, big business.

Imasco was originally created in 1970 out of Imperial Tobacco in order to diversify its profit base beyond the single problematic area of tobacco. In 1974, demonstrating the exquisite amorality of capitalism, it bought Shoppers; in 1983, it bought People's Drug Stores in the United States; and in 1986, Imasco emerged as a major player in financial services by taking over Canada Trust. In the process, it has prospered nicely, thank you.

Imasco's 1987 annual statement reports gross revenues of $5.6 billion. Imperial Tobacco accounted for 32 per cent of that, or a cool $1.8 billion. But of course tobacco was worth even more than that since what we might call a healthy share of the revenues from Shoppers itself — $144 million — would have come from cigarette sales. Oh yes, Imasco's effective 1987 tax rate was 20.6 per cent; what was yours?

Of course Imasco needs all the dough it can get to pay the high-priced legal eagles who are challenging the ban on tobacco advertising and who have created four new subsidiaries — Players Ltd., Dumaurier Ltd., Matinee Ltd., and Dumaurier Council Ltd. — to get around the government's forthcoming ban on brand-name sponsorship of special events. Consider, too, the onerous financial burdens of retaining government relations firms and of maintaining good connections with all those Liberal and Tory insiders.

I'm afraid I believe Dr. O'Brien-Bell and the CMA will be sorely disappointed if they simply wait for Shoppers to stop selling cigarettes just because of their letter. Imasco honchos need more incentive than that, and I can't imagine any group with greater leverage to provide it than Canada's 55,000 physicians. It's a terrific crusade that would do wonders for the public reputation of the CMA, and it would even make me promise not to be such a pain in the butt anymore.

* * *

1990   LITTLE KNOWN FACT NUMBER 1: The second largest
————————   contribution to the Conservative Party of Canada in
election year 1988 was $102,983.40 from a company called Nabisco
Brands. Nabisco happens to be a branch plant of the giant American
multinational RJR Nabisco, whose then president, Winnipeg-born F.
Ross Johnson, emerged as one of the egregious symbols of Ronald
Reagan's America. The central figure in the terrific bestseller *Barbar-
ians At The Gate*, Johnson is portrayed as a vastly overrated, greedy,
heartless, unscrupulous, ruthless capitalist unleashed by the Reagan
counter-revolution, who became filthy rich building and creating
precisely nothing.

Little known fact Number 2: "Among the Johnsons' closest
friends," the book reports, "were Brian Mulroney and his wife Mila.
Mila and Laurie Johnson (Ross' wife) would prowl Manhattan,
shopping for the Prime Minister's residence." The Mulroneys stayed
at the Johnsons' Florida winter house and had the Johnsons as their
guests at official social functions. Shortly after his first victory, a
puffed-up Mulroney reassured the prestigious Economic Club of
New York that Canada was "open for business again"; Ross Johnson
chaired the meeting. Birds of a feather?

Little known fact Number 3: Ross Johnson was the first American
corporate potentate to support publicly Mulroney's free trade initiative, and he became a key player in mobilizing powerful American
business interests on behalf of the FTA. According to Johnson's close
friend James Robinson, chairman of American Express whose own
active support for free trade seems to have won him incalculable
rewards from a grateful Canadian government, "Ross was the key
player here, the one who really got things started." Johnson also
made sure the Tories received lavish campaign contributions from
RJR's Canadian subsidiaries.

Little known fact Number 4: RJR Nabisco makes most of its money,
as one Wall Street executive summed it up, "selling cancer." One of
America's two largest tobacco manufacturers, it sold $1.6 billion
worth of Winstons, Camels and Salems in 1988, Johnson's last year
as CEO. Like its main rival, Philip Morris, RJR has in recent years
spent hundreds of millions of advertising and promotion dollars
targeting the few growth markets for cigarettes left in America —
women, blacks, the young and the poor.

The two tobacco behemoths also lobby ferociously for unrestricted
access to the markets of the Third World, where countless new

victims await seduction by specially designed RJR brands that promise to transform them into sophisticated, cigarette-loving, dark-skinned yuppies. According to the World Health Organization, 150 million children will eventually die around the world from current smoking habits — the greatest avoidable human-made epidemic in the world's history.

Another bountiful contributor to the Tories in their re-election year, to the tune of $45,000, was Canada's very own Imasco. Imasco is capitalism at its purest; it owns both Shoppers Drug Mart and the Imperial Tobacco Co., Shoppers growing ever richer selling balm to those maimed by Imperial. Indeed, despite the war on smoking, the Canadian tobacco industry has never been in better financial shape; "I know," said one analyst this spring, "of no more profitable business to be in today." Imperial had 1989 profits of a menthol-cool one-third of a billion dollars.

You see, even though they're selling fewer cigarettes, Canadian tobacco merchants over-compensate with higher prices. They also face many money-saving restrictions placed on tobacco advertising, and it costs far less to sponsor all those sporting and cultural events whose organizers are pleased to trade their souls for the filthy luchre earned by the sale of a lethal drug.

The most blatant hold-out against the anti-smoking forces in Canada are teenaged girls, 40 per cent of whom, despite everything, still take up smoking. Naturally, these kids are the calculated targets of certain cigarette brands and a great deal of ingenious, expensive promotions. In the graphic formulation of one Canadian medical authority: "Of 100,000 15-year-old smokers today, 10 will die of drug abuse before they reach 70. AIDS will claim 70. But 18,000 will die prematurely from smoking and the diseases that inevitably follow."

As it happens, the cigarette companies aren't just Tory fans. Imasco in 1988 also gave the Liberals $47,000 while Nabisco gave them $25,000. RJR MacDonald, another RJR Nabisco Canadian subsidiary, gave each another $15,000 for good luck. I don't have impossibly high expectations of these two parties. But how come they just can't say no to donations from what even Ross Johnson's cronies at RJR called "death merchants?"

✳ ✳ ✳

1991   OF ALL THE UNWORTHY, phony-baloney scams ever
─────────   tried in the age-old fight against equality and injustice,
the raging campaign against the so-called politically correct movement may take the cake.

This is a war, remember, against those who are dedicated to rooting
out racism, sexism, homophobia and just about any other form of
discrimination and bigotry in public life, beginning with universities
across North America.

Now that doesn't sound so awful, does it? Yet in one of the
cheekiest, most perverse PR capers of our time, enemies of equality
have successfully managed to discredit this struggle as "the new
McCarthyism of the left," "the new fascism," "the new intolerance."
Hardly a single North American medium has resisted the temptation
to caricature PC's — the Politically Correct — in the most twisted
possible way, or to repeat ad nauseum the same few stories of excess
for which over-zealous PC'ers have been responsible.

But a new low was reached right here in Canada last week when
Maclean's featured an entire cover story on PC with the hysterical
headline, "The Silencers: A New Wave of Repression Is Sweeping
through Universities." Certainly I agree absolutely that some PC'sers
have gone unacceptably overboard in their quest for justice. Canada's most notorious example was the unfortunate attack on the
Royal Ontario Museum for its exhibition called Into the Heart of
Africa, and the subsequent witch hunt against its curator Jean
Cannizzo.

The exhibition was, in fact, a faithful depiction of white colonial
paternalism and of violence against Africans, while the persecution
of Cannizzo was shameful and unjustifiable by any standards
imaginable.

Like all movements, alas, democratic socialism has always been
tarnished by the presence of unwelcome extremists whom my generation labelled totalitarians of the left. Their position was intolerable to me when they defended Stalinism, and it's intolerable now.

But watch out: beneath the easy attacks on PC'ers for a few
outrageous examples of excess and silliness there lurks a more
sinister and sophisticated campaign to disparage and undermine the
very principle of equality itself. After all, the assertion that so-called
PCs have significant influence beyond small, isolated incidents is
simply untrue. In fact, mostly they represent groups that have been
marginalized by the real power structure and have no systematic

power at all. Just look around you: this remains a white, male world, not least on our university campuses.

The anti-PC crusade is, as a matter of record, the brainchild of the American New Right. Among the many mean characteristics of the Reagan-Bush era has been the ugly backlash against civil rights, gay rights and women's equality. In universities, virulently right-wing academics started targeting PC'ers as their learned contribution to the Reaganite revolution against equality, accusing them of destroying a wildly idealized fantasy version of a university that simply does not exist. Other threatened teachers soon hopped on the bandwagon, followed by the entire North American mainstream media — and guess who owns and runs them?

But the big problem at North American universities isn't misguided fanatics trying sometimes too belligerently to end sexism and violence against women and a white Eurocentric way of seeing the world. It's that rampant sexism and sexual harassment still flourish. It's that in the name of teaching the intellectual and historical foundations of Western thought and life, universities routinely peddle the exploits and ideas of successful white males, all others being relegated largely to exotica or footnotes. And not least, it's that traditional old boys' network of academic hiring still overwhelmingly prevails.

That's why I get such a kick out of all those self-serving male professors who, in *Maclean's* words, "claim that hiring quotas (or affirmative action programs) are destroying merit as the principle basis for hiring and promotion."

Check your mirrors again, boys. If all the time-serving second-raters in North American universities constitute the merit principle in action, then we're really up the creek without a paddle.

Look: the fight for equality and against bigotry has always been incredibly tough, and the phony holy war against Political Correctness is just another obstacle to overcome. But as someone once said, some day we shall.

* * *

1991   ON THIS CANADA DAY WEEKEND, let me introduce you
———————   to a family that once believed in the Canadian promise.

José Alberto Garcia Estrada and his wife Antonia Funes Umanzor
are Salvadorans; they have two kids, 6-year-old Karla and 6-month-
old Jonathan. Estrada was a worker in Salvador who became
secretary of the union in his plant. El Salvador, as is well known, is
one of the most violent societies in the world, where the powerful
U.S.-trained and -funded military protects the privileges of the tiny
ruling class with any and all means available, however brutal or
sadistic.

Salvadoran trade union activists have long been a target of systematic repression and intimidation by the police, the military and their
death squads. In 1989, the offices of FENASTRAS, the Salvadoran
labour federation — its version of the Canadian labour Congress —
was bombed three times by the armed forces, the last of which killed
10 people. Last year, the International Confederation of Free Trade
Unions listed El Salvador as one of the world's eight most dangerous
countries for trade unionists.

Estrada quickly learned why. His first lesson came when military
police crashed a union meeting, accusing the participants of being
Communists. Some were taken away to join the swollen number of
disappeared Salvadorans. Estrada was badly beaten, but was left.

On a second occasion, he and other union activists were con-
fronted on the street by military police, beaten, made to lie on the
ground and walked upon. We have your photos and ID, the thugs
warned; if we see you again you'll be killed.

Then some 10 military police appeared at Estrada's home one
morning. Finding his wife alone, they announced that she would
suffer in his place. She was stabbed five times and left bleeding and
unconscious. Although badly scarred, she survived.

Finally, soldiers appeared again at the plant when Estrada happened to be absent, showed photos of the plant's seven union leaders
and promised to slit their throats when they were found. Clearly
being hunted, the family at last gave in and, as so many had done
before, fled hopefully to Canada.

In Montreal, Estrada attempted to get himself declared a legitimate
refugee. But the lawyer he found did not speak Spanish and was
simply too busy to deal properly with his new client. They met only
the day before Estrada's hearing at the Immigration and Refugee
Board and the lawyer bizarrely advised the wife not to reveal her

stabbing, a fact the board therefore never learned.

Nor, frankly, was Estrada a good witness on his own behalf. Nervous, anxious, disoriented by the process, still in partial shock, working in a foreign tongue, poorly educated, badly advised, he gave some inconsistent and contradictory responses to the board — how do you think you would stand up in his place? As a result, his request for refugee status was denied.

That's when the remarkable Canadians in the "Vigil Network" sprang into action. Estrada's only hope now was a special appeal to Bernard Valcourt, the minister of immigration, and the network exists precisely to help in cases of obvious injustice to refugees such as this. The minister was forwarded all the information that was absurdly denied the hearing board.

Sent were a letter from a Montreal physician attesting to the permanent scars Estrada's wife bore from her stab wounds; a letter from the FENASTRAS representative in Quebec confirming Estrada's horror stories; and petitions from the Canadian Bar Association, prominent Canadian trade unionists, the Inter-Church Committee for Human Rights in Latin America, and the Jesuit Refugee Service for Central America, all urgently warning the minister that deporting Estrada and his family to Salvador could well mean their deaths.

According to Bernard Valcourt's aide, the minister personally reviewed the case. On June 20th the entire family was unceremoniously kicked out of Canada. No explanation has been offered for this heartless decision.

What a government. As the Canadian Council for Refugees has pointed out, "The cold disregard for human life demonstrated by Valcourt in this case has alerted human rights activists that Canada's humanitarian reputation is in peril." That's why the case must not be allowed to rest here. Although, ominously, no one has yet heard from the family, it's fervently hoped they're still alive somewhere in El Salvador. Valcourt still has the authority to issue a permit to bring them back to Canada immediately and we must do everything possible to pressure him to do so.

Please join me in writing to Bernard Valcourt immediately, urging him to bring the Estrada family back. Let's see if we can get this government to do something decent for once. It's the least we can do to remind ourselves why we're supposed to celebrate Canada Day.

* * *

1991   MY HEART HAS GONE OUT recently to smokers, especially to the youthful male variety.

No, it's not because of the iniquitous tax burden that mean, miserable governments have imposed on them; I'm afraid not even I, with the milk of socialist compassion coursing through my arteries, can work up much indignation over the tax on cigarettes, despite the best efforts of trillions of dollars of advertising by the cancer peddlers all week.

And it's not even because these kids are maiming themselves in umpteen different ways — although I do resent the burden their tobacco-induced illnesses will add to publicly supported health facilities along the way, for which non-smokers' taxes will surely be increased.

But here's what's really heart-wrenching: these dumb clucks are ruining their sex lives. Really! Do you see the exquisite irony? As the tobacco companies' very secret, very extensive research into the attitudes of young people to smoking has shown clearly, many impressionable boys can't resist the lure of rugged manliness that so many cigarette ads artfully convey.

In the words of a 1988 advertising plan for Export A: "Very young starter smokers choose Export A because it provides them with an instant badge of masculinity, appeals to their rebellious nature and establishes their position among their peers." Yeah. Makes you a real man, right?

But has anyone told these poor suckers about the new study at the Boston School of Medicine? It indicates, in the words of its research director, Dr. Max Rosen, "that cigarette smoking is a risk factor . . . for developing significant narrowing of the penile arteries." You see, boys and girls, we'd already learned that old codgers with coronary heart disease get clogged arteries that are linked to impotence. Now, "it appears that smoking may affect the penile arteries in a select group of young men many years before the more generalized effects of arteriosclerosis are evident." Forget all the highfalutin' terminology there, kid; the meaning is clear. Your "instant badge of masculinity," the medical experts are telling you, works kind of limply, if you get my drift.

The world's such a funny old place sometimes. Tobacco companies are very generous donors to both the Tory and Liberal parties, although personally I've always felt that accepting dough from merchants of death was really pretty tacky. But even their fancy contributions couldn't prevent the government from banning cigarette advertising, and in 1989 the tobacco giants launched a court challenge against the ban. During this process, the companies were forced to submit in evidence masses of corporate documents that prove conclusively what most of us have always assumed and they have always denied: that they routinely target very young kids as new customers.

Take Imperial Tobacco's marketing plan for 1988, for example (you remember Imperial, I hope: owned by the respected Imasco, which also owns Shoppers Drug Mart, thus making their fortune both killing you and healing you). "If the last 10 years have taught us anything," the plan states simply, "it's that the industry is dominated by companies who respond most effectively to the needs of younger smokers. Our efforts on these brands will remain on maintaining their relevance to smokers in these younger groups."

In Canada, about 85,000 folk begin smoking each year; most are anxious kids around 15 trying to show they're grownup and independent. It's these chumps the cancer companies go after with malice and profits aforethought. "Since 1971," Imperial's 1985 marketing plan for Player's revealed, our "marketing strategy has been to position Player's as a masculine trademark for younger males." Shamelessness, I'm afraid, pays: in the face of all the anti-smoking campaigns everywhere, the tobacco giants have made a killing, if you'll pardon the expression, over the years.

And all at the expense of all that ill-fated, 15-year-old who just wants to be a hot-shot. But look what will really happen to him. "Of 100,000 15-year-old smokers today," medical authorities remind us, "10 will die of drug abuse before they reach 70. But 18,000 will die prematurely from smoking and the diseases that inevitably follow." And now we know he's more likely to become impotent in the bargain. Hey, maybe we've finally lucked into the one argument that might really deter the junior macho set. Just imagine the creative slogan possibilities:

Smokers? They're nothing but limp wimps.

Smoking. Keep it up or get it up.

Real men don't smoke.

The possibilities are endless. It's just such a shame it's already too late for all my middle-aged smoking pals.

* * *

1992   AMONG THE DIRTIEST LITTLE SECRETS of Canadian
history is that we've never quite been the kinder, gentler
nation that's so central to our mythology. Take trade unionism as an
example.

In his 1960s study *Times of Trouble: Labour Unrest and Industrial Conflict in Canada*, Professor Stuart Jamieson described as a "conspiracy of silence" the failure of Canadian scholars to record the extent of labour violence and conflict in the life of Canada. Jamieson's own research showed that labour-management disputes in Canada were only too likely to lead to violence.

The next decade, historian Irving Abella reinforced Jamieson's argument. "For some reason," Abella noted in *On Strike: Six Key Labor Struggles in Canada*, "Canadian academics seem to have shied away from writing about the violent aspects of our history, as if violence and strife were surely part of the American past but definitely not our own. The subjects they chose as worthy of study tended to reinforce the great theme of Canadian history — the peaceful evolution of a Canadian nation based on a spirit of order and compromise."

In each of the strikes that Abella's authorities dissected — Winnipeg, 1919; Oshawa, 1937; Windsor, 1945; Asbestos, 1949 — "the heavy hand of government . . . grinds down upon labor. In each, the state comes down forcefully and aggressively on the side of capital. Workers were to be crushed and unions destroyed whenever they posed a serious threat to business. And to support business, the full resources of the state were always available," especially the RCMP or provincial or local police forces blatantly harassing lawful strikers.

Nevertheless, the mythology of Canada as the peaceable kingdom continues, not least thanks to the role of most media which routinely ignore labour conflicts or present a largely pro-management perspective. Yet recent decades have been filled with bitter, violent strikes and lockouts that fit precisely the patterns described by Jamieson and Abella — Radio Shack, Fleck, Artistic Woodwork, the post office, Gainers: the honour roll is long and bloody. Now we can add the Yellowknife miners' strike against the Royal Oak Mine Company.

Well before the terrible tragedy of the bomb blast at the Giant mine that killed nine non-striking miners, the strike was shaping up as a Canadian classic in the most notorious sense. On the one side were 240 tough northern miners. Although they had not struck since 1980, their legitimate growing concerns about mine safety had been heightened by the Westray mine disaster in Nova Scotia in May when 26 miners died.

On the other side stood an American woman named Peggy Witte who had bought the struggling mine last year. By all accounts, confrontation was Witte's chosen style, slash and burn her tactics. The miners' fears for their safety were not on her agenda. Ruthless in cutting costs and reducing staff, Witte seems deliberately to have chosen to turn the clock back on labour relations by using well-honed American methods for strikebreaking. She did not long stand alone.

On the very first day of the strike four months ago, Witte brought in scabs, a highly unusual move in an industry where workers must be well-trained for safety reasons. "This is a very aggressive tactic, not common in Canada," she unabashedly acknowledged to her shareholders in June, citing the particular success of one Arizona mining company in breaking a strike with the help of strikebreakers and the American National Guard.

On the third day, 58 RCMP officers were flown in from Edmonton as reinforcements. From the plausible perspective of the strikers, the Mounties simply and provocatively placed themselves at the beck and call of Royal Oak, functioning as the company's private police force. "Instead of keeping the peace, they were the keepers of the corporate faith," commented *Fool's Gold*, published by the miners' union.

In videos taken by the strikers, phalanxes of Mounties march in full riot gear, with gas masks, shields and guard dogs. It's like something from a bygone era. The strikers saw it as a scene right out of South Africa.

And just to make the picture complete, Witte brought in Pinkerton guards from the States as well. Infamous in strikebreaking history, Witte was glad to have them live up to their notorious reputation, provocatively telling reporters they were experienced in handling violent labour disputes.

Through the months of innumerable violent, angry incidents for which both sides had responsibility, local authorities pleaded with the federal government, which has jurisdiction over labour relations in the North, to intervene. The minister of labour refused, then stalled. Presumably this was just another typical Canadian strike, not meriting special attention. Then it was too late.

The explosion that killed the nine workers cannot be condemned too harshly — whoever caused it. But four months of escalating conflict preceded the bombing. Someone is responsible for that, too.

✳   ✳   ✳

"*WAS ES EIGENTLICH GEWESEN.*"

Thus the great 19th-century German historian von Ranke defined the historian's craft: to reconstruct what really happened in the past. I was reminded of this ancient bit of lore recently at a moving ceremony at the University of Toronto at which Barbara Frum received a posthumous doctorate. Barbara graduated from the U of T in Modern History a year before me, and the day inevitably induced moist-eyed nostalgia, not only about her but about my own student days — where I learned that von Ranke was simply wrong.

Nobody can ever recreate history "correctly," since in scholarship, as in journalism and so many other things, nobody agrees on nuttin'. There are feminist academics, boring neutral academics, racist academics, all of whom no doubt believe they are in fact truth-seekers and that their truth is truer than yours. Each of us can easily find a persuasive school of thought that neatly fits our own biases.

After all, no one agrees about yesterday, never mind about history. A pertinent example: a conservative, law'n'order, gun-loving Toronto politician announces confidently that 99 per cent of local blacks repudiate black activist Dudley Laws and his militant approach. Stephen Lewis, preparing his report on racism for the Ontario government, found that almost every black person he met with shared Laws' overall views even if they didn't buy his tactics. Both positions cannot be true. Whom do you choose to agree with?

The truth, then, does not make you free, especially when there's no agreement on what's true. But surely it's still better to have data than not, even if they'll be interpreted in utterly contradictory, often self-serving, ways. Take statistics on race and crime. I believe it's wrong not to collect as much data in this area as possible.

Will they be misinterpreted, misused and abused by those who want to make racist points? Unquestionably. But that happens already. People of ill will continue to say whatever they want, regardless of the facts; just remember Toronto's mayoral campaign.

But for those who want to deal with real problems, we'd better know, to paraphrase von Ranke, what's really going on. If blacks, to take the obvious example, are really convicted in disproportionate numbers of certain crimes, if they do constitute a disproportionate number of our prison population, we should know it. This information can make nothing worse and might help lead to viable public policies.

Sometimes data truly illuminate. Why do blacks seem to have more schooling and employment problems than other minority groups? Andrew Hacker, in his new book *Two Nations: Black and White, Separate, Hostile, Unequal,* unearthed some remarkable data for the United States, at least. Sure, hard work and ambition still matter, he acknowledges. But there's another factor that I certainly wasn't aware of: while it's true that most newly arrived immigrants to America begin with lower incomes, many of them belonged to the middle class in their countries of origin and brought those values with them.

More than half the Asian students and one-third the Hispanic students in the States who take college entry tests have parents who attended college. This is far from the case either with black Americans or West Indian immigrants, and it makes a world of difference.

Hacker also argues that black Americans are still paying the price for having once been slaves. Recently I wrote that a conspicuous difference between Canada and the U.S. in matters racial was the absence of slavery in this country. As several disappointed readers correctly pointed out, I was dead wrong, inexcusably so.

According to Robin Winks' study *The Blacks in Canada,* slavery was very much a reality in both Upper and Lower Canada, and of course all blacks from the Caribbean are descended from slaves. So while most immigrants to Canada over the years have faced some degree of discrimination and exploitation — Irish, Chinese, Italians, Japanese, South Asians, Jews, Ukrainians — only blacks have ever known the meaning of actual slavery.

Then there's the revealing information from Statistics Canada passed on to me by Toronto economist Arthur Donner in the table below. It shows as baldly as can be that the less schooling you have, the less you'll earn and the more likely it is you'll be jobless. (Note also the wild disparities in male and female earnings.)

We know from the 1986 census that blacks are disproportionately streamed away from academic studies and into technical schooling, and only 10.9 per cent of all black Canadians have some university education. And a Toronto study has shown that when blacks and whites have precisely the same qualifications, whites have a 3:1 advantage over blacks in getting the job.

In other words, we are getting frighteningly close to replicating here the terrible, endless cycle that is the norm for black Americans.

Current StatsCan data reveal another distressing new phenomenon: during the last recession, youth unemployment exactly reflected over-all unemployment levels in Ontario. Not this time. In 1991, the over-all Ontario unemployment rate was 9.6 per cent; for youth it was 15.4 per cent. For the first five months of 1992, the respective figures are 11 and 18.2 per cent.

It appears that a serious new crisis for young people is on our doorsteps, one that inevitably will hit black kids hardest.

For Canada, unlike the U.S., it may not be too late to avoid a future of permanent racial hostility. But so long as many Canadians refuse to recognize what is happening in this country, the Americanization of Canada in yet another unwelcome way will continue apace.

SCHOOLING	UNEMPLOYMENT RATE	AVERAGE EARNING: FEMALE / MALE
0–8 years	19.8%	12,000 / 23,000
high school graduate	12.5%	16,000 / 28,000
post-secondary diploma	10.1%	19,000 / 32,000
university graduate	5.3%	29,000 / 45,000

* * *

1992   EVERYDAY, IN EVERY WAY, we become more and more indistinguishable from our American neighbors. Among the abundant examples of this unwelcome development, few are more sinister than the recent outbreak of American-style vigilantism. Whatever happened to the good old Canadian way of "peace, order and good government?"

Of course we have some way to go before we approach the lofty American standards in this area. The United States, according to a 1991 Senate judiciary committee report, is "the most violent and self-destructive nation on Earth . . . In 1990, the U.S. led the world with its murder, rape and robbery rates."

There, raw violence is commonplace; the American Medical Association considers violence in the home, which involves a staggering six of every 10 American couples, to be nothing less than an epidemic.

That's what's made Pat Buchanan such a fitting candidate for president; even though he couldn't dislodge President George Bush, his is the genuine voice of a dominant strand of American culture. Buchanan's the all-American who absolutely wallows in violence, almost for its own sake. Punching-out just about anybody he chooses has been a way of life for him since being weaned.

Now two high-profile incidents have cast serious doubts on whether Canadians continue to abhor these essentially American values. The first involved Brian Mulroney himself, as he lashed out furiously at the despicable way *Frank*, a low-life deceitful magazine, violated his daughter, Caroline. "I wanted," he announced, "to take a gun and go down there and do serious damage to those people" who were responsible.

Who could blame him? I, for one, agree wholeheartedly with the words of Suzanne Laplante Edward, whose own daughter was one of the 14 women slaughtered by Marc Lepine: "Believe me," she said, "having lost a daughter the way I did, I can empathize, and so can any parent." Yet, as she emphasized, there's an ever larger lesson to learn from Mulroney's outburst. "We can't control tempers but we can, and must, control guns. When men feel extreme anger or extreme depression, their tempers flare. And when they have access to guns, it leads to horrible incidents of violence."

Enter Norm Gardner, an elected Metro Toronto councillor and a member of the civilian police services board that oversees the Metro police force. For shooting an unarmed man who was robbing his bakery, Gardner is now reaping his 15 minutes of national fame and, I'm afraid, glory. If you follow Edward's logic, the Gardner affair was almost bound to happen. Gardner is a life-long cheerleader for the police and, hardly surprising, one of their favorite politicians. He's also a gun fetishist whose very office decor reflects this curious passion as does his guileless choice of licence plates: STRM NM.

Indeed many have long considered such preoccupations to be, at best, unhealthy ones. Nevertheless, a majority of his fellow Metro councillors have repeatedly, and knowingly, voted him onto the police services board. What they didn't know, however, was that by literally a two-in-a-million fluke, and for reasons that seem increasingly dubious, Gardner just happens to be one of 20 people among all 10 million of Ontario's citizens who has official police authorization to wear a loaded and concealed handgun. And to wear it everywhere he goes, just like Dirty Harry — even though Gardner's not a cop. And for it to be not just an ordinary old handgun but a powerful semi-automatic one at that.

The circumstances around the shooting remain unclear. But what's plain enough is the widespread support Gardner's gotten from the general public for "protecting himself and his employees" from possible danger. This outpouring of acclaim seems to be as depressing as his right to carry a gun — should I say "pack a rod?" — in the first place. For the issue is not whether Mulroney was right in his specific situation or Gardner in his. The question is whether anybody in Canada who thinks *his* particular circumstance warrants it, is entitled to shoot anyone he chooses at will.

That's why I regret that after his understandable eruption, Mulroney didn't go on to say that, however enraged he was, it is *not* tolerable in this country for anyone to do what the PM felt like doing to *Frank's* editors. Although Parliament has passed a new gun law, its effectiveness largely depends on the rigorousness of the detailed regulations that the government has yet to set.

That's because it's awaiting the recommendations of the Canadian Advisory Council on Firearms, a loaded group chosen personally by Justice Minister Kim Campbell to appease the many fervid opponents of gun control in the Tory government. According to Wendy Cukier, spokesperson for the Coalition for Gun Control, "Not only are we concerned about the dominance of gun owners on the council, we are concerned about the tremendous resources being deployed by the gun lobby in opposition to further controls." In other words, the Canadian anti-gun control lobby is marching steadfastly along the trail blazed by its American model.

Once already the Mulroney government has caved in to pressure from its western and northern Ontario MPs and backed off from passing a tough Canadian gun control law. Let's see what values our government now thinks are appropriate for this country — Canadian ones, or those of Pat Buchanan?

* * *

Culture versus Industry

1987　　NOTHING makes those of us wary of the current Canadian-American free trade negotiations more suspicious than the veil of secrecy cloaking the talks.

Nowhere is this problem more acute than in the area of so-called cultural sovereignty. Nowhere is there less clarity than when our political leaders and our negotiators vow to stand up for the integrity of Canada's culture. At the slightest Yankee hint that the cultural field must be on the table, our guys become apoplectic. It is to laugh.

The problem is that those aspects of our cultural industries that seem to vex our politicians have everything to do with industry and precious little to do with culture. This is especially true in the field of broadcasting, which should be the premium vehicle for communicating Canadian culture to Canadians in large numbers.

Yet the one broadcaster that truly performs this function, the CBC, is being cut back so that it will be featuring less Canadian drama, variety, arts, music than ever. At the same time, it is the private broadcasters, who deliver a derisory amount of the Canadian story on their highly profitable channels, who are the main beneficiaries of the provisions that are apparently being protected in the free trade negotiations.

The two that are most often mentioned are Bill C-58 and simultaneous substitution. The first provides an incentive to Canadian advertisers to advertise on Canadian stations. This naturally is a significant boon to Canadian broadcasters, but does nothing whatever for Canadian programming. On the contrary, it provides an incentive to Canadian stations to show the most popular American shows during peak viewing hours in order to attract large Canadian audiences and commensurate tax-deductible advertising.

*Members of the Task Force on Canadian Broadcasting Policy
with Minister of Communications Flora MacDonald.
Left to right: Caplan (co-chair), Fil Fraser, Conrad Lavigne,
Flora MacDonald, Finlay MacDonald Jr., Florian Sauvageau (co-chair),
Mimi Fullerton, Francine Côté.*

Simultaneous substitution goes even further. If an American and a Canadian broadcaster are both showing the same program at the same time, Canadian Radio-television and Telecommunications Commission (CRTC) regulations permit the Canadian station to have its signal substituted on cable for that of the American station. So whichever station you tune to, you're in fact watching the Canadian one — and, most importantly, its commercials. The catch here, of course, is that the mechanism functions only if an American program is being shown.

So what really happens is that our broadcasters deliberately buy — at a fraction of the cost of making a quality Canadian program from scratch — the most popular U.S. shows and schedule them at the same time as they're on in the States. In that sense, decisions affecting prime-time shows in Canada are actually made in New York, where American broadcasting executives decide what time their programs will be shown on their networks. Our broadcasters then adopt that New York-created schedule as their own Canadian schedule.

These two measures happen to be very lucrative for Canadian broadcasters. Our Broadcasting Task Force research indicated that it increased their revenues in 1984 by between $90 million and $95 million a year, or some 9 to 9 1/2 per cent more than they would otherwise have been — in return for showing more and more U.S. shows! Only in Canada, surely.

Nor do these extra revenues get allocated in any specific way toward Canadian programming. They simply increase the already handsome profits of the private broadcasters, who continue to show as many cheaply bought U.S. shows as the CRTC lets them get away with. In 1984–85, for example, private stations spent fully one-third of all their program expenditures on foreign, overwhelmingly U.S., entertainment shows, and just 10 per cent on Canadian entertainment programs.

Ottawa's spokesmen pretend the Americans don't understand this perfectly well. They do. Richard Parker, a top adviser to U.S. trade representative Clayton Yeutter, told an Ottawa seminar on free trade last year that he considered items like c-58 and simulcasting to be "barriers" to free trade and suggested they had little relationship to the goal of cultural sovereignty but were in fact "a disguised form of commercial protectionism." The powerful Motion Picture Association of America has made the same accusations against Canada to U.S. Congress.

Who can blame them? What research can our negotiators possibly possess to refute these charges? Yet, so far as we can tell, it is this commercial protection of private broadcasters that our government is committed to preserving in the free trade talks.

Wouldn't it be ironic if the government could get away with peddling itself as the saviour of Canadian culture sovereignty because it protects the profits of private broadcasters, who mostly provide us with America's culture, while it undermines the CBC, which mostly provides us with our own?

✳   ✳   ✳

1988   IT'S HIGH TIME fair-minded Canadians admitted they were wrong about the Mulroney government. For almost three years this government has been dismissed as inept, indecisive and opportunistic.

In fact, the opposite is true: It knows where it wants to go and how to get there. In fact, it is determined to get there. And the rest of us are going to be sorry every inch of the way.

Much of the agenda involves making us more like Americans, beginning by opening our country up even more to U.S. interests. So the Foreign Investment Review Agency is emasculated, so Canada is open to business from abroad. The National Energy Policy is trashed, and the free trade deal ties us all but inextricably to an American model of market-driven development, substantially pre-empting our right and capacity to run our affairs differently from our southern neighbors.

As if that's not enough, now they have doomed us to be increasingly dependent on the United States for our news. The chances are at least reasonably good that we will now not ever have a Canadian all-news channel, and that the only such channel available to news-hungry Canadians will remain CNN, the cable news network from Atlanta. Oh well, at least we can be confident CNN won't ever offend this government since it never acknowledges Canada's existence.

What has been so distasteful about the attacks against the CBC's licence to operate an all-news channel over the past two months is how dishonest and hypocritical virtually all the arguments against it

217

have been. The reality was straightforward: The Tories just plain loathe the CBC with an irrational passion, they have been whittling away its budget from the moment they gained office, and they were determined it would expand only over their dead bodies. What a choice.

Everything else was an excuse, not a reason. The argument that the CBC would now have a dangerous concentration of power is specious beyond words. As if the CBC's competition, with or without the news channel, didn't include four American television networks, the CTV network, the Global network, independent TV stations in most large cities, hundreds and hundreds of private radio stations, a hundred-odd newspapers and a dozen Canadian and American magazines. Some concentration.

But the argument was even more dishonest than that. It conjured up the nonsensical notion of a monolithic CBC with a house ideology and an agreed philosophical approach to the issues of the day. That, instead of the obvious truth that it is a house with hundreds of different rooms, hundreds of different new outlets, each of which decides quite independently how to handle each story so long as it doesn't violate the over-all requisite of balanced programming.

Nor does there exist a shred of serious evidence that the CBC is collectively biased in a left-wing or anti-Tory direction. The accusation is made repeatedly and has never once been demonstrated with the kind of scrupulous study that alone could settle the issue. The truth — again — is far simpler: Good journalists, whether on the CBC or not, end up dissecting the activities of the government of the day. And no government appreciates that.

Heaven knows Jimmy Carter and Ronald Reagan and Pierre Trudeau all believed the media had it in for them. Heaven knows the New Democratic Party wouldn't be in power for 20 minutes before it fell into the same trap. Meanwhile, New Democrats continue to pray for some evidence of that socialist CBC the Tory paranoids keep swearing is right there on the tube each night.

Then the CBC-haters turned to regional discontents. Even though the CBC, as a condition of its licence, was to broadcast heavily from centres in both eastern and western Canada, and was offering extensive regional news coverage, its new channel was said to mean more and more news from Toronto.

As opposed, presumably, to the hero of the west, Dr. Charles Allard of Edmonton, whose rejected all-news application called for a staff of 280 souls, precisely 222 of whom would be based in Edmonton.

Now that's the way to end regional alienation in Atlantic Canada.

In fact, regional resentments were deliberately and provocatively inflamed to turn the issue into an anti-Toronto one. Writing in *The Star*, Bill Fox, once Mulroney's press secretary, claimed that "a cursory examination of editorial opinion across the country indicates the Toronto media mafia believes the licence must be awarded to the CBC, while newspapers that don't count Toronto's annex neighborhood in their circulation area want the decision reversed." Cute and snotty, Bill, but a little too cursory. Guess what? In Alberta itself, both the *Edmonton Journal* and the *Calgary Herald* have both strongly supported the CRTC's decision to licence the CBC, not Allard of Edmonton.

The distortions hardly ever ended. None was more malevolent than the implication that the CRTC's decision favored English Canada against French Canada. In fact, our Broadcasting Task Force explicitly advocated Quebec be recognized as having a distinctive broadcasting system because of its unique broadcasting traditions and its smaller, more geographically concentrated French-speaking audience.

And one of the differences, we demonstrated, was that an all-news channel made more sense at the present time for English- than for French-Canada.

Yes, you really have to hand it to this government. For three and a half happy years, they had not a word to say about broadcasting policy. Suddenly, over a broadcasting licence that was none of their business in the first place, they have managed to do more damage to Canada's highly regarded broadcasting system than all their predecessors in the past 55 years. They have seriously undermined the autonomy of the CRTC, a quasi-judicial regulatory tribunal, by interfering with a licensing decision that should never have been challenged by the politicians.

They have seriously threatened the hands-off relationship with the CBC, whose credibility rests on its independence from government interference. They have instructed a licensee, the CBC, how they want to see a licence application framed and organized, creating frightening future precedents.

In general, it's not too much to say that they have taken a first step toward transforming one of Canada's true historic achievements — an independent broadcasting system, an independent regulatory agency and an independent public broadcaster — into a government-dominated and government-controlled sector. Not bad for a day's work for a gang that believes in less government intervention in society. Not bad at all.

*   *   *

1989   CAN I RECOMMEND a fascinating little exercise for you?
_____   It's based on Edward Herman and Noam Chomsky's latest book, *Manufacturing Consent*, which argues that under the guise of a free and feisty press, the American mass media actually serve to reflect the special interests of the elites that run the United States.

Through their choice of topics and sources, the way they frame issues, through tone and emphasis, and by keeping debate within the bounds of certain acceptable premises, the actual role of the media is "to inculcate and defend the economic, social and political agenda of privileged groups" that dominate life in America.

This is no batty left-wing conspiracy theory: The authors know that "the U.S. media do not function in the manner of the propaganda system of a totalitarian state. Rather, they permit — indeed encourage — spirited debate, criticism and dissent, as long as these remain faithfully within the system of presupposition and principles that constitute an elite consensus, a system so powerful as to be internalized largely without awareness."

This, needless to say, is a somewhat disturbing assertion, which Herman and Chomsky massively document analyzing coverage over the years of Central America and Southeast Asia by highly influential American media: the *New York Times*, *Time*, *Newsweek* and CBS News. For my money, they demonstrate a pattern of distorted news coverage so systematically, consistently and blindly pro-American as largely to validate their terrifying hypothesis.

But you can test it yourself today with any newspaper which, given commercial realities, will inevitably be chock-a-block with American news reports and comments.

The *Toronto Star*, for example, carried a post-Christmas column by David Broder, a popular American political commentator, that could serve admirably as the text for Herman and Chomsky's next book. "The Sandinistas and the Contras have stopped killing each

Aislin editorial cartoon, The Toronto Star, April 29, 1991.

other on the borders of Nicaragua," Broder wrote, for all the world as if two morally equal groups were at play here. In fact, of course, the Contras are nothing but agents of the mighty American government attempting to overthrow the legitimate government of a tiny Third World country that refuses to kow-tow to American interests. "Yasser Arafat," Broder went on, "acknowledged the existence of Israel, clearing the way for the first direct talks between the U.S. government and the PLO." Well, literally that's so, but the clear implication is that Arafat, not Washington or Israel, has till now prevented peace, a routine American value judgment but not self-evidently objective reality.

Or take the long article in the *Globe and Mail* the same day by an American historian, "Viet Nam's road to recovery looks like a long trudge." The obstacles to economic development in Viet Nam, we learn, "are substantial . . . Viet Nam is in desperate economic straits that reduce it to one of the poorest nations on earth." All because — you guessed it — of its incompetent, dogmatic Communist government. No doubt. But what of the simple truth that Viet Nam endured 30 years of devastating war, first against France and then against the invading Americans, ending only 13 years ago?

We all know that 60,000 American boys died in Viet Nam. But did you know some 3 million Vietnamese did too? Or that "the combined ecological, economic and social consequences of American wartime defoliation operations," according to one report, "have been vast and will take several generations to reverse"? Or that 9,000 of the south's 15,000 hamlets were damaged or destroyed, while all six industrial cities in the north were damaged, three of them razed to the ground?

Yet the *Globe* article, astoundingly but typically, contains only a single bizarre reference to the war: "Having just fought a 30-year war for independence, many upper-echelon veterans of the struggle are loathe to move towards capitalism." By the way, the U.S. massively and routinely used chemical and environmental warfare across Southeast Asia in those ghastly years, which brings us to the evil Colonel Khadhafi. Of all the stories you read last week about the alleged Libyan chemical weapons plant, how many have noted that such peace-loving Canadian allies as the U.S. certainly, and Israel probably, themselves possess great stores of chemical weapons? Or that Libya is in fact offering on-site inspection of the plant, which the U.S. has flatly rejected?

And how many stories have reported the many previous American accusations against Khadhafi that proved to be utter lies and deliberately concocted disinformation?

Herman and Chomsky would assert that the media are manufacturing consent for Ronald Reagan's macho determination to leave office with American guns blazing against Libya. Let's pray they're wrong.

✳   ✳   ✳

1990   YES, IT'S GIFT-GIVING SEASON AGAIN, dear friends, and
———   why not a book to expand the mind? In fact, why not that ultimate book of books, an encyclopedia? We happen to have two available for you right this moment, both on prominent display at your friendly local booksellers.

One is the new five-volume *Junior Encyclopedia of Canada*, published by Hurtig as a successor to its wildly successful *Canadian Encyclopedia*. It's an absolutely first-rate production, and a terrific bargain at $160. No school or household with kids between diapers and graduate school can afford to do without it — except they are. It's selling poorly, yet another victim, apparently, of the depressing recession.

Or perhaps it's the competition that it's getting from a new rival, the absolutely remarkable third edition of *The Random House Encyclopedia*. The RHE is being hawked with typical American understatement. For a paltry $130, you lucky people, you get "The World's Knowledge" in 2,781 jam-packed pages, "Completely Revised and Updated for the 1990s."

Yessirree folks, here's all the world's knowledge worth knowing. Why, there's two pages on the United Nations and two on American skyscrapers, two pages on the U.S.S.R. under Stalin and two on American leisure, two pages on the 200-year history of socialism in the Western world and two on American dance — a finely balanced presentation, as you readily see. And there's more, much more. There are even references to our very own little Canada and, as an added bonus at no extra cost, two — that's right, count 'em — two whole pages called, charmingly, "The Story of Canada." And what a dazzling story it is.

Here's where you finally learn it all. That Victoria is the largest city in British Columbia. That Toronto is the second largest city in Canada. That the Ontario Science Centre was founded in 1919. That Alberta's population is 1,838,037. That Canada has Eskimos. That 44 per cent of our population is British stock and 30 per cent French. That there are 220,000 Native Indians "mostly living in the prairie states." That our provincial governments are "headed by a premier of parliament." That the population of Banff is 896 souls. That Newfoundland joined Confederation in 1948. That Mackenzie King was an outstanding leader during the "drive for independence and the early years of Confederation." That Alberta has 19 members of parliament.

Wrong! Wrong! Wrong! Every single piece of it. Truth in advertising, anyone? (For the right answers, check Hurtig's *The Canadian Encyclopedia*.)

But hold on: There's even more thrills and spills from Random House. R.B. Bennett's biography ignores entirely the Great Depression. Joe Clark's entry ends in 1983 (wishful thinking?). None of Metro Toronto's component cities are named. Dave Barrett makes it, but not Bill Davis, Bill Bennett or Peter Lougheed (a left-wing bias here? It's very suspicious.) The dates for all Margaret Atwood's books are wrong.

"The 1989 ratification of a free trade agreement (between Canada and the U.S.)," we are authoritatively told, "promised to strengthen their already close economic relations." I'll say.

But here's my all-time favorite, from page 1361: "Among the most popular Liberal prime ministers in Canada were Lester Pearson, Pierre Trudeau and" — wait for it, sports fans; that's right, you guessed it — "Brian Mulroney." The sordid truth revealed at last. Only in America.

And America, of course, is where this masterpiece was fabricated. Random House Canada told me that "it's made in the U.S. We just distribute it." The two men named as Editor-in-Chief and Editorial Director both, alas, died several years ago. In any event, an RH executive in New York told me, all the research for the Encyclopedia was prepared by Sachem Publishing Association, a small, "independent editorial packager of books" in Connecticut. Random House contracted the project to Sachem, which in turn subcontracted the work to what its chief, Steven Elliott, described to me as "specialists." Needless to say, neither Random House nor Sachem had any independent capacity whatever to judge the product each approved.

And what a product, folks. Makes your Xmas choices as simple as inventing a new country. If you want a truly intellectually challenging American product, see *Rocky V*. If you want a great patriotic giggle, *The Random House Encyclopedia* has your name on it. (I'm sending a copy to my favorite Liberal prime minister.) But if all you want is one fine encyclopedia, you can always resort to *The Junior Encyclopedia of Canada*. Enjoy.

✳   ✳   ✳

1990   MAKE NO MISTAKE ABOUT IT: The latest round of cuts to the CBC is no trivial matter. They constitute a body blow to our public broadcasting system, our major instrument not only for the enhancement of Canadian culture but of all culture in Canada, and they tear another gaping hole in one of the few remaining truly national institutions that have historically functioned to keep our absurd confederation together.

It would be serious enough if it were just a matter of losing local CBC outlets across the land. Over the years, the stations in Calgary and Sydney and Matane and Windsor have become organic, integral parts of their communities. That's where public broadcasting begins — at the community level. And now where it's ending. Sure regional broadcasting matters, but you could have regional programming on a local station. And as CBC management candidly acknowledged, "hundreds of hours per year" of local and regional programming — many of them part of the warp and woof of their communities — are now unceremoniously cancelled.

(Unceremonious may be too polite a word. The manner in which the announcements were made, and the peremptory way in which programs were terminated without even an opportunity to bid viewers adieu, provided the private sector with some nice lessons in insensitive, merciless management techniques.)

Local CBC stations have always been the cradle of some of the best talent in the Canadian television world. Throughout both the upper reaches of the CBC, and throughout the private broadcasting sector, old CBC hands proliferate. That singular training function is now substantially forfeited.

*Ottawa, 1986. Caplan and Florian Sauvageau, co-chairs
of the Task Force on Canadian Broadcasting Policy,
at the press conference introducing their report.*

So is the role of the CBC in so many communities as one of the major, and indispensable, outlets for creative and artistic talent. Heaven knows, now, how women and men of creative disposition in Goose Bay, Rimouski, Cornerbrook or Saskatoon are to find a livelihood, or how Canada's regional cultural life is to be replenished. It would be a serious mistake to underestimate the CBC's role in fostering such endeavors throughout the country, and it's also why far, far more than 1,100 CBC staff members will be the casualties of this draconian exercise.

Yet the damage to local communities is only one part of the problem. Broadcasting involves, after all, or at least ought to involve, serious creative endeavour. Even a philistine like me understands instinctively that creativity can hardly flourish at its most expansive in an ambience where the hammer suddenly falls, where today's inspiration is tomorrow's dim memory. So the very magnitude of the cuts, as well as the manner in which they were carried out, have already powerfully demoralized CBC staff across the country, even those who have so far been untouched. And, of course, the key words are "so far."

Don't believe for a single second that these cuts end the CBC's financial woes. Given the economic downturn, commercial revenues are sure to suffer. Costs will increase. Inflation is not being covered by the government. In another year — maybe next Christmas again, as a special CBC treat — deep new cuts may well be necessary. Who knows what CBC services will be deemed dispensable at that time? *The Journal?* TV dramas? *The Nature of Things?* Maybe we'll see commercials back on CBC radio? Why not? Nothing about the CBC is any longer sacrosanct.

Look, the sad truth is that the CBC has been in trouble for some years — not to put too fine a point on it, let's say since about the time Brian Mulroney first took office. I always liked the simple definition that said public broadcasting was in business to make programs while private broadcasters were in it to make profits. Yet given the government's hostile funding policies, the CBC has grown, inevitably, more and more dependent on advertising revenues, with all the attendant consequences. Those who want to denigrate the CBC love to talk about its billion-dollar budget. The sad fact is that about two-thirds of the operating budget of its English TV network comes from ad revenues. This is public broadcasting?

Credit where credit is due. The Mulroney government has made great strides in its determined efforts to dismantle this country.

Quebec's about gone. North-south trading links are replacing east-west ones in every region of the nation. The national airline is gone. The national passenger railway is gone. Now the CBC, the most important single institution for creating a common sense of Canadianism, is unravelling a mile a minute. Congratulations, Prime Minister. A job well done.

* * *

1990   ONE OF THE ALL-TIME LOW POINTS in American history came during the 1988 presidential campaign when Michael Dukakis refused publicly to associate himself with the dreaded L-word. Even today in America, nothing but the most insipid, apologetic middle-of-the-road liberalism is acceptable dinner-party conversation in respectable company.

Yet, at the same time, across the United States, small bands of courageous progressives perform yeoman duty in exposing the excesses and outrages of American capitalism. Everywhere there are one or two little groups, perennially starved of funds, often the objects of illicit FBI scrutiny or vigilante terrorism, actively monitoring the activities of religious fanatics, human rights violators, racial hate mongers, and other such charmers who proliferate south of the border.

Then there are progressives who scrutinize the behaviour not of the extremists but of the mainstream corporate elite. Among these is an important little group called FAIR — Fairness and Accuracy in Reporting — a U.S. media-watch organization that focuses on "the narrow corporate ownership of the press, the media's persistent Cold War assumptions, their insensitivity to women, labor, minorities and other public interest constituencies." The contents of FAIR's excellent journal, *Extra!*, often help explain why the left has so little currency in the U.S.

In two recent issues, for example, *Extra!* examined the guests who appear on two well-known public affairs shows, ABC's *Nightline* with Ted Koppel, and the *MacNeil-Lehrer NewsHour* on PBS. The findings were disturbing enough for ABC but unnerving for the vaunted PBS program; guests on both shows overwhelmingly constituted an elite of white males reflecting the political spectrum all the way from the moderate centre to the far right. Often as not, conservative ideologues were introduced as experts rather than propagandists. Rare indeed was the dissenter from orthodox American foreign or domestic policy. In short, both programs functioned as unbalanced ideological bulwarks of the American status quo.

Now *Extra!* has released the results of an in-depth study analyzing newspaper and television coverage of working people and unions in the United States in 1989. The findings? The lives of working people "are being routinely ignored, marginalized or inaccurately reported in the media." Issues such as child care and workplace health and safety, for example, received little more than two per cent of the total air time of the three network evening news programs, while union coverage almost invariably means news of the latest messy strike, even though most labour-management disputes are settled through negotiation.

In Canada, *Media Watch* often does invaluable work from a feminist vantage point. Some right-wingers toil away at demonstrating the crypto-commie sympathies of the CBC, but there is no real equivalent of *Extra!* here, no rigorous ongoing assessment of balance and bias within the media in Canada.

Clearly, in some important ways, there's greater political balance in certain Canadian media as compared to the U.S. Most television political commentary, as I well know, happens in panels representing all three parties, giving social democrats exposure of a kind unthinkable down south. A few Canadian newspapers, you may have noticed, run commentaries by a tiny stable of pinkish writers, though conservatives from the moderate to the silly-right are infinitely more common in the Canadian press.

But when it comes to coverage of business and labour, I wonder if we're any less biased than in the States. Former Winnipeg MP David Orlikow has turned himself into a one-person monitor of media ideological prejudice, focusing especially on our own public broadcaster. Contrary to some unfounded right-wing prejudices, Orlikow believes the CBC habitually gives us highly biased coverage of business news, complaining that in covering so-called business or financial issues the CBC regularly turns to "experts" who are not detached or neutral but clearly pro-business.

During the 1988 election, for example, *Morningside's* regular business panelists were unanimously pro-free trade, leaving it to host Peter Gzowski to raise the concerns of the majority of troubled

Canadians. And where is *Morningside*'s panel on and with labour, working people and the left? In fact there's not now a single labour show on Canadian television outside some community cable channels. And where's the newspaper section labelled "ordinary working people," for those whose cranks aren't turned by the latest corporate appointment or Dow Jones index.

Seems to me a little *Extra!* would go a long way on this side of the border as well.

✳   ✳   ✳

1992   DEAR DENNIS ROSENBERG:

Thank you for your latest letter. I'm sure, as division manager for a giant cable monopoly like Rogers Cablesystems, you're a very busy fellow and I'm grateful you've taken the trouble to keep us subscribers up to date on the changes you're making — especially since we never even asked.

So if I understand what's up — and I confess I find all the channel changes this week quite baffling — you guys have just introduced something called Full Cable Service, which is weird because I thought I already had full cable service.

In fact, you tell me that what I now already have, as of this week, is this Full Cable Service — unless I prefer something else called "new basic cable service" which I can only get if I call and ask you to disconnect the new channels you just connected even though I never asked for them at all and even though they'll soon cost more than the service I now have. Do I have that straight, Mr. R?

And here's another question, sir. Your letter is just chock-a-block with assertions about how little all these terrific extra services will cost. So what does *this* throwaway sentence mean: "Annual rate adjustments will take place in January"? And why does it make me feel just a teensy bit nervous?

Can we scrutinize for a mo' the four new channels you've just generously injected into my home? Am I right in believing that three are from the United States and that the only one with any Canadian content is entirely in French? That's just swell. If there was anything we lacked around this house it sure was more American TV programs.

Then there's the separate category of Pay TV. You list about seven channels in your $15 pay TV package, making about 15 channels in all named in your recent letters. And the only English Canadian channel in the entire bunch is TSN (The Sports Network), which you only mention in order to tell me it's *no longer* going to be available on the basic service. In other words, the only English Canadian channel you refer to is one you're taking away from many of us. Ah, you cable guys are slick marketers, all right.

Of course, absolutely everybody knows you're the bold champions of the consumer, guardians of the rights of the couch potato, just making an honest buck by giving us bozos what we want. As your spokesperson told the CRTC last week at a hearing on re-licensing CBC Newsworld, he was speaking "on behalf of the over 6 million subscribers that my members serve." Now let's look at that claim, Mr. R.

In your letter to me you refer to the "popular U.S. superstations" from Atlanta and Chicago that are part of your pay TV package. And then you announce that this week you'll add to that package — be still my heart — "the much requested Boston superstation" as well. Now stop right there, Dennis. There are seven so-called American superstations, of which the most popular has 57 million American subscribers, the second *least* popular has 2.2 million, and the very least popular has 600,000. Yep: good old Boston. So by whom exactly was it "much requested?" And when CRTC chair Keith Spicer noted that I had earlier in the hearing challenged the alleged popularity of these superstations, your man couldn't produce a jot or tittle of evidence in response.

Here's another question, Dennis: Have you ever written all your loyal subscribers to explain that the reason we have to endure the egregious presence of the home shopping channel on TV is because Rogers happens to own it? The consumer, my Aunt Fanny.

Here's something else I better get off my chest while I'm at it. I read the cable monopolies' brief to the CRTC opposing a price increase for CBC Newsworld. Since you guys insist you just love Newsworld to death, how come you're seeking the right to take it off the basic tier that everyone with a converter gets and run it on a higher tier that's going to cost extra?

Even more ominously — please forgive my suspicious mind — you recommend that "cable consumers" should be able to get CNN "even in markets where cable operators have determined their subscribers would oppose the addition of Newsworld." Do words mean what

1991 — The CTV *political panel — "The Pundits" — in a benefit conference at the Royal York Hotel for the Stratford Festival. Caplan is in the back row, second from right. Others present include Hal Jackman, Bob Rae, Arlene Rae, Don Herron, Ian Scott, Michael Kirby, David Crombie, Rita Zekas, Mel Lastman, Hugh Segal, and Mike Harris.*

they seem, Dennis? Are you birds really hoping to offer some of us the American all-news channel and *not* the Canadian one at all?

And they say too that you're also pressuring MuchMusic to accept being on the second tier — you know, the one that'll have, as you wrote, "annual rate adjustments . . . in January." So this new second tier will have Newsworld, Much, TSN — all the channels we now get simply with basic cable and a converter. Sorry, but I'm confused. I don't see how the consumers you claim to champion can possibly make an informed decision about what you're really peddling with the smoke and mirrors in your letters.

Nor do you seem hellbent on making any notable contributions to Canadian television.

This country's going to have huge problems in the next few years figuring out how to preserve a Canadian broadcasting system at all, Dennis. Seems to me we might've expected just a tad more help from our all-Canadian cable monopoly.

YOURS SINCERELY, ETC

＊　＊　＊

1992   THESE ARE BONANZA DAYS for sports-obsessed TV couch potatoes. Having been saturated all spring with almost nightly Stanley Cup games, we're now in the season of double delights: Thursday nights throughout the summer and into the late September it's the Canadian Football League, while every Friday night and — be still my heart — on some Wednesday and Saturday evenings, too, it's the Jays themselves.

And if that's not good enough, last Saturday morning you could've caught the British Open golf tournament — it's a lot more gripping than those usual dreary Saturday kid's programs — and on a recent Saturday afternoon we were treated to the American golf classic, the PGA, direct from the States. Happily, it lasted so long that the dreary old 6 p.m. news was delayed.

Of course, by now it's an old story — trying to find the news on CBC-TV on any given night of the year. And what's important about the above lineup is that it wasn't on TSN but on the good old Mother

Corp itself, playing havoc with the *National,* the *Journal* and all other regularly scheduled programs.

CODCO might amuse intermittently, but the funniest moments on CBC these days are when Peter Mansbridge tries to explain with a barely straight face the changes in tomorrow night's CBC schedule across each of the country's various time zones because of one sports event or another.

So when CBC president Gerard Vielleux announces proudly that the *National* and *Journal* are going to be moved from 10 to 9 p.m. as part of the network's new "repositioning," old-fashioned CBC devotees know it just means that now the news won't be on at 9 instead of not being on at 10; public broadcasting has, apparently, come to mean massive coverage of sports events plus news and current events whenever they can be squeezed in.

I guess this will appeal to the wall-to-wall white males who run the Corp, in gross and flagrant violation of this country's employment equity laws. And it's true: sports broadcasts happen to be highly lucrative for the CBC, but what it's got to do with public broadcasting is beyond me.

But then, much of what goes on at the CBC these days is not easy to fathom. Why reschedule the *National* and *Journal* at 9 p.m., the heart of prime time, when you've got CBC Newsworld operating throughout the evening? Why give us more news at peak viewing times when Canada's greatest need remains high quality Canadian drama?

The president says that CBC-TV must be clearly distinctive from anything else on the tube, just as CBC radio is. I guess that's why he's concentrating on sports and news; if that ain't distinctive Canadian TV, what is? As for drama, says the busy little president, "I really haven't addressed that yet."

In fact, public broadcasting in general seems to be about the last thing on the CBC's agenda these days. Placating its political masters in the government seems a prime driving force for whatever's going on. Meeting financial constraints is another.

But anything like a coherent vision of the CBC as a public broad-caster worth its name is sadly lacking. Vague promises of classy programming sandwiching the new 9 p.m. news hour is not exactly reassuring, coming from these boys.

It's important for champions of the CBC to know that, as one frustrated, dedicated staffer told me this week, "fear and loathing" are rampant throughout the corporation. "There's paranoia everywhere," said another. "Everyone's terrified of speaking out."

This is a fine atmosphere for the kind of creativity and synergy that CBC desperately needs. In the recent words of David Kaufman of the Association of Television Producers and Directors, "It appears that president Vielleux has created an atmosphere of intimidation surrounding this process [the new 'repositioning' initiative] and is determined to exert absolute control over every stage of the exercise." So we have a CBC in the hands of a tiny boys' club consisting of a president with no broadcasting experience, an enormously influential PR flack recruited directly from the private sector with, of course, no broadcasting background, and a head of English TV who is not about to remind his boss why so many Canadians feel so passionately about the Corp.

This is the team that has monopolized the task of refashioning public broadcasting in Canada.

At a time when we've never been in greater need of the CBC to remind us what we Canadians hold in common, we have a dispirited, demoralized, fractured corporation that can no longer figure out its own reason to exist. The CBC has always been a potent symbol of this country. Its present state augurs poorly for our future.

✳　✳　✳

1992　MY CHERISHED FRIEND BARBARA FRUM died yesterday. So did Barbara Frum, renowned star of radio and TV and one of Canada's genuine celebrities: The Queen, as her husband Murray called her with loving mockery, but also accurately describing her role in Canada's cultural life.

It is already clear to me that while Canadian public life will suffer enormously from Barbara's sudden and unexpected death, my own loss will be almost entirely personal, and enormous; it's the departure of my friend Barbara that I'm already having trouble coping with.

To the world, we seemed an odd couple. There she was, the glamorous star, the household name, the universally recognized celebrity, the interviewer and associate of the entire Canadian Who's Who, and there was I, the lifelong outsider, the cheerleader for Canada's third political party, as permanently distanced from power through most of my life as she was a natural member of the power elite. An unlikely pairing to be sure and one of the two or three most enduring and precious relationships of my life.

For behind the public star — "Good evening, this is Barbara Frum" — lay the private star — "Ger? It's Barbara." And the reason I loved her was because the natural woman, the off-stage, non-performing woman, had at least as many genuine star qualities as the public celebrity, and even, I'm confident in saying, many more.

The Barbara I came to know over 30-odd years was a staggeringly complex person. Above all, perhaps, this was a woman who loved life and lived it intensely, not least in the long 18 years since she was first diagnosed as having leukemia. It was part of her contagious *joie de vivre* that she never succumbed to the fear that rarely left her, never surrendered to bitterness at the likelihood that she would be cheated out of a long, full life — even though, as she once told June Callwood, she regretted she'd never be a great old lady. And with her endless energy and her great courage, few people understood how ill she in fact was — which is why yesterday's news of her death set off shock waves of disbelief and dismay from one end of Canada to another.

Few understood this private anguish. And perhaps equally few knew that behind the public persona stood an absolutely private family woman, at home with the prides of her life: her inseparable partner Murray, her children and first grandchild, her mother, her siblings and their kids. Even I, as close to being an honorary member of the family as just about anyone not related by blood, was only permitted occasional glimpses of this Barbara, hair down, all self-consciousness thrown out the window, as natural and comfortable with the world as she could ever be. It was a rare sight for an outsider and one I esteemed almost immoderately.

Then there was Barbara the concerned, caring, tender friend to a vast and diverse chunk of humankind — so wildly at odds with the tough personality that so many TV viewers considered her. Probably no one but Murray knows all the different afflicted individuals to whom she reached out, often to their astonishment and pleasure, over the decades. These were no acts of charity or even haughty philanthropy, but simple empathy for those who were enduring the same nightmares she knew only too well. Dozens of friends each know about a few such cases but it was part of her glory that these were intensely private deeds on her part for which she never sought appreciation or recognition.

Homage of course must also be paid to Barbara, the hostess with the mostest. A Saturday night seat at the Frum's table was for years the most coveted ticket in town and just about everyone who was anyone at one time or another made their appearance. Fine food, generous wine, but above all, stimulating conversation among elites from every conceivable walk of life: The Frum soirées were an institution in their own time. And if you think I minded standing out like a sore thumb as the lone socialist in such lofty gatherings, you would of course be dead wrong. Unreservedly, I loved every minute of them.

But none of these are the Barbaras that will leave an unfillable void in my life. That is reserved for the Barbara of Barbara and Murray, half of one of the magical love affairs, one of the remarkable marriages, one of the exemplary partnerships of this or any other era. The relationship between Barbara and Murray was the envy of all the rest of us. They liked each other, loved each other, trusted each other, respected each other, listened to each other, learned from each other; as impressive as each was alone, together they were greater than the sum of their parts. And on those evenings we spent alone, just my wife and I and the two of them, the sheer pleasure of watching them together, of sharing in their endless debates and discussions, made for moments of such exquisite exhilaration that we couldn't stop commenting about it and marvelling at it for days on end.

Those nights remain among the most prized and memorable of my entire life, and the certain knowledge that they can be no more overwhelms me with a melancholy no words can possibly convey. One of these days, there may be another public star like Barbara Frum. But I don't expect there to be another private one — at least not in my life.

* * *

Socialist Dreams & Nightmares

1988   TWENTY YEARS AGO this week, Soviet army tanks rolled into Czechoslovakia to annihilate its Prague "spring," that exciting but abortive attempt to liberate the harsh totalitarianism that characterized Czechoslovakia as it has all the puppet governments of Eastern Europe.

I happened at the time to be in Cuba. The Cuban press, rigidly controlled then as it is now, allowed only a glimpse of the invasion to be made public. But even that was sufficient for every Cuban one met to draw the obvious parallel between Moscow invading Prague and Washington invading the Bay of Pigs. They could barely wait for Fidel to give voice to the anger and bitterness they felt for their ostensible Soviet compañeros.

Imagine the shock, then, when Castro applauded the invasion as necessary to save Czechoslovakia from some preposterous counter-revolutionary threat or other. It was another miserable milestone in the terrible history of the so-called Communist countries since the original Russian revolution of 1917.

For a democratic socialist like myself, the two words were organically linked: Socialism without democracy was a contradiction in terms. But such refined scruples seemed merely puerile to large-C Communists. Lenin himself created the structures that Stalin easily turned to his own monstrous purposes. The very Leninist concept of a vanguard party was a betrayal of democratic principles, and could lead only to the kind of privileged dictatorial elite of party leaders, government bureaucrats and secret police that in fact emerged through the Soviet bloc.

Today, the Soviet population is being stunned with endless revelations of the nightmares they have endured for the past seven decades.

But these ghastly truths have long been only too familiar to Western socialists. Nor did we need venomous and reactionary red-baiters as our tutors; we had decades earlier our own wealth of disenchanted but honorable left-wing sources: Koestler's *Darkness at Noon* with its exposé of the sadistic treason trials of the late 1930s; the remarkable group of Western intellectuals who described their disillusionment with the Soviet Union and its fanatical Western partisans in *The God That Failed*; Chaim Greenberg's devastating essays dissecting Trotsky's cruelty; Orwell's disclosures of Soviet treachery during the Spanish civil war in *Homage to Catalonia*.

Little of the horror went unexposed. The slaughter of the Krondstat sailors, protesting in the name of communism. The forced industrialization and collectivization and the appalling consequent famine that killed countless millions. The heartless prison camps and gulags. The endless purges. The Kafkaesque confessions of counter-revolutionary deeds by loyal revolutionaries. The extermination of the top military leadership on the eve of World War II. The ultimate cynicism of the Ribbentrop-Molotov pact, freeing Hitler to attack Poland in 1939. The rabid Soviet anti-Semitism leading to the executions of innumerable Jewish doctors. The invasion of Hungary. The attack on independent Polish trade unions. Afghanistan.

And always there were, in the West, devout comrades and wilfully myopic fellow travellers with an amoral rationalization for the latest crime against humanity. In a book I wrote umpteen years ago on left-wing Canadian politics in the '30s and '40s, I traced some of the warped contortions that Canadian Communists underwent to remain loyal to the ever-changing party line as dictated by the Kremlin. It was a demeaning performance.

Instead of the noble expectations of Marx, Soviet communism fulfilled the most brutish visions of Hobbes. The sheer magnitude of the evil, combined with its disgraceful justification by Western apologists, has had the double impact of slaughtering not only millions of Soviet citizens but millions of dreams and illusions as well.

Now Castro's Cuba stands as yet another bitter monument: a rudimentary welfare state, to be sure, but devoid of liberty and democracy, characterized by stultifying regimentation and soul-numbing mismanagement. No *glasnost* or *perestroika* here, you can be confident.

For some 200 years socialist thought was couched expansively in terms of a new society, inhabited by the new man and the new woman devoted to a higher value system. Socialists dreamed of utopias in which banal material needs were automatically satisfied and human creativity could therefore have free reign. Thanks to Soviet communism, its clones and sympathizers, all such dreams are dead. The modest goal of making tomorrow a little better has replaced the boundless faith of a more innocent age. That's why so many of us are so wary of the Gorbachev reforms. It seems almost too much to hope that after all these wretched decades a Communist government will finally not betray its long-buried ideals.

*　*　*

1991　　AS A LIFE-LONG DEMOCRATIC SOCIALIST, I joyfully con-
———— fess to finding the humiliating public demolition of communism in the U.S.S.R. especially sweet. As absurd as it now appears, one of history's most acrimonious rivalries once pitted Soviet Stalinism against democratic socialism in a struggle to determine which would eventually supplant an iniquitous capitalist system.

In a world where the pursuit of egalitarianism has virtually disappeared; where the viability of social democracy, let alone democratic socialism, must constantly be demonstrated; where the left is in such disrepute that George Bush can put the entire Democratic party on the offensive by accusing Democrats of being liberals: such a world will not easily remember the great promise that the Soviet Revolution once held for millions of people around the globe.

"I have seen the future and it works," exalted American John Reed from Russia during its revolution, and the very possibility that a new form of political economy was taking shape based not on private property and the profit motive but on public ownership and communal values, was enough to terrify the elites of the entire capitalist world.

It is in one key sense misleading to compare the 10 momentous days of August, 1991, in the Soviet Union with those of October, 1917. While the world enthusiastically applauded the return of Gorbachev last month, three-quarters of a century ago the world powers united to do all in their might to reverse the Communist victory.

The Great War had caused appalling damage to Russia, which was soon exacerbated by the terrible civil war that czarist forces launched against the Lenin government. The major capitalist powers, led by Britain and America, intervened militarily against the Communists. Before its final bloody victory, the new Bolshevik state was in tatters.

It was no doubt inevitable that well-meaning but weak-minded Western socialists would fall into the easy trap of sympathizing with the Soviet's onerous plight, of lauding Soviet reconstruction in the face of overwhelming adversity, while politely tut-tutting its disrespect for democracy and liberty. Totalitarians of the left, we called these fellow travellers, prepared in the name of socialism to excuse the inexcusable and justify the unjustifiable.

I became politically conscious at the feet of those who were already disillusioned by the abject betrayal of the magnificent Communist dream. Chaim Greenberg, the great labour Zionist intellectual, taught me about Lenin's penchant for dictatorship, as in the Communist party he created, and Trotsky's for ruthlessness, as when he massacred the protesting Kronstadt sailors. Arthur Koestler, in *Darkness at Noon*, exposed the grotesque show trials of the 1930s designed to eradicate any slight vestige of free thought and free speech.

The prominent Western intellectuals who bared their souls in *The God That Failed* provided a litany of horror stories of the ways in which the Soviet government or the Communist party had betrayed the faith each had passionately cherished. George Orwell in *Homage to Catalonia* showed the duplicity, the reckless opportunism of Soviet policy in Spain during the Spanish Civil War. My own research on the Canadian left revealed the bare-faced treachery carried out by the sycophants in the Canadian Communist Party at the whim of the Kremlin.

Of course, events spoke for themselves. The great purges. The vicious anti-Semitism. The wilful famines. The Gulags. The slave labour. The nightmare of the KGB. The ultimate cynicism of Stalin's 1939 pact with Hitler. The invasions of Hungary and Czechoslovakia. The institutionalization of tyranny. The ultimate refinement of totalitarianism.

But I rejected then, as I do now, certain conventional wisdom about the Soviets. Stalinism was an internal abomination, but for the past four decades Soviet imperialism has been less destructive of world peace and human development than American imperialism. The record — as opposed to a half-century of deliberate Western disinformation and propaganda — is clear.

Nor is it remotely plausible that the salvation of the U.S.S.R. lies simply in the free play of the market. The situation is infinitely more complex than the simple-minded neo-conservative nostrums of Western leaders would indicate. While market forces often create economic growth, without active state intervention they always lead to uneven, inequitable and environmentally catastrophic development.

To write off socialism because of the collapse of Soviet communism makes no sense. The failed command economy in the U.S.S.R., a product of Stalinism, has nothing whatever in common with the precepts of Western socialism. Nor does the death of Soviet communism signify the moral triumph of Western capitalism. While capitalism — when it doesn't cause depressions — has given us some unprecedented benefits, its inadequacies and failures remain appalling and monumental. The elusive pursuit of a third way — of some variety of a democratic socialist way — continues to be among the greatest goals our society can strive for.

*　*　*

1993   IT'S PERHAPS the most distressing legacy of the era of Reagan-Bush and Reagan-Mulroney that the democratic left now finds itself on the run.

For a dozen years in the United States and 8 1/2 years here, unashamed conservatives have controlled government and unleashed upon us unfettered capitalist values and capitalist economics. The results are something less than inspiring. Yet the left has been driven to adopt some of the very conservative priorities that are responsible for the debacle in the first place.

Aren't those right-wing guys supposed to be such fabulous managers? Aren't they the ones obsessed with cutting deficits? So how come Ronald Reagan and George Bush managed the unparalleled feat of saddling their country with a debt of almost $4 *trillion*? How come American productivity sagged even in the face of the most humongous war budgets in world history, a form of Keynesianism vigorously promoted by an administration and a weapons industry that endlessly genuflected to the virtues of the market and non-interfering governments?

Meanwhile, thanks to little initiative or effort of their own, the merely rich got unimaginably richer, courtesy of the greatest redistribution of wealth in recorded history.

Reagan's crackpot policies were lavishly promoted by an entire universe of learned economists, prestigious think tanks, respected pundits and trusted media, all of whom were out to lunch. But that enormous underclass of Americans who have been left behind in the wake of applied Reaganism needs no experts to understand the condition of post-conservative America.

Nor need Canadians be reminded of the shape of Canada after nearly a decade of faithful Tory implementation of the agenda of the Business Council on National Issues. The government faithfully privatized, deregulated, gave tax breaks to the rich, cut social services, signed the free trade deal, sanctioned high interest rates and a high dollar.

The result: the greatest economic mess in half a century. The corporate and Tory solution: more of the very policies that got us into this pickle in the first place, and about which Prime Minister Mulroney spoke so proudly in his resignation statement.

Throughout these cruel, rapacious years, the genius of neo-conservative governments was appropriately complemented by the performance of the private sector itself. In all human history, have so many expectations of so many leaders of society ever been so crushingly disappointed?

The record of North American private enterprise since it was unleashed by Reagan has been one of ineptitude, corruption and inhumanity on a scale rarely before witnessed. Preaching the hard-nosed rationality of the bottom line, in fact the corporate world was driven by egomania and greed without limit.

Before the looting and pillaging came to an end, a generation of American and Canadian business giants had become rich beyond the dreams of avarice, often having created little of value, risked next to nothing of their own, yet causing chaos wherever they intruded and ruining the lives of hundreds and thousands of their fellow citizens as an almost incidental by-product; call it collateral damage.

Yet, even when their paper empires lay in tatters, they remained rich as Croessus. These, of course, are the very same rocket scientists who insist that governments must operate on business-like principles. If public sector managers screwed up even half as badly as the executives who ran General Motors or IBM, we'd be really up the creek without a paddle.

As it is, we emerge from a decade of voodoo economics to be instructed that deficits and debts are so destructively gargantuan they can be combated only with the very tools that have exacerbated them. So even though the corporate emperors have been found to have no clothes, even though corporate planning has become the great oxymoron of our time, we continue to defer to the dreary nostrums of the executive class.

As if most of the simplistic business clichés of recent years have not been palpable nonsense, as if so many mouthy executives have not proved abject failures at running their own enterprises, let alone having the *chutzpah* to tell politicians how better to run entire countries.

Here's the real bottom line. Brian Mulroney, like Reagan and Bush, leaves a cruel legacy of short-term pain for longer-term pain. It's the awesome task of social democrats to work within ever narrower constraints to offer policies that can rescue us from the holy mess we're in without adding to the world's burden of injustices. It ain't going to be easy.

*   *   *

1993   ONCE UPON A TIME, many years ago, there lived a magnificent dream called democratic socialism.

The socialist vision was expansive, idealistic, bounteous. Its premise was the unlikely notion of human perfectibility, or at least a view of the human condition best reflected by the Jewish teenager Anne Frank, who hid from the Nazis during World War II in a Dutch attic. "In spite of everything," she told her diary just before she and her family were discovered and murdered, "I still believe that people are really good at heart." In spite of everything, in spite indeed of overwhelming evidence to the contrary, so did those who embraced the socialist faith. And faith is what you needed.

The more evil in the world, the more the inhumanity of man against man (and woman), the more urgent was the need to replace the capitalist system with its unworthy profit motive and dog-eat-dog morality. Socialists yearned for a world where humankind was motivated by its noblest, not its basest, instincts. People before profits

244

was the neat slogan. In place of competitive individualism, conflict, exploitation, racism, oppression, acquisitiveness, greed, selfishness, envy, the new Jerusalem would feature social justice, equality, democratic participation, co-operation, caring, peaceableness.

Not only would we study war no more, life would be characterized by perfect racial, gender, ethnic, religious and class harmony — if classes endured at all — while world government would happily supplant the deadly scourge of violently competing nationalism. In spite of this ennobling vision — or, perhaps, because of it — the socialist dream was never more than the chimera of a small minority of idealists and utopians. A few kibbutzim aside, capitalism and its cut-throat ethics continued to prevail.

A compromise was necessary if any progress was to be made toward the promised land. So the prophets of the socialist movement gave way to the politicians of social democratic parties. Here the envied models were Sweden and tiny Saskatchewan, and the goals were infinitely more modest: the creation of a just market system, the humanizing of capitalism. For decades Scandinavian social democrats ran governments that enabled their societies to become both economically productive and socially equitable, and even today there are valuable lessons a market-obsessed world can learn from the Scandinavian "middle way."

But in neither East nor West is there an appetite for the pragmatic techniques of successful social democrats. In the flush era after World War II, a fragment of social democratic thought took hold in the Western world in the form of some rudimentary welfare statism, its level depending on each individual country. But with the victories of Reaganism and Thatcherism — the true radicalism of our time — even those small steps toward a moderately more decent society were unceremoniously reversed. Putting profits before people became the first commandment.

But neo-conservatism not only legitimized greed and selfishness as acceptable driving forces in a civilized world. It not only crushed the hopes and expectations of untold millions of people around the globe for a more tolerable existence. It also so profoundly undermined the economies of so many nations that, while its victims palpably needed social democracy as rarely before, it seemed — irony of ironies — that only neo-conservative policies could deal with the crisis neo-conservatism had created. Spooked by threats of capital strikes, social democratic administrations from New Zealand to France, Australia to Saskatchewan, embraced neo-conservative policies combined with whatever small change remains for social justice.

Perhaps nothing else is possible, and bad luck for the dreams unrealized, the causes forsaken. Maybe there will never be a time when we have both the resources and the will to build a more humanistic society, though plainly we always have enough cash on hand to finance the next war. But I foresee a day when the original flame of democratic socialism is rekindled.

As we witness the ravages of war, nationalism and religious fundamentalism; as we reflect on the ever-growing universal gap between rich and poor, the abuse of women, exploitation of children, devastation of the environment; when we're sufficiently demeaned by our own selfishness and dishonored by injustice everywhere — maybe then the boundless idealism of the old socialist prophets will make sense again.

The dark side of human nature will remain an eternal quandary for utopians. But the pursuit of a more just and equal society can't be the most ignoble way to live our lives.

*   *   *